Mining Encounters

Also available:

Overheating:
An Anthropology of Accelerated Change
Thomas Hylland Eriksen

Identity Destabilised:
Living in an Overheated World
Edited by Thomas Hylland Eriksen
and Elisabeth Schober

Boomtown:
Runaway Globalisation on the Queensland Coast
Thomas Hylland Eriksen

Mining Encounters

Extractive Industries in an Overheated World

Edited by
Robert Jan Pijpers and
Thomas Hylland Eriksen

First published 2019 by Pluto Press
345 Archway Road, London N6 5AA

www.plutobooks.com

British Library Cataloguing in Publication Data
A catalogue record for this book is available from the British Library

ISBN   978 0 7453 3837 8   Hardback
ISBN   978 1 7868 0375 7   PDF eBook
ISBN   978 1 7868 0377 1   Kindle eBook
ISBN   978 1 7868 0376 4   EPUB eBook

This book is printed on paper suitable for recycling and made from fully managed and
sustained forest sources. Logging, pulping and manufacturing processes are expected to
conform to the environmental standards of the country of origin.

Typeset by Stanford DTP Services, Northampton, England

Simultaneously printed in the United Kingdom and United States of America

Contents

Figures and Maps

Preface

When the European Research Council (ERC) Advanced Grant project 'Overheating: An anthropological history of the early 21st century' started in 2012, we – the researchers – did not anticipate the centrality of mining and the resource industry in the overall project. In the event, virtually all the subprojects, including one by the Principal Investigator (Eriksen), two PhD projects, four postdoctoral projects and altogether 15 ethnographically based MA projects partly funded by 'Overheating' included a mining element, directly or indirectly. The economic boom of the early years of the twenty-first century, the crisis of 2007–8, the recovery of the subsequent years and the downturn in countries like Australia, Venezuela and Norway from around 2014 were all directly connected to the extractive industries, as is the phenomenal economic growth of certain countries, China being the most obvious example, in this period of accelerated change or overheating. Mining, as it slowly dawned upon us, is key to understanding the momentous changes shaping politics, social identities, economic relations and trade patterns in this turbulent age.

Based on a workshop taking place in Oslo on 27–29 April 2015, this book follows previous Overheating publications on knowledge and power, destabilised identities, sustainability and growth, and the different facets of accelerated change in our day and age. Bringing together scholars approaching resource extraction from different perspectives, from the legal to the symbolic, from the environmental to the economic, what holds the contributions to this book together is the ethnographically informed emphasis on what we call the *mining encounter*, the interface, interaction and interpretations of the different actors and stakeholders brought together in extractive projects. As processes of negotiation within these encounters are placed centre stage, particular attention is drawn to the changing dynamics, the inequalities and the fluidity of extractive practices. In doing so, the various authors in this volume bring to light the tensions, negotiations and disparities between different actors in the extractive industries.

The contributions of the editors and the process leading up to this publication have been funded by the ERC Advanced Grant project 'Overheating', ERC Grant number 295843. We, the editors, would like to thank the ERC for its belief in our sprawling research project. Moreover, we would like to extend a special thanks to the contributors-cum-workshop participants, and to Pluto Press for their encouragement and support.

Robert Jan Pijpers
Thomas Hylland Eriksen
Oslo, 10 February 2018

1. Introduction
Negotiating the Multiple Edges
of Mining Encounters

Robert Jan Pijpers and Thomas Hylland Eriksen

INTRODUCTION

Whereas the extraction of raw materials has been a human concern in all times, certain periods are more intense than others in this respect. Today's world definitely finds itself in the middle of such a period, with 'resource booms' and 'busts', taking place in all continents; new extraction sites are developed, closed mines are being reopened, foreign investors compete for leases, millions of people are engaged in artisanal and small-scale mining, and the global trade in resources such as coal, copper and iron ore has grown enormously since the turn of the millennium, not least due to China's industrial development and its quest for resources (see, for example, Brautigam 2009; Alder et al. 2009). In the case of Africa, Bryceson and Jønsson (2014: 3–5) even identify the current 'era of mineralisation' as one of the continent's three major mining eras of the twentieth and early twenty-first centuries, following an era of 'apartheid mining in Southern Africa' and of 'conflict mineral mining'. And indeed, human extraction and consumption of mineral resources have increased steadily since the Industrial Revolution, but never as fast as today.

Within the context of the current expansion of the extractive sector, questions related to unequal economic growth, the local distribution of benefits, development, global commodity chains, taxation, sustainability, livelihoods issues, local resistance and climate change, among others, are becoming more and more pertinent for an understanding of resource extraction's multiple effects. After all, the extractive sector (involving both large-scale industrial as well as small-scale artisanal operations) has the allure, capital and power to trigger changes across societal domains: it attracts large numbers of people, either searching for employment in industrial operations or engaging in artisanal mining; it requires, shifts and generates capital, and may contribute to local economic development through spill-over effects; it brings together a variety of stakeholders with different and sometimes opposing interests;

it turns over soil and impacts upon global as well as local socioeconomic, political and ecological systems in sometimes very dramatic ways. Due to the nature of the extractive sector, the kinds of accelerated change it triggers can often be characterised as veering between bringing about positive development by creating jobs, improving infrastructure or providing national income through taxation, and prompting crisis through land acquisitions and privatisation, displacement, exploitation or environmental destruction. This double-sided character of the effects of resource extraction emphasises that resource extraction is indeed 'contentious and ambiguous' (Bebbington et al. 2008). Moreover, at first sight it seems to correspond well to the two dominant categories in which resource extraction has often been placed: those approaches that propagate resource extraction as a blessing and those that qualify extraction as a 'curse'[1] (Gamu et al. 2015). Nonetheless, whereas extraction's effects are perhaps double-sided, they do not necessarily pose a question of either/or. On the contrary, as Pijpers (2018) argues elsewhere, while being constantly renegotiated by different combinations of actors, the effects of resource extraction, and the rapid changes it may trigger, are fluid and multifaceted, simultaneously accommodating both positive and negative dynamics. A crucial question is, therefore, how different actors position themselves vis-à-vis each other and negotiate the multiplicity of potential effects of resource extraction.

Just as the extractive sector is expanding, so is the interest among social scientists in the implications of this expansion. While being rooted in a long and rich tradition, the recent growth in studies and publications on resource extraction (we will turn to several of them shortly), indicates that this is not only an increasingly important field of study but also that there is considerable ongoing concern to seek a better understanding of extractive practices and their social, economic, political and environmental effects around the world. Consequently, this volume seeks to contribute to this research agenda and to further our understanding of the extractive sector. It does so by centralising the numerous '*mining encounters*' through which the multiple edges of resource extraction are negotiated.

Mining encounters, as we see it, can be understood as the negotiations and frictions between individuals and groups with different agendas, worldviews and aims within the context of mining operations, from the early stages of exploration and development to the final phases of closure and aftermath. By taking up this approach, we are looking at extractive practices as fields of connection and negotiation, of frictions and contradictions, between different actors who have a particular interest in extraction. This allows us to focus better on how the multifaceted effects of resource extraction, referred to above, are constantly (re)negotiated in a field consisting of a disparate variety of actors. This approach directly implies a perspective that does not limit itself to definite impact, that is, to binary assumptions regarding the effects of extraction, but takes a more dialectical and multifaceted approach, thereby giving voice to all actors in specific landscapes of resource extraction, whether these are powerful and visible or marginal and hidden. *Mining encounters*, which bring together different scales of operation, resources (including oil and gas) and life worlds, enable an approach that scrutinises processes of negotiation through the study of specific events, people and discourse, while connecting them to larger-scale processes.

The perspective cultivated here thus takes the global analysis of the resource industry as a premise, but has its substantial focus on the *mining encounters* best studied ethnographically by anthropologists. In doing so, our perspective situates resource extraction in the particular sets of histories and social, political and economic relations of specific localities (Gilberthorpe and Rajak 2017) – an approach which corresponds with and builds upon that of the anthropology of resource extraction more broadly (see, for example, Ferguson 1999; Luning 2012; Geenen 2015; Welker 2014; Weszkalnys 2016; Leonard 2016; Golub 2014; Rajak 2011; Kirsch 2014; Luning and Pijpers 2017). The *mining encounters* studied in this volume, all unfold in, or generate, spaces of accelerated change; spaces where power relations are destabilised, new livelihood activities develop, existing livelihoods are challenged, new inequalities are created and the lure of fast money in large quantities is omnipresent. Frequently, these spaces and the processes unfolding within them are marked by tension, friction and 'overheating' (Eriksen 2016), which is another central concern of this volume. Before discussing the idea of overheating and why it is especially pertinent in an exploration of resource extraction, however, we will first elaborate on some aspects of the study of extractive practices in more detail.

STUDYING MINING: TOWARDS COHABITATION

'Despite its antiquity, the miner, like Geertz's peasant, was recently discovered by anthropologists,' writes Richard Godoy (1985: 199) in 'Mining: Anthropological Perspectives'. Although anthropological studies of mining came, apparently, relatively late in the development of the discipline, they were certainly timely, with the energy and environmental crisis of the 1970s and 1980s making people more aware of the finite supply of resources and limits to industrial growth (Godoy 1985; Meadows et al. 1972). These earlier studies of mining often focused on the economics of mining, its ecological and economic impact, mining communities, colonial mining projects, rituals and ideologies, migration patterns and industrial and social transformations. Naturally, several of these studies became well known and laid a solid foundation for contemporary work on natural resources, not least with regard to the effects of the arrival and establishment of (foreign) mining operations.

The works of June Nash and Michael Taussig, for example, both deal with Bolivian tin miners and their integration in a global capitalist economy. In *We Eat the Mines and the Mines Eat Us* (1979), Nash studies processes of cultural transformation among Bolivian tin miners, arguing that 'they have transformed themselves from a peasant population with a localised world view to a proletariat aware of the world market in which the product of their labour is sold and from which they buy many of their consumption needs' (1979: 2). Nash shows how the reproduction of a big part of miners' pre-conquest identity, including particular traditional values and beliefs, has strengthened workers' solidarity. Taussig, also concerned with the effect of Bolivia's increasing (if unequal) incorporation in the global market in *The Devil and Commodity Fetishism in South America* (1980), focuses on how the devil signifies people's social experience of alienation in an emerging capitalist mining society. Across the Atlantic, Raymond Dumett (1998), who was also interested in the role of the penetration of foreign mining capital, studied the gold frontier in Ghana, illustrating how foreign companies and locals engaged in dynamic interactions in pushing the mining frontier in a country which had long been engaged in the extraction of gold.[2]

Yet, perhaps the most significant body of earlier work dealing with the role of foreign mining operations in generating local processes of change is the work of the Rhodes-Livingstone Institute,[3] later the 'Manchester School', especially those focusing on the Copperbelt in former Northern Rhodesia (now Zambia). Many of these studies (see for example, Wilson 1941; Epstein 1958; Mitchell 1956; Gluckman 1961) examined the transformative power of industrial development and the wide range of dynamics of social change it spurred, thereby particularly emphasising the transition from a tribal/rural to a modern/urban mode (Falk Moore 1994: 50–1). Social change, it transpired from these studies, was considered to be embedded in processes of industrialisation, urbanisation, migration and the development of new class structures and lifestyles, which were predominantly associated with the establishment and expansion of large-scale mining projects. This strong emphasis on change, and especially the transformative role of industrial mining in these processes, was later critiqued, for example by Ferguson (1999: 24), who characterised this area as the 'anthropological topos for the ideas of "social change" and "urbanisation"', and by Gewald (2009), who shows that the processes of change in the Copperbelt were also rooted in longer histories of mobility. Especially the argument of Gewald (2009) shows that the effects of mining are produced in dialogue with wider social, economic, political and historical dynamics, a perspective that is also central in this volume on *mining encounters*.

Since Godoy's 1985 review of anthropological studies on mining, academic interest in natural resources and their extraction has, as we indicated earlier, expanded and diversified. Acknowledging the multiple aspects of resource extraction, and their role in spurring the diverse effects of extraction, social scientists have turned more and more to the role of, for example, corporate social responsibility (Dolan and Rajak 2016; Rajak 2006), materiality (Richardson and Weszkalnys 2014), creation of identities (Welker 2014; Golub 2014), temporality (Ferry and Limbert 2008; Halvaksz 2008; D'Angelo and Pijpers 2018), resistance to mining projects (Kirsch 2014; Coumans 2011), gender (Lahiri-Dutt 2015), global geopolitics and national political discourse (Mitchell 2011; Batty 2013; Emel et al. 2011) and governance of space (Appel 2012; Ferguson 2005). In doing so, these studies show that resources and their extraction – whether this concerns gold, oil, diamonds, copper or gas – are embedded in a complex social, economic and political field. This field, which is thus crucial for our understanding of the dynamics of global resource extraction, connects specific extractive practices to a multitude of local, national, regional and global phenomena, including developments on the global commodity market, local histories of extraction, policy frameworks by continental and global institutions, local land-use practices and national development agendas.

In addition to the diverse studies on resource extraction mentioned above, one field of study that has attracted considerable academic attention is that of artisanal and small-scale mining, a development predicted by Godoy in 1985. Whereas the focus had predominantly been on situations in which large-scale, industrialised mining occurred (see the examples above, with the exception of Dumett), the dynamics of small-scale mining were given less prominent attention.[4] Yet, artisanal mining was in fact the sphere in which Godoy's antique miner operated. After all, artisanal mining has been an important part of pre-industrial economies all around the world: gold was extensively mined in the Ashanti kingdom for the production of, for example, ornaments and decorations; in Sub-Saharan Africa, extensive trading networks existed based on an exchange of gold from West Africa with salt from the Sahel region; in South East Asia, mining of copper, gold and silver served the production of Buddhas and utensils for the royal families; and the golden wealth and the metallurgical skills of the Aztecs continue to speak to the world's contemporary imagination of these ancient societies. Naturally, artisanal mining is not only an historical fact, but is of crucial importance to the lives of many people in the contemporary world. In 1999, the International Labour Organization (ILO) estimated, for example, that approximately 13 million people were *directly* engaged in artisanal and small-scale mining globally, with the number of those indirectly engaged being many times higher (estimated between 80 million and 100 million). Nowadays, this number is significantly higher, given that already, in the case of gold mining alone, 16 million people directly depend on artisanal and small-scale extraction (Seccatore et al. 2014).

Not surprisingly, given its importance, attention to artisanal and small-scale mining has become substantial (as has the study of extraction in the social sciences in general), covering topics such as mining technologies (Verbrugge and van Wolputte 2015; Arnaldi di Balme and Lanzano 2016), the role of women and gender (Graulau 2001; Werthmann 2009), local imaginaries of the underground (D'Angelo 2014), mobility and migration patterns (de Theije 2014), policy regulations and conflict (Verbrugge 2015), miners' social networks (Walsh 2008; Grätz 2009) and environmental pollution (Veiga and Hinton 2002; Hilson and Monhemius 2006). In addition, also in questions concerning 'development' and poverty alleviation, the role of artisanal mining has been thoroughly analysed and taken up in policy debates (see for example ILO 1999; Hentschel et al. 2003; UN Economic and Social Council 1996). Another significant perspective that has become incorporated in studying artisanal mining is its relation and interaction with other land users, including large-scale industrial miners (Hilson 2002; Aubynn 2009; Luning and Pijpers 2017). This development reflects, among other things, a general trend in studies of mining environments, that is, the increasingly diversified understanding of which actors combine to form what is understood as the mining community.

The Mining Community and Negotiating Cohabitation

Although the idea of the mining community was initially limited to a binary relation between states and companies, as Ballard and Banks (2003) point out, the incorporation of local communities as key players in resource extraction (through the institutionalisation of impact assessments to be conducted by large-scale companies, see Vanclay and Bronstein 1995; O'Faircheallagh 1999) gave rise to a three-legged or triad stakeholder model, consisting of the three central categories of state, corporation and community (Howitt et al. 1996). However, these three categories did not allow for detailed analysis of the complex dynamics that develop in spaces of resource extraction (Clark and Clark 1999) and the concept of the 'mining community' had to be further differentiated, for example by the incorporation of non-governmental organisations (NGOs), characterised as the 'fourth estate', and different agents affiliated to the three principal stakeholder categories (Ballard and Banks 2003: 304), in addition to the aforementioned artisanal mining communities. This expanding and diversified notion of the mining community is not surprising, considering the increased speed with which mining operations develop and the accumulating awareness of extraction's integration into wider social, economic and political dynamics. Moreover, as Ballard and Banks rightly note, 'as a sense of this broader mining community has developed, so too is there an increasing awareness of the internal complexity of what had previously been considered the monolithic entities of community, state, and corporation' (2003: 289). The work of Rajak (2011), which explores the mechanisms of corporate social responsibility and how it is used to accumulate and exercise power, and Welker (2014: 2), who shows how people 'enact corporations in multiple ways, and that these enactments involve struggles over the boundaries, interests, and responsibilities of the corporation', are excellent examples of this increasing awareness.

With the differentiation of different kinds of actors in the mining community, who often have conflicting interests, as well as their internal complexities, more and more attention is also dedicated to how processes of negotiation, for example over access to and control of resources, give shape to the establishment of forms of cohabitation, which can be understood as the ways in which different stakeholders work out ways of cohabiting in a mining area (Panella 2010). Hardin (2011), for example, develops the concept 'concessionary politics' in analysing Central African forest management, especially the competition between conservation and logging practices. This perspective illuminates how 'social and territorial struggles for control of natural resources, labour and knowledge' (Hardin 2011: S115) unfold in the 'microcosm of the logging or mining town' and 'unites widely disparate actors on intimate if unequal terms' (2011: S119). Similarly, the work of Geenen (2016), who analyses gold mining governance practices in Ghana, uses the idea of hybrid governance (one which resonates with Hardin's work), in order to show that negotiations between different groups (she focuses on companies, local and central government, and communities) constantly shift, thereby including or excluding different groups of actors at different points in time. Correspondingly, Luning (2012) details how neoliberal gold exploration in Burkina Faso affects 'relationships among stakehold-

ers, and how stakeholders value, define and redefine their identities'
(2012: 25), showing how interactions between an international exploration company and a local earth-priest in Burkina Faso are embedded
in a wider field of customary and modern authorities. This field, Luning
demonstrates, is marked by contestation, which the company capitalises
on by, for example, replacing 'one authority with another as *the* representative of the local community' (2012: 35; italics in original).

In negotiating forms of cohabitation we thus see how different actors
position and reposition themselves within the mining community in
order to safeguard their interests. Consequently, the focus on cohabitation and on its foundational negotiation processes in particular, provides
an opportunity to see mining operations beyond the 'impact' of mining
and a binary approach to either positive or negative effects. Instead, it
enables a more nuanced perspective on processes of change within
mining environments and acknowledges the agency of different stakeholders, while being sensitive to their power differences. Subsequently,
the way in which these processes are given shape can be fruitfully studied
by a focus on mining encounters, as exemplified in this volume. After
all, these encounters – which may involve staff of mining corporations,
local entrepreneurs, artisanal miners, farmers, politicians, civil servants,
NGOs and various (members of) local communities – are instances in
which processes of cohabitation are negotiated and given shape, and
through which the entanglement of local life worlds and global developments in spaces of resource extraction are made visible.

Besides building upon the rich bodies of literature on resource
extraction, to which we have referred, our approach also takes significant inspiration from Faier and Rofel's (2014) analysis of what they call
'ethnographies of encounter'. These ethnographies, Faier and Rofel argue
(2014: 364) consider how 'culture making occurs through everyday
encounters among members of two or more groups with different
cultural backgrounds and unequally positioned stakes in their relationships'. Moreover, the notion of encounter, brings 'attention to the
interactive and unequal dynamics of power that shape culture making
across relationships of difference' (2014: 364). In the case of transnational
capitalism, which is one of the main domains in which Faier and Rofel
observe an encounters approach, these approaches emphasise 'contingency, unexpected outcomes, and articulations of multiple practices that
make capitalism an ongoing process of creation and destruction rather
than a singular, deterministic structure' (2014: 378). Translating this to
a context of resource extraction, habitually marked by (trans)national
capitalism, we observe that it is through the multiple encounters between
actors – with unequal power positions and different agendas, worldviews

and aims – that resource extraction projects, and their disparate effects, are negotiated, produced and eventually materialise.

ACCELERATED CHANGE SEEN AS OVERHEATING

Not coincidentally, given the (often) conflicting agendas of those actors involved, and the considerable effects of resource extraction on people, the economy and the environment, mining encounters are habitually marked by friction and may result in forms of 'overheating', a phenomenon described as 'unevenly paced change where exogenous and endogenous factors combine to lead to instability, uncertainty and unintended consequences in a broad range of institutions and practices, and contribute to a widely shared feeling of powerlessness and alienation' (Eriksen 2016: 16).

Overheating is not a phenomenon exclusively associated with resource extraction, although this activity does bring together a number of overheating phenomena. Overheating is a far more comprehensive phenomenon, identifiable in many areas, from transportation to media consumption. Across the world, there is a widespread feeling that we humans live in a time of transition, although there is no general agreement, among social scientists or others, as to what kind of transition we are currently experiencing. And, not least, there is no general agreement about to whom attributions of responsibility or blame for the changes should be addressed, and what should be done about their consequences. This is not just about climate change, although that is arguably the most momentous and consequential change humanity is facing unless we change course: it goes without saying that resource extraction is linked with climate change.

Accelerated change can be identified in a number of areas. There are more of us, and each of us is on the average more mobile and active, and has more connections with others – is hooked up to more networks – than ever before. Earlier eras were, without exception, slower eras for the majority of humanity. In this sense, we presently live on an overheated planet. In physics, heat is closely connected to speed, and translated into the language of social science, overheating can be glossed as accelerated change. Moreover, it has long been recognised that the changes brought about by modernity have unintended, often paradoxical consequences, and when changes accelerate, so do the unintentional side effects of changes.

The most striking graphic representation of the processes of change characteristic of the current era is the exponential growth curve (Eriksen 2001). In its most familiar version, it depicts world population growth, brought to the attention of policy makers not least through the Club of Rome's commissioned report *Limits to Growth* (Meadows et al. 1972), which advocated population control and reduced consumption as two of several methods for preventing serious resource scarcity in the future. From a global environmental perspective, the concern expressed by the Club of Rome is easily understandable. From the time we were anatomically modern, it took *homo sapiens* about 200,000 years to reach a population of 1 billion around the year 1800. It subsequently took only a little over 100 years to reach the second billion (achieved in 1920) and less than another 100 years to increase world population from 2 billion to 7 billion. It does not seem likely that it is ecologically and economically feasible to offer those 7 billion people (and global population has not yet peaked) material security and a way of life compatible with the promises of consumerism. Quite the contrary, the scenarios described by activists, politicians and planners include acceptance of widespread poverty, bracing for an ecological catastrophe, promoting population reduction, and/or replacing consumerism with one or several alternative models for the good life.

At the same time, in spite of temporary downturns and slowdowns (including those that are characteristic of the boom and bust cycles of the extractive industries), growth remains near-exponential in a number of realms, and population is not growing nearly as fast as a number of other phenomena. It is trivially true that the proportion of the world's population with access to the internet has grown extremely fast since 1990, since only a few million used the embryonic internet at the time. But even the rapid growth of the online world has accelerated since the turn of the century. As late as 2006, it was estimated that between 1 and 2 per cent of the Sub-Saharan African population (with the exception of South Africa) had reasonably regular access to the internet. By 2015, the proportion was estimated at over 20 per cent (Internet World Stats 2016). The simple explanation is that millions of Africans now have smartphones (which contain numerous mineral resources), with easy access to the web and email.

Numerous other examples could be given to illustrate the processes of change that unfold at a global scale: transnational migration in areas which 'feel the heat' of heightened mobility; the sharply upward pointing growth curve of websites, international organisations (as well as international conferences and workshops), mobile telephones, TV sets, private cars and text messages and the rapid emergence of Facebook (from non-existence in 2003 to about 1.1 billion user accounts ten years later). Or take the enormous increase in energy consumption: In 1820, each of us used, on an average, 20 Gigajoules (GJ) a year. Roughly two centuries later, the figure is 80 GJ, chiefly owing to the technology making it possible to exploit fossil fuels on a large scale. The unintended consequences are well known, with pollution and environmental deterioration being the most visible and subject to immediate experience. The long-term, large-scale effects, more difficult to observe and understand, are changes in the global climate.

The contemporary expansion of the extractive industries is simultaneously a cause and a result of accelerated change and overheating. The increased demand for fossil fuels, metals and precious stones concurrently indicates global economic growth, spurs it, *and* contributes to, for example, climate change on the global scale, the growth of boomtowns locally, heated conflicts between farmers and miners, competition between corporations and local controversies over landownership and mineral rights. Indeed, mining could be said to be the quintessential overheating phenomenon, crystallising many strands of global accelerated change and its contradictions, from migration and hopes and desires for the future, to new inequalities to environmental degradation, in one compact packet of socio-material reality.

Overheating and the Extractive Industries

In the extractive industries processes of accelerated change and overheating come to the fore prominently in extraction's multiple temporalities (cf. D'Angelo and Pijpers 2018), not least in its boom and bust cycles.

The past two decades of global gold mining provide an excellent example of these boom and bust dynamics. Due to a prolonged period of global financial instability and geopolitical uncertainty, gold prices rose steeply from 2006 to 2012, thereby spurring a drastic increase in gold mining operations. Yet, with gold prices going down again afterwards, the number of operations also seriously diminished, a trend characteristically described by the CEO of a gold exploration company in Ghana who claimed that 'with gold at US$ 2,000 an ounce, the whole of Ghana is going to be turned over; at $250 all projects go into mothballs' (Luning and Pijpers 2017: 764). The case of Project Phoenix in Southern California, as discussed by D'Angelo and Pijpers (2018), provides another illustration of the fluidity and boom and bust character of mining operations. Having been one of the primary sources of rare earth minerals globally since the 1960s (Klinger 2015) the Mountain Pass Mines operated by Molycorp closed down in 2002 due to, first, an environmental disaster which caused a temporary stop in production and, second, the drop of global market prices for rare earths due to the increase in Chinese rare earth minerals production (Castor 2008). However, as the market slowly recovered, the operation eventually reopened in 2010 under the name Project Phoenix (Wiens 2012). In artisanal mining too, we see similar boom and bust dynamics, with periods of high intensity of extraction, being alternated with 'slower' and 'cooler' periods; a dynamic which is related to, among other things, developments in the market price of mined resources, as well as competing resources (such as certain cash-crops), the influence of the seasons (with mining being relatively difficult in the wet season) or the discovery of rich deposits and the subsequent influx of artisanal miners in these potentially rich sites.

Moreover, the multiple temporalities (cf. D'Angelo and Pijpers 2018) at play do not always align. Leonard (2016), for example, shows in the context of oil production in Chad, there was a two-speed complication causing problems in ensuring that oil production would contribute to development: the highly accelerated speed with which the oil industry developed its facilities, started production and generated revenues, did not match the speed of government institutions in trying to develop the appropriate infrastructure for managing these oil revenues. While the diverging speeds of activities and actors in one particular moment may be out of sync or even conflicting, so are the practices and effects of extraction not necessarily occurring at the same moment. A point in case is the abandoned Giant Mine in Yellowknife, Northwest Territories, Canada. This mine used to be an 'emblem of prosperity' in the area and a 'visible reminder of the city's [Yellowknife's] origins as a gold mining town' (Sandlos and Keeling 2016: 7). However, more recently the 'Giant Mine has also come to symbolise the destructive long-term environmental impacts of mining due to the arsenic contamination the mine had produced' (2016: 7). Pollution and contamination are excellent examples of the 'slow violence' (Nixon 2011; Sandlos and Keeling 2016) that extraction can cause. Correspondingly, Sandlos and Keeling's example of slow violence illustrates how positive effects can be succeeded by negative ones. The effects of extraction are indeed not limited to the moment of extraction itself: expectations may arise well before extraction takes place (see Weszkalnys 2008) and local communities living in the surroundings of former extraction sites may continue to experience the legacies of closed mines, while perhaps anticipating their reopening (see, in addition to Sandlos and Keeling 2016, Halvaksz 2008).

In sum, the extractive industries are characterised by diverging processes of acceleration and deceleration, including the (sometimes sudden) emergence and closure of extraction operations. These movements may cause significant changes in the life worlds and environments of people living in sites where extraction emerges or departs, as mentioned earlier in this introduction. In some cases, the movements, and the multifaceted effects of extraction in general, may contain over-heating phenomena, including experiences of instability, uncertainty and a feeling of powerlessness and alienation (Eriksen 2016). What is of particular interest is when, why and how overheating phenomena emerge, as they can be observed almost everywhere in the world, but in different domains and expressed very differently due to variations in local circumstances, both material and social and cultural. How are overheating responses formulated and to whom can they be addressed? Subsequently, crucial questions are what movements trigger overheat-ing: is it acceleration or deceleration, the opening or closure of a mining operation? The slow violence of contamination discussed above suggests that overheating effects may occur, or intensify, particularly when acceleration stops and mines are abandoned. Moreover, one could ask whether it is the movement itself that triggers overheating or whether it is people's potential exclusion from (influencing) these movements and the subsequent changes, as Pijpers' (2016) research on the reopening of an iron ore mine in Sierra Leone suggests. These questions can be studied by focusing on specific encounters. This allows us to see why extractive practices create overheating in some cases, but not in others. It also enables us to detail what it is exactly that brings about overheated mining encounters: unrealistically high expectations, the change of the environment, loss of livelihood opportunities, challenges faced by people to get access to employment opportunities, the shifting positions of local power holders, resistance to the opening of a mine or the closure of a mine where continuation was hoped for or awareness of environmental contamination surfaces.

MINING ENCOUNTERS ACROSS THE WORLD: ETHNOGRAPHIES OF RESOURCE EXTRACTION

As shown in some detail above, the use of the concepts *mining encounters* and *overheating* allows us to think of spaces of resource extraction (minerals, as well as oil and gas) as spaces of accelerated change, charac-terised by fast-changing life worlds, an increased density of connections, growing stakes, and multiplying challenges and opportunities. Within this fluid and multifaceted environment, the emphasis on encounters allows us to be sensitive to the multiple and diverging interests and stakes within these rapidly changing environments, as well as to the ways in which different stakeholders position themselves vis-à-vis others and manoeuvre within a web of connections and relations. Moreover, this emphasis on encounters allows for studies of mining that approach processes of negotiation with regard to resource extraction through the study of specific events, people and discourse, while connecting them to larger-scale processes. In this volume, we bring together a wide variety of mining encounters, precisely to be able to study larger processes in different localised contexts, indeed to study the specific local articulations of global phenomena like natural resource extraction.

The chapters in this volume contribute in different ways to this debate, but all draw upon the richness of different local contexts, while sharing the approach of overheating and encounters. The first two chapters take up the question of responsibility for conflict-ridden mining environments. While Alex Golub (chapter 2) draws our attention to the position, role and responsibility of the anthropologist in the context of encounters that are often fraught with inequality, thereby developing an ethics of mining encounters, Catherine Coumans (chapter 3) discusses the discourse of remedy and responsibility generated by an international apparatus consisting of companies, NGOs, media, academics and United Nations (UN) bodies. These chapters thus highlight the discourses of responsibility that are generated through the encounters between different stakeholders. Subsequently, the chapters by Sabine Luning and Marjo de Theije (chapter 4), Robert Pijpers (chapter 5) and Kim de Rijke (chapter 6), take a more spatial approach, showing how the negotiation processes between different actors result in particular forms of spatial governance. Equally spatially grounded, Patrik Oskarsson and Nikas Kindo's chapter (chapter 7) analyses how infrastructural politics emerge over the extraction and especially transport of coal in India. Interestingly, the coal sector under study in this chapter brings together various scales of coal extraction. Lorenzo D'Angelo (chapter 8) brings an important temporal perspective to the discussion of mining encounters. His chapter emphasises the temporal aspects of mining and develops the concept of 'temporal encounters', which enables D'Angelo to look at artisanal diamond mining as a transformative practice that accelerates the encounter between a variety of rhythms and temporalities. Lastly, Kesküla's chapter (chapter 9) brings us back from the artisanal to the large scale, and details the mining encounters between a Kazakhstani coal mining community and an international mining company that privatised the mines in 1996. Her analysis draws our attention to the double-bind in which different employees with relations and responsibilities to both communities and the mine find themselves.

* * *

All these chapters, situated in different regional and thematic contexts, bring new perspectives and insights to the core questions that this volume discusses. How do processes of resource extraction materialise?

Which stakeholders emerge, become dominant or marginalised? How does resource extraction transform landscapes? Why do extractive projects so often emerge as both promises and problems? And for whom does resource extraction pose new challenges or possibilities? Which stakeholders propagate what kind of views on extraction and how do they position these views in a political landscape? How does resource extraction give rise to a highly socialised infrastructural politics? In a fast-changing world, where resources and their extraction are key to growth and development, as well as environmental and social disasters, understanding the processes of change through the numerous encounters of people with different views and interests is crucial. Moreover, the question is not just about who wins and who loses, but about how and why some win and others lose. In addressing these questions, this volume aims to shed more light on how different kinds of mining encounters bring about forms of accelerated change, be it in the realm of environment, economy, politics and/or social identity, and how struggles over access, power and control are given shape. Through this focus on mining encounters we highlight the complex nature of resource extraction in an increasingly connected world.

REFERENCES

Alder, C., D. Large and R.S. de Oliveira. 2009. *China Returns to Africa: A Visiting Power and a Continent Embrace*. New York: Columbia University Press.

Appel, H. 2012. Walls and White Elephants: Oil Extraction, Responsibility, and Infrastructural Violence in Equatorial Guinea. *Ethnography* 13(4): 439–65.

Arnaldi di Balme, L. and C. Lanzano. 2016. Mud, Gold and Women. Leftovers, Value Creation and Changing Relations of Production in Artisanal Mining (Burkina Faso). Paper presented at the workshop 'Artisanal and Small-scale Mining in Africa: Socio-economic Change and New Research Perspectives', Nordica Africa Institute, Uppsala 10–11 November.

Aubynn, A. 2009. Sustainable Solution or a Marriage of Inconvenience? The Coexistence of Large-scale Mining and Artisanal and Small-scale Mining on the Abosso Goldfields Concession in Western Ghana. *Resources Policy* 34: 64–70.

Auty, R.M. 1994. Industrial Policy Reform in Six Large Newly Industrializing Countries: The Resource Curse Thesis. *World Development* 22(1): 11–26.

Ballard, C. and G. Banks. 2003. Resource Wars: The Anthropology of Mining. *Annual Review of Anthropology* 32: 287–313.

Batty, F. .2013. Enacting the Mines and Minerals Act (2009) of Sierra Leone: Actors, Interests and Outcomes. *African Studies* 72(3): 353–74.

Bebbington, A., L. Hinojosa, D.H. Bebbington, M.L. Burneo and X. Warnaars. 2008. Contention and Ambiguity: Mining and the Possibilities of Development. *Development and Change* 39: 887–914.

Brautigam, D. 2009. *The Dragon's Gift: The Real Story of China in Africa*. Oxford: Oxford University Press.

Bryceson, D.F. and J.B. Jønsson. 2014. Mineralizing Africa and Artisanal Mining's Democratizing Influence. In D.F. Bryceson, E. Fisher, J.B. Jønsson and R. Mwaipopo (eds), *Mining and Social Transformation in Africa: Mineralizing and Democratizing Trends in Artisanal Production*. Abingdon:: Routledge, pp. 1–22.

Castor, S.B. 2008. Rare Earth Deposits of North America. *Resource Geology* 58(4): 337–47.

Clark, A.L. and J.C. Clark. 1999. The New Reality of Mineral Development: Social and Cultural Issues in Asia and Pacific Nations. *Resources Policy* 25: 189–96.

Coumans, C. 2011. Occupying Spaces Created by Conflict: Anthropologists, Development NGOs, Responsible Investment, and Mining. *Current Anthropology* 52(S3): S29–S43.

D'Angelo, L. 2014. Who Owns the Diamonds? The Occult Economy of Diamond Mining in Sierra Leone. *Africa: The Journal of the International African Institute* 84(2): 269–93.

D'Angelo, L. and R.J. Pijpers. 2018. Mining Temporalities: An Overview. *The Extractive Industries and Society* 5 (2): 215–22 (special issue, L. D'Angelo and R.J. Pijpers, eds, *Mining Temporalities: Extractive Industries and the Politics of Time*, https://doi.org/10.1016/j.exis.2018.02.005).

de Theije, M.E.M. 2014. Small-scale Gold Mining and Trans-frontier Commerce on the Lawa River. In E.B. Carlin, I. Léglise, B. Migge and P.B. Tjon Sie Fat (eds), *In and Out of Suriname: Language, Mobility and Identity* (Caribbean series). Leiden: Brill.

Dolan, C. and D. Rajak. 2016. Introduction. Toward the Anthropology of Corporate Social Responsibility. In C. Dolan and D. Rajak (eds), *The Anthropology of Corporate Social Responsibility*. New York: Berghahn Books, pp. 1–28.

Dumett, R.E. 1998. *El Dorado in West Africa*. Athens, OH: Ohio University Press and Oxford: James Currey.

Emel, J., M.T. Huber and M.H. Makene. 2011. Extracting Sovereignty: Capital, Territory, and Gold Mining in Tanzania. *Political Geography* 30: 70–79.

Epstein, A.L. 1958. *Politics in an Urban African Community*. Manchester: Manchester University Press.

Eriksen, T.H. 2001. *Tyranny of the Moment: Fast and Slow Time in the Information Age*. London: Pluto Press.

—— 2016. *Overheating: The Anthropology of Accelerated Change*. London: Pluto Press.

Faier, L. and L. Rofel. 2014. Ethnographies of Encounter. *Annual Review of Anthropology* 43(1): 363–77.

Falk Moore, S. 1994. *Anthropology and Africa: Changing Perspectives on a Changing Scene*. Charlottesville, VA: University of Virginia Press.

Ferguson, J. 1999. *Expectations of Modernity: Myths and Meanings of Urban Life on the Zambian Copperbelt*. Berkeley: University of California Press.

—— 2005. Seeing Like an Oil Company: Space, Security and Global Capital in Neoliberal Africa. *American Anthropologists* 107(3): 377–82.

Ferry, E.E. and M. Limbert. 2008. *Timely Assets: The Politics of Resources and their Temporalities.* Santa Fe, NM: School of Advanced Research Press.

Geenen, S. 2015. *African Artisanal Mining from the Inside Out: Access, Norms and Power in Congo's Gold Sector.* Abingdon: Routledge.

—— 2016. Hybrid Governance in Mining Concessions in Ghana. IOB Working Paper/2016.05. Antwerp: Institute of Development Policy, University of Antwerp.

Gewald, J.B. 2009. People, Mines and Cars: Towards a Revision of Zambian History, 1890–1930. In K. van Walraven, S. Luning and J.B. Gewald (eds), *The Speed of Change: Motor Vehicles and People in Africa, 1890–2000.* Leiden: Brill, pp. 21–47.

Gilberthorpe, E. and D. Rajak. 2017. The Anthropology of Extraction: Critical Perspectives on the Resource Curse. *Journal of Development Studies* 53(2): 186–204.

Gluckman, M. 1961. Anthropological Problems Arising from the African Industrial Revolution. In A. Southall (ed.), *Social Change in Modern Africa.* London: Oxford University Press.

Godoy, R.A. 1985. Mining: Anthropological Perspectives. *Annual Review of Anthropology* 14: 199–217.

Golub, A. 2014. *Leviathans at the Gold Mine: Creating Indigenous and Corporate Actors in Papua New Guinea.* Durham, NC: Duke University Press.

Grätz, T. 2009. Moralities, Risk and Rules in West African Artisanal Gold Mining Communities: A Case Study of Northern Benin. *Resources Policy* 34(1–2): 12–17.

Graulau, J. 2001. Peasant Mining Production as a Development Strategy: The Case of Women in Gold Mining in the Brazilian Amazon. *European Review of Latin American and Caribbean Studies* 71: 71–106.

Halvaksz, J.A. 2008. Whose Closure? Appearances, Temporality and Mineral Extraction in Papua New Guinea. *Journal of the Royal Anthropological Institute* 14(1): 21–37.

Hardin, R. 2011. Concessionary Politics: Property, Patronage, and Political Rivalry in Central African Forest Management. *Current Anthropology* 52(3): S113–S125.

Hentschel, T., F. Hruschka and M. Priester. 2003. *Artisanal and Small-scale Mining: Challenges and Opportunities.* London: International Institute for Environment and Development and World Business Council for Sustainable Development.

Hilson, G. 2002. An Overview of Land Use Conflicts in Mining Communities. *Land Use Policy* 19: 65–73.

Hilson, G. and A.J. Monhemius. 2006. Alternatives to Cyanide in the Gold Mining Industry: What Prospects for the Future? *Journal of Cleaner Production* 14: 1158–67.

Howitt R., J. Connell and P. Hirsch. 1996. Resources, Nations and Indigenous Peoples. In R. Howitt, J. Connell and P. Hirsch (eds), *Resources, Nations and*

Indigenous Peoples: Case Studies from Australasia, Melanesia and Southeast Asia. Melbourne: Oxford University Press, pp. 1–30.

ILO (International Labour Organization). 1999. *Social and Labour Issues in Small-scale Mines*. Report TMSSM/1999. Geneva: International Labour Organization Office.

Kirsch, S. 2014. Mining Capitalism: The Relationship between Corporations and Their Critics. Berkeley: University of California Press.

Klinger, J.M. 2015. A Historical Geography of Rare Earth Elements: From Discovery to the Atomic Age. *The Extractive Industries and Society* 2: 572–80.

Lahiri-Dutt, R. 2015. The Feminization of Mining. *Geography Compass* 9(9): 523–41.

Leonard, L. 2016. *Life in the Time of Oil: A Pipeline and Poverty in Chad*. Bloomington, IN: Indiana University Press.

Luning, S. 2012. Processing Promises of Gold: A Minefield of Company–Community Relations in Burkina Faso. *Africa Today* 58(3): 23–39.

—— 2018. Mining Temporalities: Future Perspectives. *The Extractive Industries and Society* 5(2): 281–6 (special issue, L. D'Angelo and R.J. Pijpers, eds, *Mining Temporalities: Extractive Industries and the Politics of Time*, https://doi.org/10.1016/j.exis.2018.02.005).

Luning, S. and R.J. Pijpers. 2017. Governing Access to Gold in Ghana: In-depth Geopolitics on Mining Concession. *Africa* 87(4): 758–79.

Meadows, D.H., D.L. Meadows, J. Randers and W.W. Behrens. 1972. *The Limits to Growth*. New York: Universe Books.

Mitchell, J.C. 1956. *The Kalela Dance: Aspects of Social Relationships among Urban Africans in Northern Rhodesia*. Rhodes-Livingstone Papers, No. 27. Manchester: Manchester University Press.

Mitchell, T. 2011. *Carbon Democracy: Political Power in the Age of Oil*. London: Verso.

Nash, J. 1993. *We Eat the Mines and the Mines Eat Us*. New York: Columbia University Press.

Nixon, R. 2011. *Slow Violence and the Environmentalism of the Poor*. Cambridge, MA: Harvard University Press.

O'Faircheallaigh, C. 2002. *A New Approach to Policy Evaluation: Indigenous People and Mining*. Aldershot: Ashgate.

Panella, C. 2010. Gold Mining in West Africa – Worlds of Debts and Sites of Co-habitation. In C. Panella (ed.), *Worlds of Debts: Gold Mining in West Africa as an Interdisciplinary Field of Study*. Amsterdam: Rozenberg Publishers, pp. 1–14.

Pijpers. R.J. 2016. Mining, Hope and Turbulent Times: Locating Accelerated Change in Rural Sierra Leone. *History & Anthropology* 27(5): 504–20.

—— 2018. Navigating Uncertainty: Large-scale Mining and Micro-politics in Sierra Leone. PhD Dissertation, University of Oslo.

Rajak, D. 2006. The Gift of CSR: Power and the Pursuit of Responsibility in the Mining Industry. In W. Visser, M. McIntosh and C. Middleton (eds), *Corporate Citizenship in Africa. Lessons from the Past, Paths to the Future*. Sheffield: Greenleaf Publishing, pp. 190–200.

—— 2011. *In Good Company: An Anatomy of Corporate Social Responsibility*. Stanford, CA: Stanford University Press.

Richardson, T. and G. Weszkalnys. 2014. Resource Materialities: New Anthropological Perspectives on Natural Resource Environments. Introduction. *Anthropological Quarterly* 87(1): 5–30.

Sandlos, J. and A. Keeling. 2016. Toxic Legacies, Slow Violence, and Environmental Injustice at Giant Mine, Northwest Territories. *Northern Review* 42: 7–21.

Seccatore, J., M. Veiga, C. Origliasso, T. Marin and G. De Tomi. 2014. An Estimation of the Artisanal Small-scale Production of Gold in the World. *Science of the Total Environment* 496: 662–7.

Spiegel, S.J. 2009. Resource Policies and Small-scale Gold Mining in Zimbabwe. *Resources Policy* 34: 39–44.

Taussig, M. 1980. *The Devil and Commodity Fetishism in South America*. Chapel Hill: University of North Carolina Press.

Teschner, B. 2013. How You Start Matters: A Comparison of Gold Fields' Tarkwa and Damang Mines and Their Divergent Relationships with Local Small-scale miners in Ghana. *Resources Policy* 38: 332–40.

UN Economic and Social Council. 1996. *Developments in Small-scale Mining*. Report of the Secretary-General, E/C.7/1996/9 (https://documents-dds-ny.un.org/doc/UNDOC/GEN/N96/071/83/PDF/N9607183.pdf?OpenElement).

Vanclay F. and D. Bronstein (eds) 1995. *Environmental and Social Impact Assessment*. Chichester: Wiley.

Veiga, M.M. and J.J. Hinton. 2002. Abandoned Artisanal Gold Mines in the Brazilian Amazon: A Legacy of Mercury Pollution. *Natural Resources Forum* 26: 15–26.

Verbrugge, B. 2015. Decentralization, Institutional Ambiguity, and Mineral Resource Conflict in Mindanao, Philippines. *World Development* 67: 449–60.

Verbrugge, H. and S. van Wolputte. 2015. Just Picking Up Stones: Gender and Technology in a Small-scale Gold Mining Site. In A. Coles, L. Gray and J. Momsen (eds), *A Handbook on Gender and Development*. New York: Routledge, pp. 173–82.

Walsh, A. 2008. The Grift: Getting Burned in the Northern Malagasy Sapphire Trade. In K.E. Browne and B.L. Milgram (ed.), *Economics and Morality: Anthropological Approaches*. Lanham, MD: AltaMira Press.

Welker, M. 2014. *Enacting the Corporation: An American Mining Firm in Post-authoritarian Indonesia*. Berkeley: University of California Press.

Werthmann, K. 2009. Working in a Boom-town: Female Perspectives on Gold-mining in Burkina Faso. *Resources Policy* 34: 18–23.

Weszkalnys, G. 2008. Hope and Oil: Expectations in São Tomé e Príncipe. *Review of African Political Economy* 35(3): 473–82.

—— 2016. A Doubtful Hope: Resource Affect in a Future Oil Economy. *Journal of the Royal Anthropological Institute* 22: 127–46.

Wiens, K. 2012. A Visit to the Only American Mine for Rare Earth Metals. *The Atlantic*, 21 February.

Wilks, I. 1982. Wangara, Akan and Portuguese in the Fifteenth and Sixteenth Centuries. 1. The Matter of Bitu. *Journal of African History* 23(3): 333–49.

——1993. *Forests of Gold: Essays on the Akan and the Kingdom of Asante*. Athens, OH: Ohio University Press.

Wilson, G. 1941. *An Essay on the Economics of Detribalization in Northern Rhodesia*. Rhodes-Livingstone Paper No. 5. Livingstone, Northern Rhodesia: Rhodes-Livingstone Institute.

NOTES

1. The term 'resource curse' was coined by Auty (1994) as a container concept for the negative consequences of resource extraction, with a main emphasis on growing inequality and social unrest, not – as would seem more relevant today – the ecological implications of resource extraction.

2. Interestingly, the mining frontier in Dumett's work on Ghana is informed by the presence of foreign actors, notwithstanding that gold mining has long played a role across the Sahara (Wilks 1982, 1983) and one can therefore hardly speak of a frontier (for a discussion of and critique on the concept of frontier see Luning 2018).

3. The Rhodes-Livingstone Institute in Northern Rhodesia (Zambia) was founded in 1937 by Godfrey Wilson. In the early 1940s, Max Gluckman succeeded Wilson as director, establishing a research programme focused on studying social change in British colonial Africa. Gluckman was also the link between the Rhodes-Livingstone Institute and what would become known as the Manchester School as he founded the Department of Anthropology at Manchester University in 1947. Under his direction, this department focused on studying social change in situations of social problems, such as those under colonisation.

4. Mining occurs at different scales and in different ways, ranging from large-scale industrial mining, habitually targeting the ore deposit by either open-cut or deep-shaft mining, to artisanal and small-scale mining – labour-intensive and low-technology resource extraction and processing – targeting both ore deposits directly, but often also searching for alluvial sources (sources that have been transported from their origin to new locations by water).

2. From Allegiance to Connection

Structural Injustice, Scholarly Norms and the Anthropological Ethics of Mining Encounters

Alex Golub

There is no end to the intricate chain of responsibility and guilt that the pursuit of even the most arcane social research involves.

—Cora DuBois

Thomas Hylland Eriksen (2016) and the other members of the over-heating project have produced an ambitious vision of the contemporary world. In this chapter I seek to develop and extend their vision of clashing scales, runaway processes and contemporary double-binds by applying their model to the anthropology of 'mining encounters' (Pijpers and Eriksen, this volume). What are the ethical responsibilities of anthropologists who study mining encounters? What affirmative duties do we, as professionals, have to the stakeholders who are our research respondents? Are we not ourselves stakeholders? In this chapter I attempt to answer these questions by developing the groundwork for a secular, liberal ethics which anthropologists and other scholars can use to explore these issues in our contemporary overheated world.

In proposing how we might develop a robust professional ethics of mining encounters, I am not seeking to describe the ethical conduct of participant observation (Lederman 2013; Fluehr-Lobban 2013), to demonstrate the scientific credibility of participatory action anthropology (Johnson 2010), to retheorise fieldwork as a form of connectivity (Faubion and Marcus 2010), to delineate the conditions of grievability (Butler 2009) or to do an anthropology of everyday ethics (Lambek et al. 2105). Rather, this chapter hopes to locate a space between these other, adjacent literatures in which the ethical dilemmas of anthropology can be addressed.

What's more, this chapter does more than just fill a niche in an under-theorised area. I will argue that mining encounters have broad implications for the ethics of anthropology because they are just one species of a much larger form of social process which anthropologists study. Mining encounters, I suggest, represent a sort of 'elementary form' of anthropology's ethical situation because of their scale and indeterminacy. Known variously as 'structural violence' or 'structural injustice', these processes have features which make moral deliberation difficult, even as they make it necessary. I argue that creating an ethics of mining encounters forces us to understand how we can conceptualise harm when we think in terms of processes, not actors. They ask us to think against – rather than with – the corporate form. And they force us to discuss responsibility in the context of large-scale processes when our moral language encourages us to focus on the individual person and the discrete act.

In this chapter I will argue that an anthropology of mining encounters needs an explicit account of scholarly responsibilities. I will discuss the parameters we might use to deliberate about what those duties will be, and I will discuss how norms external to the discipline inform the formation of professional ethics. In particular, I will draw on Iris Marion Young's 'social connection model' of justice and demonstrate how it gives us empirical and ethical purchase on mining encounters. Drawing on Young, I will argue that we need to shift from an 'allegiance' model of ethics to a 'social connection' model of ethics. Existing approaches to the ethics of mining encounters, I claim, equate ethical behaviour with alignment to one group of stakeholders or another. The social connection model I discuss here, on the other hand, asks not: 'Which stakeholder ought I ally myself with?' but rather 'How can I make the social processes surrounding mining encounters more just?' My goal is to conceive responsibility as an ongoing duty to make existing structural social processes more just, not (or, 'not only') a judgement of guilt regarding a single action done in the past by a single actor. The chapter does not enumerate a set of duties for anthropologists, but rather suggests a set of parameters which anthropologists should use in the future to consider their own situations and, I hope, eventually develop a robust disciplinary ethics.

MINING IN PAPUA NEW GUINEA AS A LEAPING OFF POINT FOR AN ETHICS OF MINING ENCOUNTERS

The sort of mining encounter I wish to address is relatively specific: large-scale corporate mining projects and their relationships with other stakeholders, especially communities which host the mine. I am inspired by my own history with the mining industry, where large-scale mines such as Bougainville (Lasslett 2014), Ok Tedi (Kirsch 2014), Porgera (Golub 2014) and Lihir (Bainton 2010) have been key parts of unjust social situations, including state crimes, environmental pollution and human rights abuses.

There have been roughly two ethical approaches to the study of mining encounters in Papua New Guinea. Some anthropologists, such as Stuart Kirsch, see mining as a 'harm industry' in which 'profit is predicated on negative environmental impacts and risks to human health' (Kirsch 2014: 266) and 'harm is part and parcel of their normal functioning' (Kirsch and Benson 2010: 461). For Kirsch, and many others, the only reasonable approach in such a situation is an engaged scholarship which combines anthropology and activism.

Others, such as the Centre for Social Responsibility for Mining (CSRM) at the University of Queensland, feel it is important to 'work with companies, communities and governments in mining regions all over the world to improve social performance and deliver better outcomes for companies and communities' (CSRM website). Here, the proper role of the anthropologist is collaboration with all stakeholders – including corporations – and active engagement in, rather than protest against, mining development. This position can be described as instrumentalist, in that it sees anthropology as a means to an end and is willing to be active from 'within' mining encounters.

Colin Filer has labelled these the 'radical' and 'moderate' positions: the 'radical' position 'assumes a radical and irreconcilable opposition of interest between strong and weak stakeholders' and anthropologists who hold it seek to mobilise 'opposition to the main source of this community's oppression or disadvantage by "advocating" their cause before some kind of global jury ... generally identified with a middle-class "environmental lobby" in the "developed countries"' (Filer 1999: 90). In contrast, Filer argues that a 'moderate' approach (which he himself holds) takes 'the position of the moderator, the mediator, the negotiator' and 'prefers a pluralistic conception of the policy process' in which the anthropologist 'function[s] as a messenger whose messages are justified primarily by the contribution which they make to various kinds of "agreement" over the terms and conditions of the development process' (Filer 1999: 90).

More recently, Ballard and Banks note that those who chose to collaborate with mining companies are often criticised for choosing 'an illusory neutrality, which states and corporations are best positioned to exploit' (2003: 306). There is probably a lot of truth to this claim. It would be better to describe these positions as an 'externalist' versus 'internalist' approach. The distinction here is not so much between the intensity of involvement – 'moderate' or 'radical' commitments – as it is a choice between different stakeholders. The 'radical' position recognises mining conflicts as political conflicts in which one inevitably aligns one side or another – and in general, with grassroots stakeholders rather than large-scale mining companies. The 'moderate' view claims that the political conflicts of mining encounters are not so intense as to inevitably force the anthropologist to align with one stakeholder against the other. But this 'illusory neutrality', as Ballard and Banks put it, often means a willingness to pursue change from 'inside' powerful stakeholders such as the government and corporations. At the heart of this debate, then, is an allegiance model of ethics: anthropologists consider the substance of ethical debate to involve a choice of collaboration and solidarity with one set of stakeholders over and against another set.

Filer has noted that whether anthropologists adopt 'radical' or 'moderate' positions will depend on the unique nature of the mining encounter they find themselves in, and he argued that 'it is necessary for the discipline to develop something akin to a "code of practice", whereby the necessity or desirability of movements between the radical and moderate position can also be negotiated, within particular political settings' (Filer 1999: 89). Indeed, in their 2003 review article on mining, Ballard and Banks note only that 'the ethics of engagement will vary considerably from one mine site to another, over time at the same site, and from one perspective to the next within a project' (Ballard and Banks 2003: 306). However, so far this is a nettle that few have been able to grasp. We need a robust ethics of mining that will allow us to ask: Why will it vary? How will it vary? What are the parameters that will cause ethical responsibilities to alter from one mining encounter to the next? In order to move beyond the assertion that our ethical stance depends on our circumstances, we need a concrete account of how and why the dynamics of mining encounters shape our ethical choices.

PROBLEMS OF ALLEGIANCE AND LIABILITY

Many anthropologists have made personal decisions to align themselves with actors in mining encounters. In the Papua New Guinea case, for instance, one can find scholars who have worked on behalf of grassroots communities (Kirsch 2014) as well as for mining companies and the government (Goldman 2007). And, to be sure, there are many mining encounters in which no moral dilemmas are raised, either because the anthropologist entangled in them has a strong personal moral sensibility, or because the mining encounter's moral contours are clear and straightforward, or for other reasons. But the simple fact that some people have moral clarity regarding mining ethics does not mean that we can escape the task of theorising mining ethics.

First, many anthropologists who study mining encounters experience a pressing sense of moral immediacy combined with an inability to determine what, specifically, they should do about it. There may not be a clear moral intuition about what to do with the mining encounters one encounters, merely a sense that something must be done. In situations which are both fraught and ambivalent, researchers (especially junior researchers) need guidance. Second, these questions are important enough that they should not be left to the intuitions of individual researchers. Rather, anthropologists should make their decisions in light of a robust, widely shared scholarly ethics about responsibility in mining encounters.

The concept of responsibility has a long history which, in philosophy, centres around questions of free will and determinism (Appiah 2003: 365–77). Anthropologists and social thinkers have also addressed the concept of responsibility (see reviews in Hage 2012; Trnka and Trundle 2014). Most secular liberal theories of responsibility (that is to say, the hegemonic form of ethics globally) make the individual the locus of responsibility. One is responsible for actions that one has willed, not ones done by others or over which you had no conscious control. The individual agent, then, is central to an account of ethics.

The allegiance model draws on this tradition of theorising responsibility. However, such an approach is, in general, insufficient to ground an anthropological ethics of mining encounters because it relies on an imaginative world populated by what I have called 'leviathans' (Golub 2014) – a world in which broader social processes are reified as action taken by individual (but collective), agentive actors like 'the state' or 'customary landowners'. Such an approach operated with what Iris Marion Young (2006: 115) has called the 'liability' model of responsibility, which stresses the culpability of an agentive individual. In reality, mining encounters feature agency distributed across actors, processes where causality is difficult to discern, institutional forms that deflect accountability, and scenarios that run counter to taken-for-granted narratives of political conflict.

According to Young, the liability model of moral responsibility is inadequate because it requires 'that we trace a direct relationship between the action of an identifiable person or group and a harm' (2006: 115). But often, for instance in mining encounters, 'injustice consists in the *way* they [structures] constrain and enable, and how these constraints and enablements expand or contract individuals' opportunities' (2006: 114). As a result, Young claims that 'identification of the wrongs that individual actors perpetuate ... needs to be supplemented with an account of how macro-social processes encourage such wrongs, and why they are widespread and repeated' (2006: 115). Liability models, on the other hand, isolate responsibility in the individual rather than in macro-scale social processes, assume that background conditions do not favour some actors over others, and are 'backwards looking' – that is to say, 'the harm or circumstance for which we seek to hold agents responsible is usually an isolatable action or event that has reached a terminus' (Young 2006: 121) and on which the individual actor is judged. Such a view, she argues, equates responsibility with guilt.

This liability model is inadequate to the study of mining encounters for several reasons. First, mining encounters often do not feature actors with a sufficiently coherent identity such that they can bear responsibility for their actions. On the surface, narratives of mining encounters appear to involve agentive actors such as corporations, tribes, non-governmental organisations (NGOs) and so forth. These leviathans appear at first to be responsibility-bearing agents. But in fact, this is not the case. Like many social processes, mining encounters do not involve 'a world of socio-cultural billiard balls, coursing on a global billiard table' (Wolf 1982: 16). The leviathans in mining encounters are not externally bounded or internally homogeneous. In fact, as a number of authors have demonstrated, corporate forms are construed as part of a political process, not an entity that engages in it (see Welker et al. 2011 and other papers in the same special issue).

This is not a new insight. Ballard and Banks argue that there has been 'an increasing awareness of the internal complexity of what had previously been considered the monolithic entities of community, state, and corporation' (2003: 289), and that as a result traditional triad stakeholder models of state, company and community are no longer adequate for understanding mining encounters. At the same time, they argue that contemporary mining – what Pijpers and Eriksen (this volume) would call 'mining in our overheated world' – has introduced a 'new global cast of agents and a novel range of interconnected locations' (Ballard and Banks 2003: 289). And yet, this is an insight that social scientists are always at risk of losing because it gainsays our everyday assumptions that corporate actors are easily reckoned with, ethically and empirically. Thus, for instance, one popular documentary (Bakan 2003) treats corporations as schizophrenic – a diagnosis which buys their coherent identity only by misrecognising their inherent instability as a form of mental pathology.

When leviathans are sufficiently solidary to act as singular agents, their internal organisation often serves to diffuse responsibility. As Robert Jackall (1988) has shown, bureaucracies (in this case mining companies) push decisions up the chain of command even as responsibility for actions is pushed down. This is a result of the clashing scales which Eriksen (2016) discusses. A liability model of responsibility relies on a clear causal connection between an individual's willed act and a caused effect. But the spatial, temporal and causal scale of mining encounters often involves processes where cause – and sometimes even effect! – can be hard to discern. They feature 'slow motion disasters' of environment and social change whose beginning is hard to determine and whose author is hard to discern. It takes considerable work, for instance, to determine the causal nexus that results in large-scale, long-term, often subtle danger to an ecosystem (Ross and Amter 2010). The scope of action and causality is pitched at a level which creates pervasive uncertainty about what will happen and who is responsible.

Finally, people who are socially and geographically distant from mining encounters often rely on simple, leviathan-filled narratives to understand what happens within these encounters. Despite decades of prying apart stereotypes of ecologically noble savages and their anthropological allies, mining encounters still often involve alignments of stakeholders that are unexpected to non-experts. Global news media and first world common sense are still used to convey David versus Goliath narratives of greedy corporations and exploited local communities. Yet often local communities welcome mining, provided it is done on their own terms. At the same time, global corporations which are under pressure from environmentalist groups in their home countries can be more concerned with the wellbeing of the local environment and communities than the governments which host them.

In sum, mining encounters are 'overheated' in the sense that 'exogenous and endogenous factors [...] lead to instability, uncertainty and unintended consequences' (Eriksen 2016: 16). Their large scale and the amorphous nature of the leviathans involved in them make it difficult to bring to bear a traditional, liability-focused sense of responsibility.

MINING ENCOUNTERS AS A FORM OF STRUCTURAL VIOLENCE/INEQUALITY

These features make mining encounters a subset of what anthropologists often refer to as situations of 'structural violence' or what Iris Young calls 'structural injustice', that is, a situation in which:

> social processes put large groups of persons under systematic threat of domination or deprivation of the means to develop and exercise their capacities, at the same time that these processes enable others to dominate or to have a wide range of opportunities for developing and exercising capacities available to them. (Young 2011: 52)

Many anthropologists have studied structural injustice; surprisingly few writers, however, have theorised the ethical implications of fieldwork in such situations. Paul Farmer, for instance, is one of the best-known anthropologists who has addressed the issue of structural violence. His important response to the phenomenon is to: 'reframe the problems at hand ... as social action in order to have a broad view of the inequalities in which such endeavours are grounded ... Efforts to resocialize problems allow all concerned to have a more meaningful understanding' of the experience of people suffering from structural violence (Farmer 2010: 476). On this account, the main response to structural injustice has been to make it more visible and to socialise a new generation of doctors in order to ensure they understand the role of structural violence in health disparities.

Farmer's approach can be complemented by what Young calls a 'social connection model' of justice. This approach 'says that all agents who contribute by their actions to the structural processes that produce injustice have responsibilities to work to remedy these injustices' (Young 2006: 102–3). It is thus the inverse of a liability model: it understands structural processes, not just individuals, to be subject to justice – responsibility is, in other words 'essentially shared' (Young 2006: 103). 'All the persons who participate by their actions in the ongoing schemes of cooperation that constitute these structures are responsible for them, in the sense that they are part of the process that causes them' (Young 2006: 114). Background conditions are precisely the things to be scrutinised. Such an approach is 'forward looking' in that it asks what forms of collective action are necessary to remedy ongoing injustices. 'Responsibility derived from social connection ... is ultimately *political* responsibility. Taking responsibility in a forward-looking sense ... involves joining with others to organize collective action to reform unjust structures' (Young 2006: 123). On this account, one can be responsible for remedying injustice because one is socially connected to it, even if one is not guilty of committing discrete, unjust acts.

Young argues that our individual responsibilities regarding structural injustice depend on our 'structural positioning' (Young 2006: 126) in relation to unjust social processes. In particular, Young suggests that 'persons can reason about their action in relation to structural injustice along parameters of *power, privilege, interest*, and *collective ability*' (Young 2006: 127; italics in original). Young's four parameters are useful because they can be used to break social positions into discrete components which can be examined and provide an analytic frame within which normative debate can be carried out. For instance, we often think of power, privilege and interest as being combined. A large mine, for example, may have tremendous power in shaping the regulatory environment in which it operates. Its operations, thus privileged, allow it to benefit from the profit it accrues, making it highly interested in the social processes that produce that profit. But Young's analytic also helps us parse situations in which power, privilege and interest combine in unexpected ways. Consumers of minerals, for instance, may be privileged by exploitative mining practices because of the inexpensive consumer goods they afford, but may not have the power to change unjust mining practices. Local communities may have interests strongly at odds with mining but may be powerless. By providing us with parameters for moral discussion, Young's model connects empirical social science approaches to normative deliberation.

PARAMETERS OF ETHICS OF MINING ENCOUNTERS

As anthropologists attempt to assess their responsibility for structurally unjust mining encounters, then, it may be useful for them to analyse their own social position with regard to Young's four parameters.

Power

Anthropologists have long emphasised their efficacy to change their field sites. 'Internalist' anthropologists have aspired to improve the human condition through interventions ranging from social mapping such as that done by Laurence Goldman (2000) right up to aspirations to govern entire territories, as in the case of George Murdock and the Coordinated Investigation of Micronesia (Kiste and Marshall 2000). Activist and 'externalist' approaches also aspire to incredible potency and resistance to global capitalism following role models such as Terence Turner, David Graeber or Stuart Kirsch. Whatever their political positioning, anthropologists who believe in their power to change unjust social processes are right, on Young's view, to believe that they have a responsibility to do so.

At the same time, it is important to temper anthropology's self-confident enthusiasm for its own efficacy. In some cases, there are genuine opportunities for anthropologists to affect the social processes they study, such as winning important court cases (Kirsch 2014) or raising awareness through indigenous film (Turner 1991). But anthropologists would also do well to be sceptical of their ability to radically alter the situations they encounter, especially in situations where red carpet treatment by mining companies seeking consultants can lead to an intoxicating sense of efficacy. Anthropologists would do well to remember that James Watson's adage about the military is equally true about mining companies: they are 'interested in what scientists know, not what scientists think' (Watson 2007: 345).

Indeed, Filer, in his 1999 piece, imagined a potent anthropology which brokered important decisions about mining and for a time this sort of power did exist. This is no longer the case. Indeed, Kirsch's recent work in South America is interesting because it attempts to find situations in which anthropologists can be more powerful by influencing projects at an early stage. A comparative study of mining encounters could be undertaken to examine what conjunctures increase anthropological agency.

That said, anthropological efficacy can be diffuse and difficult to detect. The Ok Tedi settlement memorialised by Kirsch and others, for instance, has had little impact on the mine's operation, and Ok Tedi continues to be a shameful example of what the mining industry can accomplish. At the same time, there can be no doubt that the Ok Tedi settlement altered global perceptions of mining and strengthened the position of anti-mine activism in the future. It altered mining activism at a broad level, not a narrow one. These sorts of ironies are common in mining encounters.

Another example of diffuse power is ethnographic representation. Anthropologists should not underestimate the power we have as ethnographic authorities. Although we may not always be institutionally empowered in mining encounters, our descriptions of them can be influential. Indeed, we are often at our most potent when we act as conduits of information about mining encounters to people outside of them. Despite cynicism about how rarely we are read, we must acknowledge our power to shape public opinion about mining encounters (Clark 2010; Bessire 2014).

Where anthropologists are efficacious, responsibility increases. This means that anthropologists who work within corporate structures cannot legitimately claim that they are 'not part of the system' or deny responsibility for the deeds of the leviathans they work with. Anthropologists who collaborate with corporations should recognise that they must own corporate actions, and increasingly so the more deeply they coordinate with leviathans – it is their social connection, not their individual liability, which fixes their responsibility.

Privilege

While anthropologists on the whole are not very powerful actors in their field sites, they are often uniquely privileged ones. There is by now a significant and growing literature on how structural injustice creates and maintains privilege (Kimmel and Ferber 2016). Many of our research communities suffer tremendous deprivation, deprivation from which many first world academics escape due to their own colonial and post-colonial privilege. Additionally, we are afforded tremendous amounts of time and effort, both from corporations but especially from local communities who host us. This increases our responsibility.

Furthermore, anthropologists make careers out of mining encounters. Much of this success is structural: academic anthropologists rarely profit from the sales of their academic publications. But hiring and promotion are critically connected to publications which result from fieldwork. Grant funding is also socially connected with field sites where our mining encounters occur. And we ourselves benefit greatly from the knowledge and wisdom of the local community where we work. It is, indeed, a privilege to study with them.

Recognition of our privilege should affect what sort of work we do. We cannot generate normative accounts of responsibility without generating empirical accounts of overheating processes. In American anthropology, overheating is often seen as an invitation to genre experimentation. I value the avant-gardist impulses of anthropology, but I don't think there is something specific about our contemporary world that requires them. On the contrary, explanation – dare I say 'causal inference' – is necessary to understand the world. Explanation – not just description – should be back on the menu. As Bessire (2014) has convincingly demonstrated, some fieldwork situations oblige us to pursue some research projects and not others.

Interest

Anthropologists have a widely varying set of interests in mining encounters. Academic anthropologists who conduct research on mining encounters rely on access to their field site in order to obtain grants, publish and advance their careers. However, they do not have a direct stake in the outcome of mining processes. At best, this means that university-based anthropologists paid mainly to teach can offer a prudent, impartial and disinterested account of mining encounters. At worst, however, this mixture of privilege and disinterest can lead to a sort of quietistic anthropology which benefits from structural injustice but does little to stop it. There is a danger here of producing 'disaster porn', which can be just as exoticising as classical 'savage slot' ethnography. Alternatively, academic anthropologists may find themselves empowered to effect change in their mining encounter, perhaps by sitting on a board or providing consultancy, but will not feel the negative (or positive) effects of the changes they bring about. Anthropologists who engage in consultancy work or who are employed by stakeholders in mining encounters are, clearly, highly interested. Anthropologists with family members or close friends who are entangled in mining encounters may also have a strong interest in outcomes in mining encounters. In these situations, responsibility is particularly important, as is the temptation to pursue one's self-interest over and above the demands of justice.

Interestingly, anthropologists who have an attenuated interest in mining encounters perhaps should not always take upon themselves personal responsibility for decisions made in mining encounters. When new waste dumps are approved or new hiring policies put in place, it is typically not the anthropologist who will be hired, or whose ancestral territory will be destroyed. Recognising a *lack* of anthropological interest in mining encounters is key to respecting the autonomy and responsibility for local stakeholders to make their own decisions. An analysis of the parameter of interest, then, may reveal that simply because an anthropologist has the power to intervene in a mining encounter does not mean that they should do so. Recognising our own disinterestedness may be key to avoiding a patronising or colonising attitude to the mining encounters we study and the local stakeholders within them.

Collective Ability

What abilities do anthropologists have to engage in collective action and to organise new collectivities to combat structural injustice? Young recommends that a first step in correcting structural injustice is:

> not to blame the powerful ... but rather to publicly hold them to account ... political contestation about structural injustice entails making arguments that some of the sufferings of people is ... caused by processes in which many participate, and then demanding on moral grounds that those with a particular power to alter the processes do so. (Young 2011: 149)

This is what she calls exposing the 'structural fissures' between 'powerful agents' that 'have an interest in the status quo and ... others' who have 'an interest in change' (Young 2011: 148).

A political anthropology of mining encounters is clearly analytically well-suited to this task. Scholarly work in this vein not only needs to be produced, it needs to be made open and accessible in order for it to have greater effect. In addition to specialist work, anthropologists need to engage in popular/public anthropology to broaden awareness of mining encounters.[1]

Anthropologists who expand their audience and write in multiple genres not only meet the demands of responsibility but also become more socially connected to mining encounters, and thus have increased responsibility for them. For many anthropologists from rich countries who only occasionally visit the poor country where 'their' mine is located, it is always easier to toil away in obscurity and simply not weigh in when 'our' mine makes national or global news. But to do so would mean disavowing the fact that we are always already connected to the extractive industries we cover. This may mean that more established – and thus more comfortable and less activist – scholars have a responsibility that increases even as their seniority makes it easier for them to shirk it. In particular, academic anthropologists with long-term job security are in a position to keep an eye on structural injustice in a way that other political actors may not be. Our long-term, in-depth knowledge of our field sites allows us a deep understanding of mining encounters that journalists might not have. The slow pace of our academic career gives us a kind of institutional memory which NGOs or development agencies may lack as they undertake short-term interventions in mining encounters.

Another form of collective ability that academic anthropologists have is the university itself. Libraries in rich countries contain specialised literature which stakeholders in poor countries do not have access to. As educators, anthropologists have a unique opportunity to promote the training and development of grassroots people in mining encounters. We can also inform first world students about mining. For these reasons, academic anthropologists have a unique ability to ground and connect collective ability that other actors may lack. Finally, to the extent that they can do so, their responsibility increases.

CONCLUSION

In this chapter I have suggested how Young's parameters for under-standing social connection and responsibility provide the flexible code of ethics that Colin Filer has called for. I believe that, as they are based in a secular, liberal philosophy, Young's parameters should be widely acceptable to anthropologists from a wide variety of personal back-grounds. They are a broad framework to guide discussion, rather than a concrete enumeration of duties. Through them, anthropologists can move from a sense that ethics is best served by aligning with one stake-holder rather than another. Rather, they should take a broader view and ask themselves what concrete steps they can take to make mining encounters more just. This may involve advocacy, consultancy, public anthropology or a variety of other actions and alignments. Recognising our political responsibility does not mean that everyone must become an activist. In fact, Young's model suggests that there is no single kind of anthropology the anthropology of mining should be. But I would argue that most anthropologists of mining encounters probably have a responsibility to their field site that is broader than they may like to admit, even if it is shallower than the responsibility demanded of them by activists.

In closing, I want to make a few broader points about the ethical project I've outlined here.

First, I believe that anthropology must move beyond the idea that an ethical stance on mining issues is purely personal. Rather, we must deliberate as a scholarly community about what concrete professional ethics we should have. Just as anthropological scholarly societies have developed codes of ethical conduct, anthropologists of mining encounters need a robust set of community ethics built out of collegial, public deliberation in which we bring our personal outlooks into dialogue. In a future publication I hope to discuss in more detail how this dialogue might happen.

Second, in this chapter I have argued that mining encounters are a form of structural injustice. But this is perhaps overly simplistic. It is more accurate to say that all social processes have a degree of structural injustice built into them. It is for this reason that thinking about anthropological responsibility for mining encounters might also be useful, because resource conflicts present an 'elementary form' of the ethical situation for anthropologists, and are thus of interest to anyone trying to think about what our anthropological responsibilities are. To this extent, ethical standards for the study of mining encounters can and should be part of a much broader discourse about scholarly and scientific responsibility, both within anthropology and across disciplines. The theoretical stakes in mining encounters, then, are quite large.

Finally, the world is not currently a just place, and it is not likely to become one in the near future. Anthropologists who struggle with the ethics of mining encounters should not give in to cynical perfectionism. We are not likely to solve the problem, but neither can we shirk it. Rather, the issue is how our actions contribute to the amelioration of currently unjust situations, even if injustice will not be rectified in our lifetime. In this chapter I have argued that existing thinking about anthropological responsibility does not do enough to engage the anthropologist as a whole person as they seek to understand mining encounters. It behoves us to move forward, as a scholarly community, to develop a robust sense of what those responsibilities are.

Indeed, in a world where structural injustice touches the lives of practically everyone in our global community, members of this community must not just participate in, but theorise, social process in order to understand their responsibility to this overheated world. To this extent, anthropology does not need to change to meet the requirements of an overheated world. Rather, in this overheated world, everyone must become – to a greater or lesser extent – anthropologists.

ACKNOWLEDGEMENTS

I wish to thank Robert Pijpers and Thomas Hylland Eriksen for their hospitality at the 'Overheating' mining conference at which this paper was originally presented, as well as their patience with the timeframe in which I developed this chapter. The chapter also benefited from presentations given at the Anthropology Department of the University of Western Ontario (hosted by Dan Jorgensen) and the Centre for Social Responsibility in Mining and the Anthropology programme at the University of Queensland (hosted by Yancy Orr). All errors and omissions are my own.

REFERENCES

Appiah, K.A. 2003. *Thinking it Through: An Introduction to Contemporary Philosophy*. London: Oxford University Press.

Bainton, N. 2010. *The Lihir Destiny: Cultural Responses to Mining in Melanesia*. Canberra:ANUPress.http://press.anu.edu.au/publications/series/asia-pacific-environment-monographs/lihir-destiny (accessed 26 July 2016).

Bakan, J. 2003. *The Corporation*, documentary film. Available at: https://archive.org/details/The_Corporation_

Ballard, C. and G. Banks. 2003. Resource Wars: The Anthropology of Mining. *Annual Review of Anthropology* 32: 287–313.

Banks, G, D. Kuir-Ayius, D. Kombako and B. Sagir. 2013. Conceptualizing Mining Impacts, Livelihoods and Corporate Community Development in Melanesia. *Community Development Journal* 48(3): 484–500.

Bessire, L. 2014. *Behold the Black Caiman: A Chronicle of Ayoreo Life*. Chicago: University of Chicago Press.

Butler, J. 2009. *Frames of War: When Is Life Grievable?* London: Verso Books.

Clarke, K. 2010. Toward a Critically Engaged Ethnographic Practice. *Current Anthropology* 51(S2): 301–12.

Eriksen, T.H. 2016. *Overheating: An Anthropology of Accelerated Change*. London: Pluto Press.

Farmer, P. 2010. *Partner to the Poor: A Paul Farmer Reader*. Berkeley: University of California Press.

Faubion, J. and G. Marcus (eds). 2009. *Fieldwork Is Not What It Used to Be: Learning Anthropology's Method in a Time of Transition.* New York: Cornell University Press.

Filer, C. 1999. The Dialectics of Negation and Negotiation in the Anthropology of Mineral Resource Development in Papua New Guinea. In A. Cheater (ed.), *The Anthropology of Power: Empowerment and Disempowerment in Changing Structures.* London: Routledge, pp. 88–102.

Fluehr-Lobban, K. 2013. *Ethics and Anthropology: Ideas and Practice.* New York: AltaMira.

Goldman, L. (ed.). 2000. *Social Impact Analysis: An Applied Anthropology Manual.* Oxford: Berg.

—— 2007. Incorporating Huli: Lessons from the Hides Licence Area. In J.F. Weiner and K. Glaskin (eds), *Customary Land Tenure and Registration in Australia and Papua New Guinea: Anthropological Perspectives.* Canberra: ANU Epress. pp. 73–96.

Golub, A. 2014. *Leviathans at the Gold Mine: Creating Indigenous and Corporate Actors in Papua New Guinea.* Durham, NC: Duke University Press.

Hage, G. 2012. *Responsibility.* Melbourne: Melbourne University Press.

Jackall, R. 1988. *Moral Mazes: The World of Corporate Managers.* New York: Oxford University Press.

Johnson, B.R. 2010. Social Responsibility and the Anthropological Citizen. *Current Anthropology* 51(S2): 35–47.

Kimmel, M. and A. Ferber (eds). 2016. *Privilege: A Reader.* New York: Westview Press.

Kirsch, S. 2014. *Mining Capitalism: The Relationship between Corporations and their Critics.* Berkeley: University of California Press.

Kirsch, S. and P. Benson. 2010. Capitalism and the Politics of Resignation. *Current Anthropology* 51(4): 459–86.

Kiste, R. and M. Marshall. 2000. *American Anthropology in Micronesia, 1941–1997.* Pacific Science 54(3): 265–74.

Lambek, M., V. Das, D. Fassin and W. Keane. 2015. *Four Lectures on Ethics.* London: HAU Books.

Lasslett, K. 2014. *State Crime on the Margins of Empire: Rio Tinto, the War on Bougainville, and Resistance to Mining.* London: Pluto Press.

Lederman, R. 2013. Ethics. In J. Carrier and D. Gewertz (eds), *Handbook of Sociocultural Anthropology.* New York: Bloomsbury Academic.

Pijpers, R.J. and T.H. Eriksen (this volume). Introduction: Negotiating the Multiple Edges of Mining Encounters. In R.J. Pijpers and T.H. Eriksen (eds), *Mining Encounters: Extractive Industries in an Overheated World.* London: Pluto Press.

Ross, B. and S. Amter. 2010. *The Polluters: The Making of Our Chemically Altered Environment.* New York: Oxford University Press.

Trnka, S. and C. Trundle. 2014. Competing Responsibilities: Moving Beyond Neoliberal Responsibilisation. *Anthropological Forum* 24(2): 136–53.

Turner, T. 1991. Representing, Resisting, Rethinking: Historical Transformations of Kayapo Culture and Anthropological Consciousness. In G. Stocking (ed.), *Colonial Situations: Essays on the Contextualization of Ethnographic Knowledge*. Madison: University of Wisconsin Press, pp. 285–313.

Watson, J. 2007. *Avoid Boring People: Lessons from a Life in Science*. New York: Vintage Books.

Welker, M., D. Partridge and R. Hardin. 2011. Corporate Lives: New Perspectives on the Social Life of the Corporate Forms: An Introduction to Supplement 3. *Current Anthropology* 53(S3): 3–16.

Wolf, E. 1982. *Europe and the People Without History*. Berkeley: University of California Press.

Young, I.M. 2006. Responsibility and Global Justice: A Social Connection Model. *Social Philosophy and Policy* 23(1): 102–30.

—— 2011. *Responsibility for Justice*. New York: Oxford University Press.

NOTES

1. The website resourceworlds.org is a good example of one such form of public anthropology.

3. The 'Shooting Fields of Porgera Joint Venture'[1]

An Exploration of Corporate Power, Reputational Dynamics and Indigenous Agency

Catherine Coumans

INTRODUCTION

At the end of a rough, winding road in the Papua New Guinea (PNG) highlands lies the Porgera Joint Venture gold mine (Porgera mine or PJV).[2] The mine's isolation likely contributed to shrouding years of the use of excessive force and violence perpetrated against local men and women by mine security and by PNG police[3] guarding the mine. Isolation does not suffice as an explanation, however, as foreign professionals, including anthropologists (Coumans 2011, 2014), lived and worked in Porgera while gross violations of human rights were ongoing.

In 2005, the Ipili of Porgera and their Engan relations from Laigam exposed the enormity of the criminal acts taking place in the shadow of the mine. As international awareness grew, various actors responded representing a wide range of interests, many aligned in one way or another with corporate strategies. The involvement of these outside agents had unanticipated impacts on the lives and agency of the indigenous activists at the centre of an escalating maelstrom. Although local Ipili and Engans were key to exposing abuses at the mine and remain engaged in pushing for remedy for the victims, they were dealt with particularly harshly in ensuing years in high-profile international narratives about violence at the mine.

This chapter reviews the history of disclosures of mine-related violence in Porgera, and responses by executives of the Canadian mining company Barrick Gold Corporation (Barrick). Non-governmental organisations (NGOs) and experts from academic human rights clinics first responded to the information provided by the local activists. Later, other actors and organisations became involved, including a burgeoning rank of consultants and advisers brought in by Barrick, other NGOs, academics, media, and United Nations (UN) bodies. Following years of denial, Barrick implemented a precedent-setting, but highly contentious, remedy mechanism at the mine to deal with a select category of victims of violence by mine security. This chapter examines how corporate power limited access to justice for the mine's victims, while shaping narratives in ways that marginalised the mine's local indigenous critics.

Welker et al. (2011: S12) note that 'countermovements to capitalism are reshaping corporate ethics and governance'. This chapter demonstrates that corporations are adept at wielding their power in new ways to achieve their goals, both when 'countermovements' appeal to corporate social responsibility (CSR) norms (Dolan and Rajak 2016), or, in this case, to claims that corporations respect human rights (OHCHR 2011).[4]

THE 'SHOOTING FIELDS OF PORGERA JOINT VENTURE'

In 2004, Ipili and Engan relatives of men allegedly killed by mine security and police guarding the Porgera mine formed the Akali Tange Association Inc. (ATA).[5] ATA's mission was to 'serve the sole purpose of being the human rights defender of the local people namely the Alluvial Gold Miners of the Porgera/Paiela Valley who have been wrongfully killed and/or have become victims of injustice act [sic] by the Porgera Joint Venture's security personnel' (ATA 2005: 104). ATA documented human rights abuses in order to engage with, and claim compensation from, the Porgera mine. ATA's work was supported by local landowners and businessmen, contracted academics at the University of PNG, the Porgera District Hospital and through fundraising by local musicians (ATA 2005: 8–9).

By April 2005, a 163-page English-language document was completed. *The Shooting Fields of Porgera Joint Venture* (ATA 2005) is a rich ethnographic source on the history and impacts of the Porgera mine from the perspective of affected indigenous men. It describes: loss of land for agricultural subsistence; loss of livelihood; loss of sacred sites; loss of potable water; social and cultural impacts; impacts on health; and environmental impacts, particularly through the wide-scale pollution of local valleys and waterways. The report details lost development opportunities that should have derived from the operation of a modern large-scale mine (ATA 2005: 58–9), and it provides insight into the culturally mediated way that legal and rights-based language informed ATA's arguments and agency.

The term 'alluvial miner' in the report refers to any person who makes part of their income from panning or searching for gold. Before the open-pit Porgera mine started operating, local Ipili panned for gold in the waterways of Porgera. This activity provided an important income supplement to largely subsistence agricultural practices and pig raising. ATA point out that the Mining Development Agreement of 1989, between the company and the local landowners, takes into consideration the effects of the mine's operations on traditional panning practices and notes that any negative impacts should be compensated by the company (ATA 2005: 58). By the time the ATA report (2005) was written, most waterways around the mine were heavily contaminated by mine waste (Shearman 2001), which, contrary to global best practice, is dumped directly into the environment, and locals were panning for gold in massive waste flows or seeking ore in the open pit. Key concerns of the landowners had turned to the high number of people drowning in the mine's waste and to excessive use of force by mine security[6] against locals[7] in, or near, the waste flows, even when they were not seeking gold. Eleven villages are squeezed up against the open pit and between the waste dumps and tailing streams. In order to reach agricultural land or other settlements some villagers are forced to traverse the dumps and waste, exposing them to mine security guards. The ATA report provides a map of the mine site showing traditional pathways used by villagers that now cross over waste dumps and go through pit areas (ATA 2005: 80).

ATA sought PGK 30 million (Papua New Guinea Kina; USD 9.18 million) in compensation explaining that '[o]ur claim's [sic][8] based on our estimate of PJV's income for one month of which PJV has stolen from the community as profit rather than spend on *reasonable precautions to prevent these ten (10) deaths*' (ATA 2005: 117, emphasis in original). One such precaution ATA mentions is resettlement. The Porgera Landowners Association (PLOA) has also long asked the mine to resettle affected communities. Consulting firm URS concluded a study in 2007 that found that living conditions 'have deteriorated to the point where they fall below what would be commonly accepted by Papua New Guinea standards' and that 'SML [Special Mine Lease] communities are currently living in over-crowded, unsanitary and potentially dangerous conditions, and have limited available land for family subsistence' (OECD Complaint 2011: 5-6).

The ATA report details activities the association will undertake to achieve its goal. ATA undertakes to, among others: 'make claims and enter into negotiations'; 'arrange for and procure for the associations or alluvial miners on such terms as the association shall deem fit, all such legal advice, expert opinion, assistance and help in connection with the matters or in defending or prosecution of the rights of Alluvial miners' (2005: 111-12). A sample 'Delegation of Authority' sets out the terms under which ATA will represent claimants upon receipt of a PGK 2,000 (USD 612) non-refundable fee. The document details that the parties agree that ATA will have 'power to control and determine what amount of money shall be made payable to both parties [ATA and claimant]' (ATA 2005: 144). This authorisation document, however imperfectly, resembles a legal retainer in form and language and forms a commentary on the lack of effective access to judicial remedy.

ATA asserts that 'trespassing is a minor offence under the Summary Offences Act and illegal prospecting for mineral constitutes fine but does not permits shooting with intend to cause death or grievous bodily harm to a person' (ATA 2005: 63). The report is a powerful indictment of the 'climate of impunity surrounding economic activities that promote or sustain conflict and human rights abuses. Porgera Joint Venture [...] operates one of the world's biggest gold mines in Papua New Guinea (PNG) beset by violence, repression, where effective governance and accountability are absent' (ATA 2005: 56).

It is noteworthy that positions taken in ATA's report (2005) concerning the human rights context of the mine, including weak governance, corporate impunity and the responsibility of the company to provide remedy, pre-empt a multi-year global exploration of these themes in a UN-led process that started in 2005.[9]

BREAKING ISOLATION AND BUILDING ALLIANCES: YEARS OF CORPORATE DENIAL AND 'SHOOTING' THE MESSENGERS

Receiving no response from the company to their report, ATA members travelled to Mt Hagen in September 2005, where internet access made it possible to seek outside help. They attached their report to a widely dispersed email with the subject heading: 'Porgera mess [sic] Killing – Require Assistance'. This led to communications between ATA members and staff at the Mineral Policy Institute, in Australia, and MiningWatch Canada (MiningWatch). By April 2006, these NGOs realised that the mine-related human rights abuses, such as ongoing killings, not only affected men[10] but also local women, who were subject to rape, gang rape and beatings by mine security and police guarding the mine (MiningWatch Canada 2006a, 2006b). The NGOs sought assistance from the International Human Rights Clinic of the Harvard Law School, which responded in collaboration with the New York University's Global Justice Clinic, and later the Columbia University Human Rights Clinic (Human rights clinics).

Locally, ATA was not alone in raising concern about the alleged killings. Chairman Mark Ekepa of the PLOA,[11] also spoke out in 2005 about 21 killings reportedly stating '[t]hey come and take gold from our land, but why kill us? [...] The most recent killing was last week. [...]

We want those responsible to be put behind bars' (Huafolo 2005). In 2008, ATA and PLOA formed a new organisation, Porgera Alliance.[12] This alliance brought together the financial resources and representational role of the landowners' association, with its focus on resettlement of the affected villages, with the concerns for victims of violence by mine security and the international connections established by ATA.[13]

From 2008 through 2010, ATA and PLOA sent delegations to Canada to attend Barrick's annual general meeting (AGM).[14] They read out statements that were unvarnished in detailing the mine-related violence: 'Since I spoke at this meeting last year, there have been 5 more killings of indigenous community members by your security guards and more women have been raped by your security guards. [...] *Will Barrick finally pay fair compensation to the families who have lost their loved ones to the guns of your security forces, to the rape victims, to the families who have lost members in your open pit and in the waste dumps and who have drowned in your river of tailings?'*[15]

Barrick executives consistently denied the accusations, while questioning the credibility of the PNG spokespeople. Shortly after the 2008 AGM, PJV's then-manager sent a letter to PLOA Chairman Ekepa stating 'we found your public allegations of our employees "gang raping" Porgera Land Owners' women to be most distasteful, to say the least as you know these allegations to be untrue' (OECD Complaint 2011: 13).[16]

Denial also characterised Barrick's response to testimony given by representatives of MiningWatch Canada and the Harvard and New York University human rights clinics before a Canadian parliamentary committee in 2009 and 2010:[17] '[w]e also reject the characterization of the company's security personnel as violent and unlawful' (Barrick 2009e).[18]

In April 2009, a police and military action called Operation Ipili '09 commenced in Porgera with strong support from the mine's management (OECD complaint 2011: 16–21; Amnesty International 2010: 5, 14). This action led to illegal evictions (Amnesty International 2010: 5) and the burning down of at least 130 houses in the near-pit village of Wuangima alone (Amnesty International 2010: 4) with associated human rights abuses. Barrick notes that Wuangima 'is an area in which PJV has historically been given little or no access by the landowners' (Barrick 2009d: 14). Prior to the house burnings, the mine's 'effort to acquire surface interests necessary to permit it to become part of PJV's operations was unsuccessful' (Barrick 2009d: 14). Mass burnings of village houses inside the Special Mine Lease area by police have occurred repeatedly since at least 1987 (Golub 2014: 104). These attacks have been justified in the name of 'peace and order' but, as Golub (2014: 104) and others (Amnesty

International 2010: 3, 6, 9, 10) have pointed out, the victims have been overwhelmingly innocent civilians.[19]

Following the house burnings, Barrick combined denial of most related allegations with acute personal attacks on the integrity of ATA, PLOA and international organisations such as Amnesty International. Allegations against Amnesty included presumptions that the organisation was acting at the behest of others: 'we are concerned that it [Amnesty] was simply acting as a conduit for the intentionally embellished and harmful allegations of third parties who were advancing their own agendas' (Barrick 2009c). Barrick directed these criticisms to UN Special Rapporteurs (Barrick 2009a), the Business and Human Rights Resource Centre (Barrick 2009b) and Amnesty (Barrick 2009c, 2009d). Barrick said a leader of ATA 'routinely embellished' (Barrick 2009a) the human rights abuses in Porgera and made 'facially preposterous public claims', 'colourful allegations' (Barrick 2009b) and 'extraordinary exaggerations' (Barrick 2009c).

Barrick's communications with Amnesty reveal the company's preoccupation with the leadership of ATA and PLOA. Barrick impugns Amnesty's professional reputation and implies bias in Amnesty's assessment of the house burnings in Porgera by repeatedly questioning Amnesty's relationship with ATA and PLOA (e.g. Barrick 2009d: 14, 15, 22).

EXTENDING THE CORPORATION: CORPORATE RELATIONSHIPS, ALIGNING INTERESTS AND REPUTATIONS

In April 2010, the chairman of the PLOA concluded the annual intervention at Barrick's AGM in Toronto with: '[w]e are tired of travelling to Canada and talking to you executives at your Annual General Meeting. We want to open up a genuine dialogue with you. Will you meet with us here in Toronto to start that dialogue?' (Porgera Alliance 2010). Around the same time, Chris Albin-Lackey of Human Rights Watch (HRW) conducted a field investigation in Porgera supported by a member of one of the academic human rights clinics working in Porgera.[20] Before publishing a report in February 2011, HRW entered into 'an extended dialogue with Barrick officials' (HRW 2011: 28) that included written exchanges and in-person meetings in North America and PNG (HRW 2011: 28). It is not known whether HRW was subjected to the same detailed interrogation regarding its relations with ATA and PLOA that Amnesty faced as there is no public record of these exchanges. HRW's researcher distances his field assessment from PLOA and ATA (HRW 2013), who were not consulted on the final text, maintaining that his research was 'treated as more credible' by Barrick as a result (Enodo Rights 2016: 11). Additionally, HRW notes that '[a]ll of Barrick's input was fully incorporated into this report' (HRW 2011: 28).

While focused on human rights abuses at the mine, HRW's report includes a number of pages that critique the financial management of the PLOA (HRW 2011: 35-7) and the arrangements made by ATA with the victims of alleged human rights abuses by mine security (HRW 2011: 45). HRW's critique of the role ATA assumes as distributor of any resources that may come from their advocacy on behalf of victims of violence by mine security, might have benefitted from Foster's (2016) analysis of how corporations attempt to occupy the space of the Melanesian 'Big Man': 'as both assume a role as arbiter of debts, gifts and moral responsibility over the community or clan, Foster shows how what is at stake in both is a question of authority' (Dolan and Rajak 2016: 15). Since the report's release, Barrick references HRW's criticisms of ATA and PLOA to justify not consulting these groups, and unfailingly credits only HRW with having opened the company's eyes to the possibility of human rights abuses at the mine.

Gaining High-level Support for an Inequitable Remedy Programme for Rape Victims

In 2011, the UN Guiding Principles for Business and Human Rights were endorsed by the UN Human Rights Council. The principal author of the UN Guiding Principles, John Ruggie, proposed that 'business enterprises should establish or participate in effective operational-level grievance mechanisms for individuals and communities who may be adversely impacted' (OHCHR 2011: 32). Ruggie set out 'effectiveness criteria' for these grievance mechanisms to ensure that the mechanisms would be rights compatible and equitable (OHCHR 2011: 34-5).

Shortly after the UN Guiding Principles were endorsed, Barrick started work on a remedy framework to address victims of sexual violence by mine security personnel. These victims posed a particularly high degree of legal risk for the company as mine security personnel cannot plead self-defence in regard to charges of rape. Barrick's narrowly focused remedy mechanism excluded many male and female victims of violence by mine personnel and by police guarding the mine. The remedy framework was designed only for victims of sexual assault by mine security, not by police guarding the mine. Mine security personnel have a direct relationship to the mine, even though the police are financially supported, housed and clothed by the mine. The mechanism was not designed for men who allege assault by mine security and police guarding the mine.[21] The mechanism did not meet the UN Guiding Principles' effectiveness criteria[22] and was not procedurally fair. In particular, the women did not have access to competent independent legal advice (Coumans, 2017; Human rights clinics 2015; Knuckey and Jenkin 2015). In a move unanticipated by the UN Guiding Principles, Barrick made the provision of compensation packages conditional on the rape victims signing legal waivers creating legal immunity for the company and its subsidiaries from civil suit by the victims. The legal waivers signed by 119 victims of rape and gang rape by mine security now form a barrier to access to judicial remedy for the women, who have expressed their dissatisfaction with the remedy they received and the remedy process they endured in a complaint to the UN Working Group on Business and Human Rights (MiningWatch Canada 2016b). Even the consultant Barrick chose to review the finalised remedy programme found that: 'successful claimants expressed near universal dissatisfaction: 60 of 62 claim that the remedies they received were not the ones they wanted and expected; 59 out of 62 believe that they were not treated fairly by the Framework' (Enodo Rights 2016: 106). Flaws in Barrick's remedy programme, in particular the lack of competent independent legal advice, are accentuated as EarthRights International represented 11 rape victims, who, it is widely reported, received a settlement worth four times what the 119 rape victims ultimately received through the company's remedy programme (Enodo Rights 2016: 5, 26).

As Barrick was developing its remedy framework for Porgera in 2012, John Ruggie, lead author of the UN Guiding Principles, became a special adviser to a newly created CSR Advisory Board to Barrick's board of directors, a position he continues to hold. In addition to lending his reputional status to the company, Ruggie also defended the company with regard to its use of legal waivers.[23] In response to criticism regarding the legal waivers (MiningWatch Canada 2013; MiningWatch Canada et al. 2013), Barrick turned to Ruggie, who had provided input on the remedy framework's design (Enodo Rights 2016: 52). Barrick reported that Ruggie had 'expressly confirmed' that Barrick's remedy framework design, in regard to the waivers, conformed to Principle 29 and related Commentary in the UN Guiding Principles (Barrick 2013: 7). Principle 29 of the UN Guiding Principles notes that: 'Operational-level grievance mechanisms [...] should not be used to preclude access to judicial or other non-judicial grievance mechanisms' (OHCHR 2011: 32). In a personal communication, Ruggie said: 'If there were a "no waiver" stipulation, how many companies do you think would set up grievance mechanisms? My suspicion is very few' (personal communication 22 August 2013).

Subsequently, the Office of the High Commissioner for Human Rights (OHCHR), which is also advised by Ruggie on issues related to the UN Guiding Principles, issued a disputed (Knuckey and Jenkin 2015: 812) opinion regarding the use of waivers, noting that there should be a presumption against the use of waivers in non-judicial mechanisms, but that this presumption can be set aside on the basis of corporate desire for a waiver (OHCHR 2013: 8).

MARGINALISING LOCAL INDIGENOUS AGENCY

Barrick (2016) uses HRW's (2011) critique of ATA and PLOA to justify having marginalised these local organisations from the formation and implementation of the company's remedy programme. The OHCHR (2013) relied on HRW's opinion (2011, 2013) to conclude that exclusion of ATA and PLOA from consultation on the creation and operation of the remedy programme was acceptable, even while recognising that '[t]hese two organizations [ATA and PLOA] were among those who consistently raised concerns about sexual abuse from an early stage' (OHCHR 2013: 12–13). The chairman of the PLOA wrote to the OHCHR to indicate a willingness to participate in a review of the remedy mechanism as recommended by the OHCHR (2013: 10):

> We are writing to you for the first time now to tell you directly what we know about Barrick's remedy program and to speak for ourselves as we notice that too often others are speaking about us. [...] We hope that in the future you will contact us directly if you will write about us. We are always open to dialogue. Finally, we strongly support your recommendation for an independent review of the Porgera remediation programme. (PLOA/ATA 2013).

Barrick did not take the OHCHR's advice. Rather, Barrick brought in a consulting firm, BSR, to carry out a review while the programme was ongoing but did not release the resulting report. Barrick is a fee-paying member of BSR and the organisation's President, Aron Cramer, sits on Barrick's CSR Advisory Board with UN Guiding Principles author John Ruggie.

Upon completion of the remedy programme, Barrick hired a consulting company Enodo Rights (Enodo) to conduct a review. The review process had an External Committee of three, including Chris Albin-Lackey of HRW, who was also interviewed for the review report, as was John Ruggie. Enodo references both the HRW report (2011) and the OHCHR opinion (2013) to conclude that excluding ATA and PLOA from consultations on the remedy programme did not breach the UN Guiding Principles' effectiveness criteria (Enodo Rights 2016: 15). Enodo's review of Barrick's remedy programme for victims of sexual violence by Porgera mine security concludes that the remedy framework designed by Barrick was praiseworthy (Enodo Rights 2016: 2) and that flaws in the implementation of the programme can be largely attributed to the entities Barrick hired to carry out the programme (Enodo Rights 2016: 5), to 'international stakeholders' (Enodo Rights 2016: 2), and to ATA and PLOA (Enodo Rights 2016: 96), even as Enodo acknowledges relying on ATA's support to carry out its own field assessment (Enodo Rights 2016: 25). In a detailed critique, human rights advocates from Harvard and Columbia note that 'Enodo Rights and Barrick have threatened to undercut standards surrounding company-created remedy mechanisms designed to address corporate human rights violations' (Human rights clinics 2018).[24]

Significantly, those who engaged intensively with the human rights issues in Porgera since 2005, and did so independently from Barrick, do not concur with the marginalisation of ATA and PLOA. Knuckey and Jenkin note of these organisations that:

Many of their members have been *the* most important local stakeholders advocating an end to and redress for security guard violence. It is indisputable that these groups have been the primary actors engaged on issues of human rights at the Porgera mine, are trusted by many victims, and deserve significant credit for the fact that international groups and Barrick itself even became aware of the abuse allegations. (2015: 806, emphasis in original)

The Human rights clinics (2015) note that:

marginalizing members of the ATA/PLOA from consultation came at a high cost. [...] ATA/PLOA members were trusted by many of the victims, and members of the groups have occupied positions of authority. Indeed, many women reported cases of sexual violence directly to members of the ATA, and trusted individuals within that group to advocate for them and to inform and advise them about the mechanism; initially, some women were reluctant to use the mechanism without ATA verifying the process for them. (2015: 59)

EarthRights International (2013) addresses the OHCHR's role in marginalising and delegitimising the Porgera organisations by noting that:

OHCHR's response refers to disparaging comments made both by Barrick and Human Rights Watch about the legitimacy of our partners, ATA and PLOA, and suggests that these unfounded beliefs justified Barrick's decision to exclude them from the consultations about the remedy framework. [...] We wish to emphasize that ATA and PLOA are the only representative, community-based organizations that are independent from Barrick and work directly with the victims of sexual violence in Porgera.... They have consistently been the subject of public attacks and attempts at delegitimization by Barrick and its predecessors. [...] If your letter is read to lend credence to the attacks on ATA or PLOA's credibility and legitimacy – and Barrick's related decision to exclude them and the women they represent from the development of the remedy framework – it could have very serious consequences for their ability to work on victims' behalf both within Papua New Guinea and internationally. It would also provide a roadmap for any company that wishes to exclude its most vocal critics from the universe of 'legitimate' stakeholders, in favour of its handpicked supporters and dependents.

CONCLUSIONS

The global mining industry's quest for access to the world's remaining lucrative ore bodies is 'heating up', driving the industry deeper into landscapes where it is difficult, if not impossible, to contain toxic mine waste and where indigenous peoples and other remote communities struggle to maintain their cultural integrity and critical access to land and water. Yet, the 'encounters' between mining companies and the local populations who will bear the brunt of their activities are not restricted to these two main actors.

Local peoples are on the front lines of efforts to resist mining impacts, to avoid or minimise harm, to capture benefits, and to obtain remediation and remedy for harm done. They more often than not find themselves on the losing end of long-drawn-out and sapping power struggles, not just with the mining company but with their own governments, who often criminalise their opposition, with the outposts of home state governments – embassies whose mandate it is to protect the interests of their multinational corporations – and with a growing number of consultants, experts and corporate 'partners' who are engaged by the company and/or drawn into its ambit for their own reasons. While affected communities will, and do, reach out and seek help, as the Ipili of Porgera did when faced with extreme violence by mine security, the power differential they face remains overwhelming and the cultural and social nuances of this disadvantage are still understudied by academics entering this arena.[25]

Academic anthropologists have long engaged with the Porgera mine in various capacities. However, before Barrick acknowledged, late in 2010, that sexual violence by its personnel 'may have occurred', anthropologists had not studied and published on the issue of violence by mine security and police guarding the mine. In some cases, contracts anthropologists had with the mine would have prohibited publication of evidence of violence by mine security (Coumans 2011: S33–S35). In 2010, Barrick contracted anthropologist Aletta Biersack, renowned for her fieldwork in the Porgera Valley (Biersack 1999, 2001), to undertake a study of rape in Porgera.[26] Her study was not made public.

Anthropologist Martha Macintyre was a participant on the mine-funded Porgera Environmental Advisory Komiti (PEAK) during the years that the issue of violence by mine security was publicised by ATA and PLOA, the human rights clinics and MiningWatch Canada, but still denied by Barrick. PEAK did not address the issue. In 2011, PEAK sponsored research by anthropologist Penny Johnson on the social impact of mining on women in the Porgera area. Johnson thanks Macintyre for her 'support and feedback' and Biersack for her 'comments' (PEAK 2011: 2). The study addresses 'gender-based violence and rape' (PEAK 2011: 56–9) but, remarkably, does not mention sexual violence against local women by mine security. A single reference to the work of Sarah Knuckey of Columbia University's human rights clinic mentions that she describes 'brutal abuse and rape and grave human rights [sic] experienced by many women' (PEAK 2011: 59) while failing to mention that Knuckey's work focused on sexual violence against women in Porgera by mine security and police guarding the mine.

Anthropologist Alex Golub conducted fieldwork in Porgera in the early 2000s and was aware of house burnings (Golub 2014: 104) and of violence perpetrated by mine personnel (Golub 2014: 7, 21). Golub discusses reports of violence associated with mine security and police guarding the mine in an afterword to his book (Golub 2014: 208–13). In the text itself, Golub's two references to violence by mine security are made to illustrate other points (Coumans 2014). Golub does not further interrogate the extreme violence associated with mine security and the role it plays in limiting local agency.

As anthropologists grapple with the 'power of corporations over human and environmental life' (Welker et al. 2011: S12), consideration should be given to the roles and responsibilities of anthropologists themselves as they become aware of human rights abuses by the corporations they are engaging.

Dolan and Rajak point out that the 'politics of CSR create new domains for the exercise of corporate power' (2016: 11). This chapter considered the exercise of corporate power and strategies in the context of emerging human rights claims. Dolan and Rajak (2016: 18) also point to the way corporations choose their partnerships 'privileging certain actors, agendas and interests, while marginalizing others'. This chapter considered the interests and goals, including reputational, of the non-corporate partners in these collaborations. It exposed how external actors may consciously, or carelessly, adopt and accept a company's biases and desire to marginalise its most determined local critics. It also considered how personal and organisational agendas and interests of external actors may cause them to prioritise their own goals and reputations over the agency of local actors. More work needs to be done to understand how cultural biases may make it easier for external actors to seek to obtain the change they desire through engagements with corporate lawyers and managers in comfortable surroundings than in solidarity with remote and cultural 'others'.

In the short term, Barrick and the company's various collaborators achieved from their alignments what they sought, including, for Barrick, legal immunity from vulnerable human rights victims and marginalisation of the company's most effective local indigenous critics. However, realities on the ground have not changed. Many alleged human rights victims have yet to receive remedy and new abuses continue to be reported. In this context, local-level organising around human rights issues is thriving.[27] In November 2017, a female advocate with ATA and one of the 119 rape victims sat across from John Ruggie in his Harvard University office. 'We told him, you have listened to Barrick, now you need to listen to us.'[28] For international actors engaging in this space, be they consultants, academics or others, this urgent request is an imperative.

ACKNOWLEDGEMENTS

I would like to thank the organisers and participants of the Mining Encounters workshop in Oslo, where an earlier version of this chapter was presented, for lively and enriching exchanges. My gratitude goes out to the people of Porgera, who, even as they continue to suffer environmental and personal losses they could not have foreseen, and struggle to negotiate engagements with the mine and various outside actors and interests, ultimately root their ongoing struggle for justice in their own cultural traditions and understandings of compensation and the value of human life.

REFERENCES

Amnesty International. 2010. *Undermining Rights: Forced Evictions and Police Brutality around the Porgera Gold Mine, Papua New Guinea*. London: Amnesty International.

ATA (Akali Tange Association). 2005. *The Shooting Fields of Porgera Joint Venture: Now a Case to Compensate and Justice to Prevail*. A Compensation Specific Submission to the Porgera Joint Venture on behalf of Placer Dome Canada Inc, Durban Roodepoot Deep of South Africa and Mineral Resources Enga Ltd and the Independent State of Papua New Guinea; On the Unlawful Killings of Village Alluvial Gold Miners at the PJV Mine Site – Special Mining Lease (SML) and Lease for Mining Purpose (LMP) Areas. Available at: http://miningwatch.ca/sites/default/files/ATA_Case_Documentation.pdf (accessed 3 May 2018).

Barrick Gold. 2009a. Letter to U.N. Special Rapporteurs. 2 June. Available at: https://business-humanrights.org/en/documents/alleged-forced-evictions-at-porgera-papua-new-guinea-and-barrick-gold-response (accessed 9 December 2017).

—— 2009b. Letter to the Business and Human Rights Resource Centre. 16 June. Available at: https://business-humanrights.org/en/documents/alleged-forced-evictions-at-porgera-papua-new-guinea-and-barrick-gold-response (accessed 9 December 2017).

—— 2009c. Letter to Amnesty International. 11 May. Available at: https://business-humanrights.org/en/documents/alleged-forced-evictions-at-porgera-papua-new-guinea-and-barrick-gold-response (accessed 9 December 2017).

—— 2009d. Letter to Amnesty International. 22 May. Available at: https://business-humanrights.org/en/documents/alleged-forced-evictions-at-porgera-papua-new-guinea-and-barrick-gold-response (accessed 9 December 2017).

—— 2009e. Brief to Canadian Parliamentary Committee. Available at: https://business-humanrights.org/en/documents/testimony-before-canadian-parliament-re-barrick-porgera-jv-papua-new-guinea (accessed 9 December 2017).

—— 2013. Letter to the U.N. High Commissioner for Human Rights. Available at: http://www.barrick.com/files/porgera/Letter-to-UN-High-Commissioner.pdf (accessed 9 December 2017).

—— 2016. Correspondence between the Akali Tange Association and Barrick Niugini Limited. 8 July. Available at: http://www.barrick.com/files/porgera/Correspondence-between-the-Akali-Tange-Association-and-Barrick-Niugini-Limited.pdf (accessed 9 December 2017).

Biersack, A. 1999. Porgera: Whence and Whither? In C. Filer (ed.), *Dilemmas of Development: The Social and Economic Impact of the Porgera Gold Mine 1989–1994*. Canberra: Asia Pacific, pp. 260–79.

—— 2001. Dynamics of Porgera Gold Mining: Culture, Capital and the State. In B.Y. Imbun and P.A. McGavin (eds), *Mining in Papua New Guinea: Analysis and Policy Implications*. Waigani: University of Papua New Guinea Press, pp. 25–45.

Burton, B. 2005. Canadian Firm Admits to Killings at PNG Gold Mine. Inter Press Service, 18 November. Available at: http://www.ipsnews.net/ news. asp?idnewsp31074 (accessed 9 December 2017).

Burton, J. 1999. Evidence of the 'New Competencies'? In C. Filer (ed.), *Dilemmas of Development: the Social and Economic Impact of the Porgera Gold Mine 1989–1994*. Canberra: Asia Pacific, pp. 280–301.

Coumans, C. 2011. Occupying Spaces Created by Conflict: Anthropologists, Development NGOs, Responsible Investment, and Mining. *Current Anthropology* 52(S3): S29–43 (Supplement to April 2011 issue: *Corporate Lives: New Perspectives on the Social Life of the Corporate Form*, edited by M. Welker, D. Partridge and R. Hardin).

—— 2014. Book Review of *Leviathans at the Gold Mine: Creating Indigenous and Corporate Actors in Papua New Guinea*, by Alex Golub. *PoLAR* 37(2): November.

—— 2017. Do No Harm? Mining Industry Responses to the Responsibility to Respect Human Rights. In E. Grégoire, B. Campbell and M. Doran (eds), *Rights-based Approaches, Between Renewal and Depoliticisation*. Special Issue of *Canadian Journal of Development Studies* 38(2).

Dolan, C. and D. Rajak. 2016. Introduction: Toward the Anthropology of Corporate Social Responsibility. In C. Dolan and D. Rajak (eds), *The Anthropology of Corporate Social Responsibility*. New York: Berghahn, pp. 1–28.

EarthRights International. 2013. Letter to the UN OHCHR Regarding the Porgera Joint Venture Remedy. Available at: https://business-humanrights.org/en/doc-letter-to-un-ohchr-regarding-the-porgera-joint-venture-remedy-framework (accessed 3 May 2018).

——2016a. Many Valuable Lessons from Barrick's Remedy Framework; 'It's Cheaper to Rape Poor Women' Should Not Be One of Them. Blog, 22 January. Available at: https://www.earthrights.org/blog/many-valuable-lessons-barricks-remedy-framework-its-cheaper-rape-poor-women-should-not-be-one (accessed 3 May 2018).

—— 2016b. International Human Rights Law Does Not Support Giving Less Compensation to Claimants from Poorer Countries. Blog, 29 January. Available at: https://www.earthrights.org/blog/international-human-rights-law-does-not-support-giving-less-compensation-claimants-poorer (accessed 2 May 2018).

Enodo Rights. 2016. *Pillar III on the Ground: An Independent Assessment of the Porgera Remedy Framework*. January. Available at: http://www.enodorights. com/assets/pdf/pillar-III-on-the-ground-assessment.pdf (accessed 3 May 2018).

Foster, R.J. 2016. Big Men and Business: Morality, Debt and the Corporation: A Perspective. In C. Dolan and D. Rajak (eds), *The Anthropology of Corporate Social Responsibility*. New York: Berghahn.

Golub, A. 2014. *Leviathans at the Gold Mine: Creating Indigenous and Corporate Actors in Papua New Guinea*. Durham, NC: Duke University Press.

HRW (Human Rights Watch). 2011. *Gold's Costly Dividend: Human Rights Impacts of Papua New Guinea's Porgera Gold Mine*, February. New York: Human Rights Watch.

—— 2013. Letter to Office of the High Commissioner for Human Rights. 5 April. Available at: https://barrick.q4cdn.com/788666289/files/porgera/Letter-from-Human-Rights-Watch-to-UN-High-Commissioner-for-Human-Rights.pdf (accessed 9 December 2017).

Huafolo, A. 2005. Landowners call for mine closure. *The National* (Papua New Guinea), 30 March. Available at: http://www.minesandcommunities.org/article.php?a=1454 (accessed 3 May 2018).

Human rights clinics. 2009. *Legal Brief: Before the Standing Committee on the Foreign Affairs and International Development (FAAE), House of Commons, Regarding Bill C-300*, 16 November (Harvard Law School International Human Rights Clinic and New York University School of Law Center for Human Rights and Global Justice).

—— 2015. *Righting Wrongs? Barrick Gold's Remedy Mechanism for Sexual Violence in Papua New Guinea: Key Concerns and Lessons Learned* (Columbia Law School Human Rights Clinic and Harvard Law School International Human Rights Clinic). Available at: http://hrp.law.harvard.edu/wp-content/uploads/2015/11/FINALBARRICK.pdf (accessed 3 May 2018).

—— 2018. *Eroding the UN Guiding Principles: How the Enodo Rights Assessment of Barrick Gold's Remedy Mechanism Turns the Floor into the Ceiling*. Columbia Law School Human Rights Clinic and Harvard Law School International Human Rights Clinic.

Kirsch, Stuart. 2014. *Mining Capitalism: The Relationship between Corporations and Their Critics*. Berkeley: University of California Press.

Knuckey, S. and E. Jenkin. 2015. Company-created Remedy Mechanisms for Serious Human Rights Abuses: A Promising New Frontier for the Right to Remedy? *International Journal of Human Rights*, 19(6): 801–27, DOI:10.1080/13642987.2015.1048645

MiningWatch Canada. 2006a. Placer Dome Admits to Killings at Porgera Mine in Papua New Guinea. Press release, 8 April. Available at: http://miningwatch.ca/blog/2006/4/8/placer-dome-admits-killings-porgera-mine-papua-new-guinea (accessed 3 May 2018).

—— 2006b. Barrick Gold's Porgera Mine in Papua New Guinea Linked to Grave Human Rights Abuses, Environmental Impacts. Press release 12 May. Includes background document. Available at: http://miningwatch.ca/news/2008/5/12/barrick-gold-s-porgera-mine-papua-new-guinea-linked-grave-human-rights-abuses (accessed 3 May 2018).

—— 2009. MiningWatch Appeals to UN over Human Rights Abuses Related to Barrick Mine in Papua New Guinea. News release, 8 May. Available at: http://miningwatch.ca/news/2009/5/8/miningwatch-appeals-un-over-human-rights-abuses-related-barrick-mine-papua-new-guinea (accessed 22 May 2018).

—— 2010. Indigenous Leaders from Papua New Guinea Accuse Barrick Gold of Abuses. News release 5 May. Available at: http://miningwatch.ca/news/2010/5/5/indigenous-leaders-papua-new-guinea-accuse-barrick-gold-abuses (accessed 3 May 2018).

—— 2013. Letter to UN Commissioner for Human Rights re: Barrick Gold's 'Grievance' Procedure for Victims of Rape by Security Guards at the Porgera Joint Venture Mine in Papua New Guinea. 23 March. Available at: http://miningwatch.ca/blog/2013/3/23/letter-un-commissioner-human-rights-re-barrick-golds-grievance-procedure-victims-rape (accessed 3 May 2018).

—— 2014. Villagers' Houses Burnt Down Again at Barrick Gold Mine in Papua New Guinea. News release 11 June. Available at: http://miningwatch.ca/news/2014/6/11/villagers-houses-burnt-down-again-barrick-gold-mine-papua-new-guinea (accessed 3 May 2018).

—— 2016a. Barrick Consultant Delivers Biased Report on Inequitable Remedy Mechanism for Rape Victims. Available at: http://miningwatch.ca/publications/2016/3/15/barrick-consultant-delivers-biased-report-inequitable-remedy-mechanism-rape (accessed 9 December 2017).

—— 2016b. Video Message from Porgera Women to UN Forum on Business and Human Rights. Available at: http://miningwatch.ca/blog/2016/11/16/video-message-porgera-women-un-forum-business-and-human-rights (accessed 9 December 2017).

MiningWatch Canada, Rights and Accountability in Development and EarthRights International 2013. Rape Victims Must Sign Away Rights to Get Remedy from Barrick. Media Release, 30 January. Available at: http://www.miningwatch.ca/news/rapevictims-must-sign-away-rights-get-remedy-barrick (accessed 3 May) with attached background brief: Concerns Regarding the Remediation Framework for Women Victims of Sexual Violence by Porgera Joint Venture Security Guards. Available at: http://www.miningwatch.ca/sites/www.miningwatch.ca/files/background_brief_violence_against_wo men_with_january_30_press_release_2.pdf (accessed 3 May 2018).

National Post. 2009. Innuendo-law Will Hurt Canada. *National Post* 27 November. Available at: https://www.pressreader.com/canada/national-post-latest-edition/20091127/283987533407071 (accessed 3 June 2018).

OECD Complaint. 2011. Request for Review Submitted to the Canadian National Contact Point of the OECD Guidelines for Multinational Enterprises by Porgera Landowners Association, Akali Tange Association, MiningWatch Canada. 1 March. Available at: http://www.miningwatch.ca/sites/default/files/OECD_Request_for_Review_Porgera_March-1-2011.pdf (accessed 23 May 2018).

OHCHR (Office of the High Commissioner for Human Rights). 2011. *Guiding Principles on Business and Human Rights: Implementing the United Nations 'Protect, Respect and Remedy' Framework*. HR/PUB/11/04. New York: UN.

—— 2013. Re: Allegations regarding the Porgera Joint Venture Remedy Framework. 1 August. Available at: http://www.ohchr.org/Documents/Issues/Business/LetterPorgera.pdf (accessed 3 May 2018).

Patterson, K. 2006. A Deadly Clash of Cultures. *The Ottawa Citizen* 6 June. Available at: http://www.canada.com/ottawacitizen/news/story.html?id=26bacccd-fa28-4f96-b067-a436b6a6d881 (accessed 9 December 2017).

PEAK (Porgera Environmental Advisory Komiti). 2011. *Scoping Project: Social Impact of the Mining Project on Women in the Porgera Area.* Consultant: Penny Johnson, Emic Consultancy. Port Morseby, Papua New Guinea.

PLOA/ATA (Porgera Landowners Association/Akali Tange Association). 2013. Letter to the UN High Commissioner on Human Rights. 29 August. Available at: https://business-humanrights.org/sites/default/files/media/pla-porgera-aug-29-2013.pdf (accessed 9 December 2017).

Porgera Alliance. 2010. Statement of Mark Ekepa, Chairman of the Porgera Landowners Association at Barrick's Annual General Meeting, 28 April. Available at: http://www.porgeraalliance.net/2010/04/statement-of-mark-ekepa-chairman-of-the-porgera-landowners-association-at-barrick%E2%80%99s-annual-general-meeting/ (accessed 9 December 2017).

Shearman, P. 2001. Giving Away Another River: An Analysis of the Impacts of the Porgera Mine on the Strickland River System. In B.Y. Imbun and P.A. McGavin (eds), *Mining in Papua New Guinea: Analysis and Policy Implications.* Waigani: University of Papua New Guinea Press, pp. 173–91.

Welker, M., D.J. Partridge and R. Hardin. 2011. Corporate Lives: New Perspectives on the Social Life of the Corporate Form: An Introduction to Supplement 3. *Current Anthropology* 52(S3): S3–S16

NOTES

1. The title of this chapter is taken from a report by the Akali Tange Association Inc. (ATA 2005).

2. The Porgera mine started operating in 1990. In 2006, Barrick acquired Canadian mining company Placer Dome and therewith its 95 per cent ownership and management control of the Porgera mine. Barrick's stake in the mine was through its wholly owned subsidiary Barrick Niugini Ltd. The remaining 5 per cent is held by Mineral Resources Enga, of which 2.5 per cent is owned by the Enga Provincial Government and 2.5 per cent is owned by Porgera landowners. In 2015, Barrick sold 50 per cent of its share in Barrick Niugini Ltd to Chinese-owned Zijin Mining Group.

3. In 2005 Placer Dome, later Barrick Niugini Ltd, entered into a Memorandum of Understanding with the Royal Papua New Guinea Constabulary, the police force of PNG. Under this agreement the Porgera Joint Venture mine houses, feeds, clothes and pays salaries for reserve police who, among other things, provide security services to the mine. At times mobile police squads are also dispatched to Porgera to deal with law and order issues related to the mine. Unless specified, 'mine security' here refers to both mine personnel and police guarding the mine.

4. The 'responsibility to respect' human rights is interpreted by human rights experts as 'do no harm'. For a discussion of differences between CSR and

human rights claims on multinational corporations and corporate adeptness at using human rights tools to achieve their own goals, see Coumans (2017).

5. *Akali*, in Engan, translates as 'human being'. *Tange* in Engan translates as the 'rightful or legitimate custodians' or 'defenders' – in this case of the victims of the Porgera mine (personal communications, 31 March 2016 and 2 April 2016).

6. In 2005, Placer Dome admitted to eight killings by mine security and police, of which seven had taken place since 2000, but maintained that all were in self-defence (Burton 2005).

7. The use of the term 'locals' here refers both to the pre-mining landowner families of Porgera and those who have migrated to the mine site and live there with the permission of Porgeran landowners. Often these are people who can claim genealogical ties to the Porgeran landowners (Burton 1999; Biersack 1999, 2001). ATA notes that 'The Ipili people have very close relationship with the people of Tari/Kandep and Laiagam/Mulitaka respectively. [...] people of Laiagam, Muritaka, Kandep, Tari, Koroba, Paiela and other areas geographically close to Porgera are linked through the cognatic network and cultural similarities that qualifies them as Porgeran' (ATA 2005: 46).

8. The convention of using [sic] where quoted material contains errors has not been used in quotes from local activists apart from here.

9. In 2005, a six-year UN process to determine the human rights responsibilities of business enterprises resulted, in 2011, in the UN Guiding Principles for Business and Human Rights (OHCHR 2011), further discussed below.

10. In 2006 the first media coverage on the mine-related violence appeared in Canada (Patterson 2006). In 2007, MiningWatch sought the intervention of the UN Special Rapporteur on Extrajudicial Summary or Arbitrary Executions on alleged killings of local men by mine security or police guarding the mine (see: http://miningwatch.ca/blog/2007/12/2/urgent-appeal-united-nations-special-rapporteurs-regarding-human-rights-abuses). Shortly thereafter another local, Amos Wakali, was killed by gunfire on 27 December 2007, allegedly at the hands of PJV security guards outside of the active mining area. MiningWatch followed up with the UN's human rights officer in Port Moresby on 7 January 2008 (OECD complaint 2011: 10). On 22 July 2008, 15-year-old Gibson Umi was allegedly shot and killed by PJV security guards in the Special Mine Lease area where he lived, but outside the active mining area (OECD complaint 2011: 10).

11. The seven landowner clans of the Special Mine Lease area appointed 23 'agents' to negotiate with the mine on their behalf. The PLOA is funded through a budget derived from mine revenues. PJV pays 2 per cent of its total sales as royalties of which 12 per cent goes to the PLOA.

12. See Porgera Alliance at http://www.porgeraalliance.net

13. See http://www.porgeraalliance.net/tag/akali-tange-association/

14. These visits were largely self-funded. In addition to attending the AGM in Toronto the delegations also met with Barrick executives in 2008 and 2010 (OECD Complaint 2011: 13), issued press releases, met with Canadian

Members of Parliament and civil servants. MiningWatch assisted with logistics and some in-country expenses.

15. Jethro Tulin (2009) (italics in original): http://www.porgeraalliance. net/2009/04/jethro-tulins-testimony-read-to-barrick-shareholders-at-their-2009-annual-general-meeting/. See also *Statement of Mark Ekepa, Chairman of the Porgera Landowners Association at Barrick's Annual General Meeting* (Porgera Alliance, 2010), and MiningWatch Canada (2010).

16. Letter on file with author.

17. Catherine Coumans, *Statement of Catherine Coumans Before the Canadian House of Commons' Standing Comm. on Foreign Affairs & Int'l Dev., Hearing on Bill C-300, An Act Respecting Corporate Accountability* (8 October 2009), http://business-humanrights.org/en/documents/testimony-before-canadian-parliament-re-barrick-porgera-jv-papua-new-guinea. Sarah Knuckey, *Statement of Sarah Knuckey Before the Canadian House of Commons' Standing Comm. on Foreign Affairs & Int'l Dev., Hearing on Bill C-300, An Act Respecting Corporate Accountability* (20 October 2009), http://business-humanrights.org/en/documents/testimony-before-canadian-parliament-re-barrick-porgera-jv-papua-new-guinea. Supplementary testimony was also provided on 3 June 2010. See Sarah Knuckey and Tyler Giannini, *Statements of Sarah Knuckey and Tyler Giannini Before the Canadian House of Commons' Standing Comm. On Foreign Affairs & Int'l Dev., Meeting on Bill C-300, An Act Respecting Corporate Accountability (June 3, 2010)*, https://openparliament.ca/committees/foreign-affairs/40-3/21/the-chair-4/. The human rights clinics also tabled a detailed brief (Human rights clinics, 2009).

18. The editorial board of a national Canadian newspaper commented on testimony by Sarah Knuckey, then of New York University's human rights clinic: 'This testimony bespeaks not merely fabrication but mental derangement in the cause of anti-development. A Barrick spokesman noted that if any such charges had been made, they would be the subject of a thorough investigation' (*National Post* 2009). The editorial praises Barrick's 'comprehensive refutation of the allegations made by (...) Ms. Knuckey, and by radical Canadian anti-mining organizations such as Mining Watch' (*National Post* 2009).

19. Golub (2014: 104) speculates that the 1987 house burning was 'perhaps spurred on by the mine' as it came during a heated dispute with the landowners. Amnesty International (2010) and others (MiningWatch Canada 2009) pointed out the support the mine provided for Operation Ipili '09, which resulted in the house burnings of that year. In 2014 another mass house burning was perpetrated in the Special Mine Lease area allegedly by PNG police (MiningWatch Canada 2014).

20. Personal communication with a translator used by HRW, the human rights clinics and MiningWatch Canada, March 2013.

21. For more on the flaws of the remedy mechanism see (Coumans 2017; MiningWatch Canada 2016a; Knuckey and Jenkin 2015; EarthRights International 2016a, 2016b; Human rights clinics 2015).

22. Barrick's mechanism did not provide equitable remedy for the 119 rape victims it processed (EarthRights International 2016a, 2016b; Knuckey and Jenkin 2015: 810); was unpredictable (Coumans 2017; Human rights clinics 2015; Knuckey and Jenkin 2015); was conceived without input by the victims themselves or significant local stakeholders such as ATA and PLOA (MiningWatch Canada et al. 2013; Knuckey and Jenkin 2015; Human rights clinics 2015).

23. Ruggie's picture is prominently displayed on the company's website. See: www.barrick.com/responsibility/our-approach/csr-advisory-board/default. aspx (accessed 17 June 2016).

24. For a further critique of Enodo's assessment see (EarthRights International, 2016a, 2016b; MiningWatch Canada 2016a).

25. There are, of course, exceptions such as Kirsch (2014).

26. A. Biersack, personal communication, 20 February 2011. Biersack acknowledged that she had signed a contract with the company that may prohibit her from publishing her results.

27. The ATA is now joined by Porgera Women's Rights Watch; Human Rights Inter-Pacific Association; Porgera 119 Indigenous Woman's Association; Porgera Red Wara Women's Association.

28. Personal communication in Porgera, 12 December 2017.

4. Rubbish at the Border

A Minefield of Conservation Politics at the Lawa River, Suriname/French Guiana

Sabine Luning and Marjo de Theije

INTRODUCTION

This chapter is concerned with the relation between gold mining and nature conservation in the southern forest zone of French Guiana, since 2007, almost entirely given the status of Parc National Amazonien. These conservation politics are closely connected to an overheated socio-political arena in which a central state is trying to govern its 'periphery'. A periphery that is not only a frontier zone – in which the state is seeking more presence and governance – but also a border zone. The politics around the Parc National Amazonien are influenced by border dynamics with neighbouring countries Suriname and Brazil. Suriname, situated on the left bank of the Lawa River, plays a major role in cross-border trade, and Brazil is the country of origin of most of the immigrants searching for livelihoods in the French forest. Both the cross-border trade and the influx of migrants are triggered by one major factor: the forests in the south of French Guiana are part of a prolific goldfield.

The relation between gold mining and nature conservation is primarily concerned with questions of valuing of places and land: the relation between centres and peripheries, between claims in land and belonging, between borders and national territories, between exploitation and protection of land, between private property and collective regimes, between the individual interests of people making a living on the land and the long-term preservation of nature and wildlife. In order to bring out these valorisations of land, this chapter will analyse two conservation issues. The first concerns debates about the instauration of the Parc National in a gold field, the second is a case concerned with waste problems on both sides of the river/border. Together, the debates on the Parc National and on waste disposal bring out how overheated identity politics on the border between France and Suriname refer to past legacies and future destinies of this frontier region.

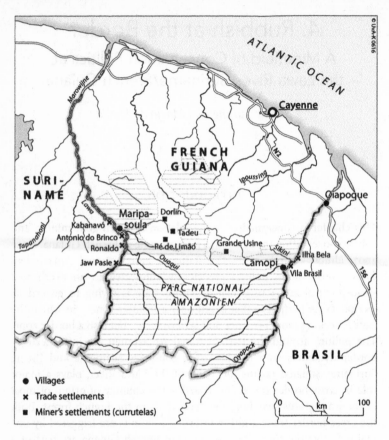

Map 4.1 French Guiana border area
Source: GOMIAM/UvA Kaartenmakers.

GOLD MINING: THE MAKING OF FRONTIERS
AND BORDERS AT THE LAWA

Korf and Raeymaekers (2013) analyse two vocabularies on the margins of the state that are often opposed: those of frontiers and borderlands (2013: 9) and argue they should be brought together. Frontiers are portrayed as zones where key social features, in particular governance practices, are lacking. Borders, on the other hand, are places marked by daily practices of cross-border smuggling, corruption and contraband operations. Whereas analytical attention focused on frontiers is mainly about political projects at the 'end of the state', the academic vocabulary of borders emphasises subversion and transgression. The region that sets the stage for this chapter has a history of marrying frontier and border politics, with gold serving as the metaphorical wedding ring.

The Lawa is a border with some very specific characteristics. This border does not constitute a clear-cut line. On the contrary, many stretches of the Maroni and the Lawa are so broad and filled with islands that both French and Surinamese policing authorities don't know how to determine where one country ends and the other begins. It is also a border that literally runs through an area that the Aluku Maroons consider as their territory. They regard the Lawa Aluku River and the waters of the Lawa, together with both banks, as their lands. For a long time, the north–south axis was dominant for the Maroons in this region: the river was the territory on which transport and access were organised and controlled.

In recent times the east–west axis has become more pronounced: the axis of crossing the river, and moving from one country to another, with Suriname on the left and French Guiana on the right bank. Korf and Raeymaekers rightly stress that border zones are 'where the action' is (2013: 9). Since borderlands are spaces on both sides of a territorial boundary with different regulatory frameworks, smuggling is often lucrative. The borderline acquires a defining feature of the spatialities of circulation across borders (2013: 11–12). Intense flows of goods and people definitely characterise the situation at the Lawa (de Theije 2014; Luning and de Theije 2015).

The borderland dynamics are influenced by the different ways in which the French and the Surinamese states deal with their frontier zones in the forest. Whereas the French are actively trying to impose regulations for access to and use of the forest, this is far less the case on the Surinamese side. This difference in itself is a major trigger for border dynamics of trade. Cross-border flows are amplified due to two regulatory features. The way the French state governs this frontier is based on European standards of policing, and in particular the formal imperative to abide by human rights, which turn out to substantially increase the cross-border flows, as we will see. The benefit of these flows for its economy appears to make the Surinamese authorities less eager to step up governance practices in their frontier at the border. This in turn makes the French attempts at governing their goldfield in the frontier a mission impossible. Trying to organise projects of governance in a frontier is one thing; doing this in a borderland is quite another.

The rest of this chapter will focus on the ways in which the French state is trying to control its frontier, how this affects and is affected by border dynamics and how this is perceived by members of an important group implicated in these dynamics: Aluku. First, we will analyse how works of territorialisation and making identities are currently affected by a mining–conservation nexus. In this nexus, conservation is not the opposite of mining since it goes hand in hand with reformulating the boundaries between legal and illegal mining. Conservation is strategically linked to legitimising specific forms of mining and criminalising other forms. The next section analyses how Aluku identified conservation politics as negative and detrimental to their own local interests, in particular in gold mining. In the last section, we will analyse how the waste problem eventually motivated several Aluku to jump on the bandwagon of conservation and join forces with French state authorities, which are pushing for this agenda. This change was an attempt to regain terrain they had lost due to environmental initiatives.

GOLD MINING IN FRENCH GUIANA: SHIFTING BETWEEN LEGAL AND ILLEGAL GOLD MINING IN THE FOREST

French Guiana is a most peculiar patch of land in South America: as a *Département* of France it is a piece of Europe that is heavily dependent upon the '*métropole*' and surrounded by 'real' South American countries. French government agents spell out their predicament: the guidelines for governing the territory are tailored to European circumstances, whereas the administrators have to work in a South American situation, influenced by the standards set by their neighbours. Suriname is characterised by corruption and a malfunctioning state and Brazil by a more violent style of policing. Under these circumstances, French officials stated time and again, making people respect the law as well as enforcing the law in accordance with international human rights standards are tough tasks. This is most apparent in the domain of regulating gold mining.

In the early 1990s, the French government was making a concerted effort to regulate and formalise the small-scale mining sector. It introduced permits for small-scale mining (Autorisation d'Exploitation – AEX) to mine an area of a maximum of 1 square kilometre on the banks of creeks where alluvial gold is deposited. The permits were handed out to Aluku with French nationality; some of them arrived from Suriname where they had fled to escape the violence of the Interior War (1986–92). The Aluku exploited their mining sites mainly with the help of Brazilian migrant workers. Aluku owned the permits and the machines, Brazilians provided labour but also their expertise. In the region, Brazilians are seen as expert miners, and in the early 1990s they were actively recruited to come and work in French Guiana. Retrospectively, many Aluku portray this period as good, peaceful and productive. For a while Aluku were able to dominate gold mining on both sides of the Lawa. Even though the states of Suriname and French Guiana formally do not recognise the land rights of indigenous and Maroon peoples in their legal systems, in practice Aluku were able to position themselves as traditional owners of land around the Lawa. As hosts they could restrict Brazilians' access to land and negotiate payments for plots they made available to miners (de Theije and Luning forthcoming).

Two factors caused the situation to deteriorate fairly rapidly. First, in 1994 several violent incidents occurred between Aluku and Brazilians at Dorlin, which caught the attention of the media.[1] The events substantially damaged the reputation of well-known Aluku gold miners in French Guiana. The second factor was the start of discussions on the ecological impacts of small-scale gold mining (Oder 2011). Both the violence and the ecological discourse have triggered policy measures that made it almost impossible for Aluku miners to continue their legal operations. Legal small-scale gold miners had to adhere to stringent environmental, social and managerial regulations, which comply with European standards. For Aluku miners it was impossible to live up to these standards.[2] Oder (2011) shows that the total number of permits decreased from 220 in 2002 to less than 100 in 2009. Some of the local Aluku gold miners have moved to Suriname, but most have abandoned gold mining altogether.

Importantly, this decrease in legal permits coincides with a period of spiking gold prices: from $250 an ounce in 2002 to about $1,800 an ounce in 2011. The combination of this surge in gold prices and the 'legal void' for small-scale mining boosted illegal gold mining. The estimated figure of 10,000 clandestine miners in French Guiana keeps recurring in various sources and conversations (Luning and de Theije 2015: 13). In conjunction with this, available indicators suggest that the number of illegal mine sites has been increasing. In 2013, the French National Forest Service counted 774 illegal gold mining sites in French Guiana. Many equate this shift from legal to clandestine gold mining to a marginalisation of Aluku and an increased number of Brazilians.

Policing strategies on this European frontier are mentioned as a major contribution to the shift in the identity of gold miners in the forest of French Guiana. The issue of how the laws are enforced and illegal mining is combated by police and military is an important topic in conversations with citizens, foreigners and government officials alike. Aluku are very outspoken on this issue: as French citizens they are at a disadvantage. If they get caught carrying out illegal mining activities they are taken to court. If Brazilians are caught they are at best expelled from the country – exiting French Guiana one day, coming back the next. Due to inequalities before the law, Aluku have been excluded from gold mining in what they consider to be their territorial patch on the French bank of the Lawa River. When the authorities closed the door on legal miners, so Aluku argue, they did not realise that people can still come in through the window. But these are different people: not French Aluku, but Brazilians.

French law enforcers informed us that arresting illegal miners is not a goal of police actions in the forest. The French authorities choose a European style and abide by a human rights framework. The rule for action stipulates: do not harm the people, focus on the goods. However, tackling illegal gold mining through the system of provisioning goods appears to fuel rather than eradicate cross-border activities. The focus of the French on strangling the provisioning of mining sites gave 'smuggling' greater prominence, with the Surinamese bank of the Lawa as the zone

Figure 4.1   Aerial view of Maripasoula and Antonio do Brinco on the banks of the River Lawa

Source: Sabine Luning.

to set up shop. The shopping hub that has emerged just across Mari-pasoula over the last ten years testifies to this. When police operations occur in the French forest, the Brazilian men and women working on the targeted site often flee to the Surinamese side, for example to Antonio do Brinco. They leave their mining equipment, refrigerators and so on behind. These materials have often been bought on credit. When these are destroyed, what are their options? The destruction of the means of production and food stocks indebt people further and make them even more dependent on each other. The only way they can recover is to start producing again, which they often do with borrowed gold. It is a vicious circle that traps people in the mines or at the border settlements, where we found so many just waiting for a chance to return or to make enough money to be able to return home to Brazil.

Shopkeepers who are providing mining equipment and consumer items on the Surinamese side can benefit from these developments (Luning and de Theije 2015; de Theije and Luning 2016). The shifts towards illegality and the approaches to tackle illegal gold mining in the French forest have drastically changed the landscape of cross-border relations. This situation on the banks of the Lawa creates both tensions and opportunities. It has given rise to border dynamics that can be identified as 'overheating'. As shown, the shift from legal to illegal gold mining was motivated by ecological arguments. These are also at the heart of the most dominant icon of nature conservation in this region: the French Parc National Amazonien.

THE PARC NATIONAL AMAZONIEN:
CONSERVATION AND MINING NEXUS

Conservation issues are always part of a political arena. The perspective we call 'political ecology' brought home that conservation initiatives are presented as relevant to the world at large, but will simultaneously serve parochial interests, on national as well as local levels (Tsing 2004; Robbins 2011). The proposal to create a park in the south of French Guiana dates back to the 1970s (Grenand et al. 2006), but it was only in the 1990s that two attempts at actually setting up the park were made. Both failed because local mining interests were strong enough to resist the creation of the park. The weakened position of Aluku gold miners as a result of shifts in legality a decade later may partly explain why the park could be initiated in the early 2000s. The park took off from the announcement made by President Chirac in 2002 at the Earth Summit in Johannes-burg. Aubertin and Filoche (2008: 165) stress that Chirac's gesture was a reaction to Brazil's declaration to create one of the largest parks in the world, the Parque Nacional das Montanhas do Tumucumaque in the states bordering on French Guiana. Parks near borders or trans-border parks are always imbued with larger geopolitical agendas (Büscher 2013) and so was the Parc National Amazonien. It was formally inaugurated in 2007. From that moment onwards debates about *métropole* and margin took a different shape.

How would this form of governance move into the forest? Two questions are pertinent: first, how would the French state recognise local populations and engage with them and, second, how would nature conservation be combined with livelihood opportunities for local inhabitants in the park?

Concerning the first issue, it is key that the French constitution only acknowledges 'citizens' and never specific collective identities ('*autochthones*'). A national park is state property and rules and regulation apply to all French citizens in the same way. An abundant literature has dealt with the formal, state-centred, assimilationist approach of France towards citizenship both in France itself (Brubaker 1992) and in its former colonies (Cooper 2014). The French colonial style of governance was called direct rule since it was characterised by attempts to circumvent local political structures. In practice, forms of hybrid governance (Geenen 2016) were worked out, but this always remained an uncomfortable marriage with the ideology of only recognising one status of citizenship. Tapping into differentiated fields of localised identities could be formalised but in a low key, with minimal governance substance and preferably incidental in nature.

This governance strategy can be seen at work in the context of the Parc National Amazonien. State officials did have to acknowledge that the space allocated to the park overlaps with historical territories of several Amerindian groups (Wayapi, Emerillon and Wayana) and Aluku Maroons. Members of these groups have to be involved in decision processes and their ways of life (*modes de vie*) have to be safeguarded. How to do that without acknowledging these groups as collectivities with claims in ancestral lands is a challenging question for the authorities trying to bring new forms of governance to this frontier.

One solution for the park is to build upon longer histories of what can be called 'informal formalisation' of customary power holders and seek collaboration with customary authorities and community leaders, notably *Capitaines* and *Grand Mans* of Amerindians and Maroons. For a long while, the French state (in the past through the Préfecture, nowadays through the Conseil général) confirms the nomination of these traditional authorities, even though their position and tasks are not formally defined or acknowledged in the legal system. In practice, traditional authorities are involved in setting dates for festivals, they are concerned with issues related to agriculture such as conflicts over land, and they perform certain tasks that come close to policing (Aubertin and Filoche 2008: 180–1). This vague form of recognition allows state agents to choose whether or not to collaborate with traditional authorities on certain issues and under specific circumstances. The case of waste management that we analyse in the next section of this chapter provides a perfect illustration of this strategy of state authorities. Following these examples, the park also opts regularly to involve traditional authorities in their dealings with social situations. This option of 'informal formalisation' is facilitated by the institutional structures of the park. The setting up of a large Advisory Council which includes among its members political figures (e.g. mayors of the four municipalities), but also representatives of Amerindian and Maroon communities, provides the staff of the park with a forum where they can engage with local groups without actually recognising them (Aubertin and Filoche 2008).

The second solution to engaging with the local population is to recognise *modes de vie*. Instead of recognising them as collective groups, the park defines residents in the park in terms of their ways of life and the use rights in land derived from these. It is crucial to note that the rights are cast in terms of *droits d'usage*, not in terms of property for groups or individuals. To limit the rights of residents of the park to 'use rights' is not merely an act of dispossession – collective and individual – it is also the crucial step in restricting what sort of uses are permitted. They are the starting point for stipulating where and how activities such as hunting, fishing and agriculture are to be carried out.

The park is a way of protecting nature against commodification. Tania Li (2010) discerns that such protection of lands and wildlife are based on the contrast between private property (inclusion in the market) and collective land rights (protection from the market). In this perspective, acknowledgements of indigenous rights and the creation of parks for conservation are put in the same category: both are ways of countering the market. But the creation of the Parc National Amazonien brings into play conflicting systems of collective property: the park as state property is a purposeful denial of indigenous collective rights for Amerindians and Aluku living in the forest. Collective ownership of the state supersedes collective claims from local groups. Subsequently, this collective right of the state leads to rules which stipulate how local inhabitants can and can not use the bounty of the forest. The ways of life acknowledged by the state are associated with *use* rights. Local residents are entitled to use value, not exchange value. This park regime is crafted on a double dispossession: first a denial of (collective and individual) property rights and, second, a prohibition of commercial resource extraction. The aims may be to protect local residents and nature against the market, but this brings into play a complex double movement beyond the one described by Tania Li's broad dichotomous division between collective and private property rights.

This analysis allows us to pursue the second question in more detail: how would nature conservation be combined with livelihood opportunities for local inhabitants in the park? And in line with that question: what is the place of gold mining in these efforts to safeguard nature and livelihoods simultaneously? The attempt to combine nature conservation with options for local livelihoods is expressed in the architecture of the park. The architecture depends upon the distinction between the Heart of the Park (*Coeur*) and four peripheral zones called *Zones de Libre Adhésion* (ZLA) in which four municipalities (Maripasoula, Saul, Papaïchton and Camopi) are located.[3] The Heart of the Park, in which mainly Wayana Indians reside, falls completely under the jurisdiction of the state and is considered to be an area that deserves the strictest possible protection: hardly any economic activities can be carried out there legally. In each ZLA, the mayor and council of the municipality can allow economic activities (such as legal gold mining), and the municipality can get access to (European) funds for sustainable development. Three of the four municipalities and ZLAs are situated on the River Lawa and Aluku Maroons constitute the majority; only Camopi, with Amerindian inhabitants, is located on the other side where the River Oyapock marks the border with Brazil.[4]

In the Heart of the Park, exploitation of the natural riches of the forest is confined most stringently. Nowadays, hardly any of the former hunting and agricultural practices of Amerindians are allowed in an unconstrained manner. When contesting these restrictions one topic always recurs: what about gold mining? In the Heart of the Park gold mining is per definition illegal, but, despite military surveillance of different sorts, it does occur on a substantial scale. Understandably, the presence of mainly Brazilian gold miners in the Heart of the Park delegitimises attempts at confining Amerindians: any form of excessive hunting or fishing pales into insignificance when compared to the pollution due to current gold mining in the Heart of the Park. This predicament forces park officials to be careful in proposing restrictions on local populations in the name of nature conservation. Moreover, in order to be credible in the eyes of Amerindians and Aluku they need to identify strongly with the fight against illegal gold mining.

The ZLAs allow municipalities to shape policy and individuals' economic space. One of the activities that could be allowed – if formalised – is gold mining. Indeed, several protagonists of the conservation agenda fear that mayors and local pressure groups may attempt to push for legalising mining within the ZLAs. In Maripasoula the lobby of former gold miners does indeed hope that gold mining may in the near future become an option once again. Aubertin and Filoche point to an interesting aspect of the current situation: the Heart of the Park is surrounded by ZLAs that are all located in border zones of French Guiana. This opens the door to what they call *transactions non contrôlées* (Aubertin and Filoche 2008: 183). The ZLAs on the Lawa do indeed already play a role in gold mining: they are part of 'where the action is', the zones where cross-border movements of goods and people are organised to facilitate illegal gold mining in the Heart of the Park. This indicates that the architecture of the park may be part of the problem of illegal gold mining rather than an avenue for solving it. Aluku and former gold miners express this view regularly. They state that the *raison d'être* of the park is the presence of illegal gold mining. Nature conservation in this part of French Guiana is primarily a battle against the greatest polluters of all: Brazilians mining for gold illegally. At the same time, the park is seen to contribute to the perpetuation of illegal gold mining rather than its eradication. This failure is the result of both the organisation of the park and its dependence upon law enforcers with 'soft' and counterproductive policing styles. In a beautiful one liner this point of view was formulated: 'The park is the concession of the illegal gold miners. We are not allowed in, but Brazilian gold miners find their way in and are able to stay in.' The park allows the Brazilians to hold their gold mining grounds, so to speak.

No wonder, Aluku are negative about this conservation initiative. They have lost terrain in the field of gold mining. Conservation discourse has restricted them, but not the Brazilians. All the more telling is that currently several Aluku are jumping on the bandwagon of conservation as a way to regain lost terrain. In this attempt they capitalise on their territorial claims: Aluku Liba, the territory made up of the river with the two banks, the left bank in Suriname, the right bank in French Guiana.

RUBBISH AT THE BORDER

The waste issue surfaced in the public debate and the media as a typically European problem. In 2010 the European Union condemned France because it did not comply with the standards for dealing with waste. Four municipalities in the forest region of French Guiana were singled out, Maripasoula, Papaïchton, Apatou and Grand-Santi. Importantly, all four municipalities are located on the right bank of the Lawa and Marowine rivers that constitute the border between Suriname and French Guiana. The European debate on proper processing and containment of waste had its origin in the European *métropole*, but it played out eventually as a cross-border issue in the Amazonian forest. In response to the threat of high fines, the *Préfecture* presented an 'urgent waste plan Maroni' that promised to allot €12 million to the municipalities in order to address the problem. The promise of these moneys forms the trigger for our case.

This case has unfolded at a particular part of the Lawa riverbanks: the municipality of Maripasoula and opposite to it, the string of shops called Antonio do Brinco situated in Suriname. Maripasoula, with only 4500 inhabitants, is the largest French municipality, with a surface of 18,360 square km. Antonio do Brinco has seen a rapid rise over the past decade. Along with Brazilian gold miners, who come either to take a rest from work in the gold fields in French Guiana or to transit between the gold fields and Paramaribo, Chinese traders have become particularly prominent. The commercial activities in the settlement generate substantial waste that is either dumped between the houses or in the River Lawa. The waste issue triggered cross-border blaming and shaming between people whose different economic activities were associated with different national and ethnic identities. One question that emerged was who produces most waste; Brazilian miners or Chinese shopkeepers? Another one was: should France take care of Surinamese waste, and who should be in charge of organising that? Or, again: can 'traditional' authorities of Aluku play a role? The prospect of reorganising waste management in Maripasoula became entangled with attempts to get more control over the situation at Antonio do Brinco.

The French authorities are unhappy with the new settlement across from Maripasoula since the possibilities for smuggling and miners taking refuge clearly undermine the campaign against illegal mining. Collaboration with Surinamese authorities is not very successful since Suriname benefits from the cross-border trade. The Surinamese government collects taxes and the commerce with Paramaribo is important. The presence of Surinamese police is half-hearted; they only intervene in cases of violence or theft, and according to some informants they are hired by Chinese to protect their shops.

In this context, the French state officials sometimes opt to play the card of the customary land rights Aluku try to exercise along the Lawa River. We have seen that the confirmation by the French of the nomination of Aluku and Amerindian Capitaines implies an 'informal formalisation' of traditional authorities. The French gendarmes consider the Aluku Capitaines to be *gens du fleuve*, with a role in controlling access to the river and to both banks of the Lawa, for example, who can help in dealing with dredges (*balsas* in Portuguese) that are 'hoovering' the bottom of the river for gold. Sometimes Capitaines help the French authorities; sometimes they use the same authority to demand concession money from the *balsa* owners. Such money can be claimed on the water and on land.

On land, money can be demanded not just by Capitaines, but also by other Aluku owners of gardens on the riverbanks (*kostgrondjes*). Any newcomer who wants access to such a place can be asked to pay, even if the garden has been abandoned long ago. This is relevant for our case at Antonio do Brinco because the shops are situated on a stretch of land that several Aluku claim as former gardens. They have asked for money from all those who have a house or a commercial operation at Antonio do Brinco. Most people pay such moneys because they are in an insecure position. In particular, Brazilians pay the fees hoping it may legitimise their residential situation.

In this situation an Aluku Capitaine tried to intervene. The issue of managing waste opened the cross-border door. Since Antonio do Brinco lacks a formal community organisation that could handle the increased waste being disposed of by shop owners in the vicinity of the houses, some Brazilian inhabitants contacted French authorities in Maripasoula to investigate the possibility of using the French waste disposal facilities to process 'their' rubbish as well. They argued their case by stating that this would also benefit the French since a lot of rubbish from the shops is simply dumped into the river. In February 2014 a meeting was organised to discuss the issue. Several Capitaines were present and one Capitaine, named Apodo, used the meeting to reproach a fellow Capitaine for taking concession money from Brazilians and Chinese. The area had not been used for gardening in the past: to charge concession money in Antonio do Brinco was not legitimate and contributed to the existence of this dustbin. The garbage issue became an arena for contestations over legitimacy and hierarchy among Aluku Capitaines.[5]

In addition to this internal strife between Aluku, the rubbish case proved explosive for cross-border relations more broadly. The request for help to the French backfired. In the meeting – so we were told – Apodo had gone on to argue that since the concession payments are illegitimate, either everyone had to leave or they had to accept Apodo's leadership in organising things. He stated that the shopkeepers should pay him and not the so-called owners of the gardens because he would connect with the French authorities to get them to clean up the place. Apodo started to present himself as the solver of the cross-border waste problem and, together with an aide, he started negotiating with people at Antonio do Brinco about the price of the service the French government would provide them with. They asked for €200 per month per Chinese shop, €150 from Brazilian restaurants and €100 from individual residents. The difference in price between the Chinese and the Brazilians was motivated by the fact that the Chinese produce much more waste with their shops. However, the discourse was outright anti-Chinese. The waste issue was cast in anti-Chinese rhetoric: 'Chinese just throw the waste in the water.' This was most painfully demonstrated during visits Apodo and his aide would pay to Antonio do Brinco. They would enter the Chinese shops not only complaining about the waste but also about goods that were sold beyond their expiry date and so on. The Chinese were treated as a menace to health.

By April 2014 it became clear that authorities on both the Surinamese and the French side contested the activities of Apodo and his aide. Surinamese policemen would not interfere openly with the visitors, but they did pose the rhetorical question: 'What are you doing here? You are French and this is Suriname.' Even though they did not intervene – the activities did not constitute a criminal offence – they strongly disapproved because of the rising tensions. Moreover, even though the gendarmes still seemed to support Apodo, other French authorities started to shy away from him. In particular, the newly elected mayor (as of March 2014), himself an Aluku, was very critical. He took a formal statist position: as French citizens they had to refrain from interfering with the situation at the other side of the border. Collaboration with traditional authorities and the Surinamese police would be valuable, but the waste issue should be tackled under the guidance of formal French and Surinamese authorities.

Eventually, the activities of Apodo and his aide came to be criticised in Maripasoula more broadly. People from the park pointed to the hypocrisy of blaming the Chinese: all residents from Maripasoula cross the river to buy their groceries at these shops because it is cheaper. Moreover, let us solve our own problems first, they argued. We are the dirtiest part of Europe, and now that the government has made funding available, all the efforts should focus on that. Of course this does not mean that the waste problem in the creeks and at the other side of the river should be neglected. Waste pays no regard to borders, certainly not when it is floating on a river that serves as a national border.

In March 2015, when we returned to the region for further fieldwork, the affair appeared to have died down. The main protagonist, Apodo, had left the public scene for health reasons, and the Brazilians were disappointed that the Aluku had mainly been interested in money and had been making false promises. At Antonio do Brinco the affair had sharpened the relations between Brazilians and Chinese. Many Brazilians think the Chinese shops are the major source of pollution but shouting about that in rude ways had not helped. Perhaps it would be best if the Surinamese authorities could eventually be persuaded to help out.

Why had the Brazilians asked for French help in the first place? Our interlocutors at Antonio do Brinco argued that this had seemed the best option to deal with a situation that needed to be taken care of quickly. Not everyone trusts this motive of the Brazilians. Some Aluku hinted at opportunism on the part of Brazilians. Pointing to the waste in Antonio do Brinco puts Chinese pollution in the limelight, and this may distract from the real polluters: the illegal Brazilian gold miners in the forest. No doubt relations between Brazilians and Chinese at Antonio do Brinco are uneasy. Brazilians who lose their equipment during French police raids in the forest may become trapped: they cannot go home and have to borrow again to set up new mining operations. The Chinese shop-keepers, on the other hand, appear to gain from the destruction of goods and an increase of indebted Brazilians. This does appear to trigger overheated border dynamics fuelled by identity politics.

CONCLUSION

The relation between gold mining and nature conservation is above all concerned with questions of valuing places and land. The debates centre on how to balance the relation between exploitation and conservation of land, and between the individual interests of people making a living on the land and the long-term preservation of nature and wildlife. Moreover, in the context of the Guianas (groups of) people participating in the debate position themselves vis-à-vis others by contrasting *métropole* and margin, and in reference to ethnic and national territorial claims. Given the specific location at the border with Brazil and Suriname, our analysis required distinguishing frontier from border dynamics in order to see how these two sets of dynamics affect each other. Indeed, we have shown that the River Lawa as a border 'where the action is' partly derives from the specific features of governance practices at a frontier. The way the French state has opted to move into the forest has created overheated border dynamics. Four aspects are key: changes in mining regulation and instauration of the park motivated by the agenda of nature conservation; the 'European' style of policing; the ideological take of the French state on dealing with its citizens; and the choice to work out contingent forms of hybrid governance. Together these aspects appear to have fuelled forms of discontent of people living at the French frontier, the acceleration of circulation of goods and people at the border, as well as tensions between people living on the border.

The mining regulations intended to fight violence and pollution provide interesting insights into identity politics and citizenship. Aluku feel disenfranchised, despite their long territorial legacy, and see their French citizenship as a major cause of disadvantages when compared to Brazilian gold miners. Gendarmes confirm that their style of policing does increase mobility of Brazilians mining illegally: the police may force them to move out of French Guiana, but they will be back again. French Aluku do not have this option and will be prosecuted when mining illegally.

Identity politics are also a major element in the way the park has been put into place; the non-recognition of collective identities is combined with informal-formalisations. This leads to hybrid governance practices that are characterised by contingency, since French officials may sometimes opt to collaborate with traditional authorities and not at others. For the traditional Aluku authorities this has an upside because it gives room for initiatives, for trying out new domains to craft hybrid governance. The rubbish case illustrates this perfectly. Aluku can capitalise on their historical legacies to do territorialisation work across the border in ways that the French state cannot. As a result, their water and land territory is sometimes acknowledged, although it seems to benefit only the male Capitaines.

We have also stressed major downsides of non-recognition of collective rights on local territorial legacies. This chapter analyses how collective state ownership of the park overrules collective territorial claims of Amerindians and Aluku. The different types of collective rights interact with and modify each other. The non-recognition of any property rights, collective and individual, comes with recognition of ways of life. However, these *modes de vie* are associated with use rights, rather than rights to commercial exploitation of the land. Extending and nuancing Tania Li's analysis, we have identified the double movement that aims to protect nature and local inhabitants from the market. For local populations the park affects a double dispossession: exclusion from property rights in land and from commercial resource extraction. Furthermore, we have seen that restricting Amerindians and Aluku to use rights over land is accompanied by restrictions on ways of using the forest, in particular in the Heart of the Park. These rules are literally undermined: as long as illegal gold mining occurs how can Amerindians be expected to reduce hunting? The architecture of the park is intended to grapple with the balance between local livelihoods and preservation of nature. But the distinction between the Heart of the Park and ZLAs has turned out to be problematic. Not only is illegal gold mining delegitimising the attempts at nature conservation in the Heart of the Park, the ZLAs serve as bridges in the border dynamics facilitating illegal mining.

Cross-border trade, that is the transnational mobility of goods and people, is key to the mining–conservation nexus analysed in this chapter. Nature protection at the park takes place in close collaboration with police who are trying to eradicate illegal mining. This links violence used by the state to conservation practices. However, the 'European' style of policing, targeting traffic in goods rather than people, appears to stir up border dynamics. It has developed into a major cause of the perpetuation of illegal mining and the smuggling associated with it. This chapter shows how governance practices of the state fuel border dynamics marked by subversion and transgression. The state co-produces social overheating at its border. This is the case when the state is trying to function by following its formal rules of governance, but also when it is trying to craft its work on hybrid forms of governance.

The 'rubbish' case brings out the predicament of governing nature at the intersection of frontier and border dynamics. In defending nature for the world at large hybrid forms of governance appear to fuel parochial interests and tensions. Such governance allowed specific Aluku to try to regain lost terrain by taking on the rhetoric of conservation. They started to intervene in the arena of Brazilian, Surinamese and Chinese actors organising illegal gold mining based on cross-border provisioning of goods and services. Their initiative reinforced practices of shaming and blaming: Aluku blaming Aluku; Aluku blaming Brazilians and Chinese; Brazilians accusing Chinese and Aluku. When social overheating continued, Surinamese and French authorities tried to curtail the cross-border room for manoeuvre of the Aluku protagonists. They should not be allowed to act beyond national borders; they had to be boxed back into France. The case, even now that it has died down, encapsulates how the discourse on conservation can be instrumental in overheated social situations. It also shows the precarious position of French officials at the crossroads of frontier and border dynamics. At this patch of the 'end of the state' (Korf and Raeymaekers 2013), the French authorities seem to be at their wits' end in terms of knowing how to deal with the mining–conservation nexus.

REFERENCES

Aubertin, C. and G. Filoche. 2008. La création du parc amazonien de Guyane: redistribution des pouvoirs, incarnations du 'local' et morcellement du territoire. In C. Aubertin and E. Rodary (eds), *Aires protégées, espaces durables*. Marseille: IRD, pp. 163–85. Available at: http://horizon.documentation.ird.fr/exl-doc/pleins_textes/ed-06-08/010045269.pdf (accessed 5 April 2015).

Bilby, K. 1989. Divided Loyalties: Local Politics and the Play of States among the Aluku. *New West Indian Guide/Nieuwe West-Indische Gids* 63(3/4): 143–73.

Brubaker, R. 1992. *Citizenship and Nationhood in France and Germany.* Cambridge, MA: Harvard University Press.

Büscher, B. 2013. *Transforming the Frontier: Peace Parks and the Politics of Neoliberal Conservation in Southern Africa.* Durham, NC: Duke University Press.

Charte du Parc Amazonien de Guyane. 2012. 20 July. Available at: https://documentation.outre-mer.gouv.fr/Record.htm?idlist=82&record=191239921 24919411749 (accessed 31 May 2018).

Cooper, F. 2014. *Citizenship between Empire and Nation: Remaking France and French Africa, 1945–1960.* Princeton, NJ: Princeton University Press.

de Theije, M. 2014. Small-scale Gold Mining and Trans-frontier Commerce on the Lawa River. In E. Carlin, I. Léglise, B. Migge and P. Tjon Sie Fat (eds), *In and Out of Suriname: Language, Mobility and Identity.* Leiden: Brill, pp. 58–75.

de Theije, M. and S. Luning. 2016. Small-scale Mining and Cross-border Movements of Gold from French Guiana. In G. Collomb and S. Mam Lam Fouck (eds), *Mobilités. ethnicités, diversité culturelle: La Guyane entre Brésil et Suriname.* Cayenne: Ibis Rouge: pp. 141–59.

de Theije, M. and S. Luning. forthcoming. Uncertain Mining Encounters: Migrant Miners, Border Men, and the Contest for Gold at the Banks of the Lawa River (Suriname, French Guiana) (under review).

Dupuy, F. 2012. Un territoire, deux peuple: autochtonie, histoire, légitimité dans le sud-ouest de la Guyane. Available at: http://www.collectif2004images.org/3-5-septembre-2012-Entre-Creolisation-et-autochtonie-memoires-ambigües-et-reponses-creatives-dans-les-mondes-tropicaux_a830.html (accessed April 2014).

Geenen, S. 2016. *Hybrid Governance in Mining Concessions in Ghana* (No. 2016.05). Universiteit Antwerpen, Institute of Development Policy and Management (IOB).

Grenand, F., S. Bahuchet and P. Grenand. 2006. Environment and Peoples in French Guiana: Ambiguities in Applying the Laws of the French Republic. *International Social Science Journal,* 187: 49–58.

Korf, B. and T. Raeymaekers (eds). 2013. *Violence on the Margins: States, Conflict, and Borderlands.* New York: Palgrave Macmillan.

Li, T. 2010. Indigeneity, Capitalism, and the Management of Dispossession. *Current Anthropology* 51(3): 385–414.

Luning, S.W.J. and M. de Theije. 2015. *Small-scale Mining and the Routes Travelled by Gold that Is Illegally Produced in French Guiana.* Amsterdam and Cayenne: GOMIAM and WWF-France.

Oder, J. 2011. Vers la structuration d'une filière aurifère 'durable'? Etude du cas de la Guyane française. *EchoGéo* 17: 1–26.

Robbins, P. 2011. *Political Ecology: A Critical Introduction.* London: Wiley Blackwell.

Tsing, A. 2004. *Friction: An Ethnography of Global Connection.* Princeton, NJ: Princeton University Press.

NOTES

1. See e.g.: http://www.tonkeul.com/guyanefarwest.html.
2. Regulations include the obligation to regenerate mined areas, and the requirement to have €200,000 investment funds. In 2005–6, virtually all titles were withdrawn and the equipment of Aluku operators who were not following the letter of the law was massively destroyed. Under the new regulations these local miners may again apply for a permit but few – if any – have the capital available for exploration and exploitation.
3. Maps showing the architecture of the park in detail can be found in the Charte du Parc Amazonien de Guyane (2012), https://documentation.outre-mer.gouv.fr/Record.htm?idlist=82&record=19123992124919411749
4. Camopi is the only municipality that has refused to sign the Charter of the Park. Since Camopi is not a border community with Suriname, we refrain from discussing details about the conflicts in this community.
5. These contestations have to be understood in the context of longer histories of competition over leadership between Aluku groups based on matrilineal descent, so-called *lo* (Bilby 1989; Dupuy 2012), recently influenced by conversion to Protestantism and gold mining. The Capitaine who is taking concession money comes from the *lo* of the Protestant village Wakapou.

5. Territories of Contestation
Negotiating Mining Concessions in Sierra Leone

Robert Jan Pijpers

INTRODUCTION

The map of the London Mining iron ore concession (Map 5.1) in Marampa, Sierra Leone, presents it in a clear and straightforward way. On the map, thick black lines indicate the concession boundaries as they have been agreed upon with the Sierra Leonean state, clearly delineating what is inside and what is outside the concession. Furthermore, within the black lines, the map distinguishes different kinds of space: some areas are clearly marked, such as the final pit, the plant area or the Chaindatha (on the map spelled as 'Chendata') waste dump, whereas other areas within the black lines seem to be more 'open', such as the area north-west of the Konta waste dump. Moreover, different communities are indicated on the map; some of them inside the concession and close to planned operations, such as Chaindatha, others on the fringes

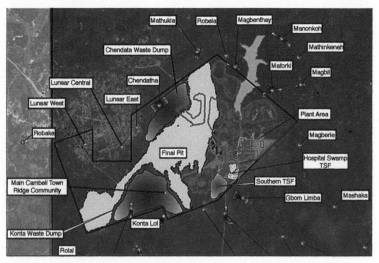

Map 5.1   London Mining concession map

Source: London Mining, personal communication.

of the concession, such as Magbenthey (spelled as Magbenthay) and Konta Lol, and again others further away, such as Manonkoh. All in all, the map communicates the general image of a concession as desired by the company: a well-organised and controlled space. Yet, while the map offers a clear plan, the location of several villages simultaneously suggests that a variety of encounters take place within and on the borders of the concession. Subsequently, conflicts of interest may easily develop, as different usages, values and ownership structures of land intersect with those proposed by London Mining. As a result, a crucial question that needs scrutiny is what happens when a concession map is translated into practice, involving actual people and physical space. How do concessions look in practice? Are they isolated and restricted spaces, or are they more porous and penetrable? And in what ways do different actors, people living in the vicinity or within these concessions in particular, face, challenge or influence the making of a concession?

In this chapter I take on these questions by focusing on the ways in which the boundaries and accessibility of the London Mining concession were contested and negotiated through a multitude of *mining encounters*, conceptualised in the introduction to this volume (Pijpers and Eriksen) as 'the negotiations and frictions between individuals and groups with different agendas, worldviews and aims within the context of mining operations, from the early stages of exploration and development to the final phases of closure and aftermath'. The analysis focuses on the dynamics in the northern parts of the concession as they unfolded in 2013–14 when London Mining's production was expanding. It is situated in a point in time where agreements between company and state had been negotiated, maps had been created and plans for extraction developed (although these too are ongoing processes), but where the organisation of certain areas within the concession was still (or again) in progress. Taking the London Mining concession in Marampa Chiefdom, Sierra Leone, as an ethnographic example, this chapter shows that, rather than being disconnected from their surroundings (a perspective implicit in enclave theories), mining concessions are marked by the presence of different activities and people and embedded in broader social, economic, political and environmental dynamics. Consequently, mining concessions can be seen as dynamic social configurations, as they are actively negotiated, enforced and challenged through series of encounters.

MARAMPA CHIEFDOM: A STORY OF IRON ORE MINING[1]

The London Mining concession is, as indicated above, located in Marampa Chiefdom in the Northern Province of Sierra Leone. Marampa has a long history of iron ore mining, which started in the early 1930s following two geological surveys initiated by the British colonial government, whose interest was to supply Great Britain with raw materials for the military industry (D'Angelo 2015) and diversifying Sierra Leone's declining agriculture-based national economy (Kaniki 1973). Whereas the first survey (1919–22) did not meet expectations, the second one, between 1926 and 1930, was more successful: besides registering the country's gold, platinum, diamond, uranium and rutile deposits, the Masaboin hills in Marampa Chiefdom were assessed as extremely rich in iron. Soon after this second survey, Marampa Chiefdom witnessed the birth of a mining industry with the establishment of the Sierra Leone Development Corporation (DELCO) and its first shipment of iron ore to the UK in 1933 (Forde 2011: 30).

The emergence of this new mining industry triggered significant developments in Marampa (as well as in other mining areas in the country). The mines and surrounding towns offered employment, and, as the population nearby mining operations grew due to internal migration, the demand for agricultural products, construction, crafts, manufacturing, trade and transport increased (van der Laan 1965: 169; see also Jarrett 1956; Gamble 1963). Simultaneously, the departure of the male workforce from their farms to labour in the mines diverted attention from agriculture to mining operations (Jarrett 1957), meanwhile propelling previously unemployed workers into productivity on the now available land (Conteh-Morgan and Dixon-Fyle 1999). However, besides spurring growth, economic development and a variety of opportunities, the iron ore mining industry also had more worrying effects. The demand for land, for example, increased to such an extent that it was 'no longer possible for an inhabitant to secure land unless he is a native of the area, and preferably a Temne' (Jarrett 1956: 157). Moreover, there were concerns that the town was underdeveloped compared to the mining compounds and that social tensions were rising due to the mixing and juxtaposition of too many ethnic groups (1956: 157).

Whereas the dynamics during the DELCO period were ambiguous, on average this time is positively remembered and referred to by contemporary inhabitants of Marampa. Perhaps not surprisingly, given that the closure of DELCO in 1975 symbolised (locally) the emergence of a nationwide period of economic decline and socio-political turmoil. Also the brief reopening of the mines in the early 1980s by the Australian company Austrominerals did not turn the tide in Marampa Chiefdom and the situation worsened so severely that eventually Marampa found itself in 'the wilderness' and Lunsar became a 'ghost town', as the chiefdom's Paramount Chief Bai KobloQueen II formulated it in 2014. Ultimately, years of widespread discontent and frustration in Sierra Leone led to the outbreak of a civil war in 1991, which would last until 2002. After the war a process of reconciliation and reconstruction started. People in Marampa, like everywhere else in the country, had to rebuild their lives, and several initiatives tried to contribute to this project: non-governmental organisations (NGOs), like the Cotton Tree Foundation, initiated rural development projects; the Catholic Mission ran important operations, not least in the form of secondary and vocational education, and a larger-scale mechanised rice cultivation project, Genesis Farms, was established, creating employment opportunities and contributing to agricultural development. Yet, it was the re-establishment of the mining industry that really accelerated the speed of change in Marampa once again.

With the arrival of London Mining in 2006,[2] a common feeling of excitement was injected into the area and a promising future seemingly lay ahead. 'People are happy. In every house there are workers. When they cook, the rice will be shared and maybe they give some money to the children for school', an inhabitant of one of the villages around Lunsar, Marampa Chiefdom's main town, told me. Expectations of development rose rapidly as the chiefdom started to experience multiple changes, such as the improvement of infrastructure, the opening of restaurants and shops, electricity supply, increased motorised transport facilities and a significantly growing number of jobs. Around 2010, the year that iron ore production really started, Marampa had turned into a landscape of accelerated change; coming out of decades of crisis, including a civil war, good times were now being experienced, and even better times were expected. Yet, simultaneously, some aspects of Marampa's transformation seemed to create concern. The high influx of people, for example, resulted in encroachment on the town cemetery to give way to the construction of houses. Local people complained that companies employed people from outside the chiefdom and abroad. Moreover, certain changes in the landscape (intended or not) caused new challenges. In Magbenthey, one of the villages just outside of the London Mining concession, for example, people indicated that due to the operations of London Mining they had 'no place to walk any more' and that due to a serious flooding issue their crops and houses were damaged and they had 'entered in the world of suffering'. In other words, mining, as it often does, had a dominant, yet ambiguous, influence on the contemporary landscape in Marampa Chiefdom.

As this brief overview illuminates, Marampa's social, economic, environmental and political structure is entangled in its mining history, present and future. In this sense, Marampa's landscape of resource extraction can be seen as a *minescape*, which according to Ey and Sherval is a 'representational tool that underscores the intricate ways in which extractive processes are imbued with complex socio-cultural dynamics, and powerful material and discursive elements' (2016: 1). Focusing on spaces of resource extraction as minescapes puts at the centre the interplay between various actors, and their disparate social, economic and political interests, in the establishment of extractive processes. This interplay materialises and becomes visible through mining encounters, for example those that concern the establishment of a crucial element of minescapes: mining concessions.

THE LONDON MINING CONCESSION:
FROM ENCLAVE TO COHABITATION

At the time field research for this chapter was conducted, in 2013–14, the London Mining concession was approximately 14 square km in size. The legally binding rights and responsibilities of London Mining towards its concession area are formulated in the Mines and Minerals Act of Sierra Leone (Government of Sierra Leone [GoSL] 2009) and the Mining Lease Agreement between the Government of Sierra Leone and London Mining (GoSL and LMC Ltd 2012). These laws and agreements grant the company the right to organise the mining lease area (the concession) in ways that facilitate a successful mining operation. This includes the construction of infrastructure, the stacking or dumping of minerals/ waste products, the utilisation of resources such as water, the removal of buildings, the hiring and maintenance of an unarmed security force and the resettlement of villages. Naturally, this authority is subject to other laws and guidelines. As the agreement makes clear, the company cannot, for example, appropriate land that has been used for dwelling, agriculture or public infrastructure without the consent of the owners. However, when reasonable justification is not provided for withholding such consent – a judgement made by the minister responsible for mineral resources – the minister can enforce a company's rights to use of the land.

Both the lease agreement and the concession map (Map 5.1) presented at the beginning of this chapter point towards the company's authority inside the mining concession and communicate the idea of a company-controlled territory of resource extraction which can be detached from its wider environments. But how can we look at the social materialisation of maps and agreements and how can they be related to the actual landscapes in which they materialise? After all, the concession map also indicated several villages inside and on the borders of the concession.

Is the establishment of a concession a fixed moment in time ratified by an agreement between state and company which generates an enclave, or can we see the concession as a result of ongoing social processes (including 'enclaving' strategies) and as a dynamic and porous territory open to contestation?

Mining Enclaves

A perspective that has gained increasing traction in the literature to analyse the (limited) linkages between mining operations and their surroundings is that of 'enclave economies' or 'extractive enclaving'. In 'Seeing Like an Oil Company' (2005), for example, Ferguson provides an influential account of extractive enclaving. Responding to Scott's idea of the homogenising and standardising state (Scott 1998), Ferguson proposes a perspective that takes in the ways in which 'recent capital investment in Africa has been territorialised, and some of the new forms of order and disorder that have accompanied that selectively territorialised investment'. Investments (Ferguson focuses on oil companies) have been concentrated in secured enclaves, with little or no economic benefit to the wider society, a phenomenon called 'extractive enclaving' (Ferguson 2005: 378). In order to support this argument, Ferguson demonstrates how, drawing upon a colonial distinction of *l'Afrique utile* and *l'Afrique inutile* (usable and unusable Africa; Reno 1999: 35), investments divide space into the useful and the non-useful: 'Capital does not "flow" from London to Cabinda, it hops, neatly skipping over most of what lies in between' (Ferguson 2005: 379). The parts that capital skips over are unusable, those where it alights (the mineral-rich spots) are usable. This, he argues, undermines the contiguous and bounded nature of national territories. Extraction, in other words 'produces classic enclave economies that are, at one and the same moment, both deeply integrated into the global economy and also fragmented from national space' (Bridge 2009: 5). Appel (2012) builds upon this idea of the enclave in her work on oil companies in Equatorial Guinea, discussing collaborations between those in power and oil companies, especially in terms of the state's granting corporate sovereignty within enclaves, and the labour applied by oil companies to disconnect oil from its source. Although it can be questioned whether, and to what extent, companies gain 'sovereignty' within their concessions, through their enclaving nature, companies engage in a process of disentanglement from local processes, as Appel argues (2012: 442). Akiwumi translates this view on enclaved oil territories to mining companies in Sierra Leone, observing that 'mining companies in Sierra Leone operate as self-contained foreign entities and interact minimally with local people and their traditional socioeconomic structures' (Akiwumi 2012: 588).

Such perspectives on the disentanglement of mining operations from their surroundings are at times also reflected in local discussions. In November 2013, for example, a new bank opened in Lunsar – a major event attended by prominent local and national authorities such as the paramount chief, the director of the National Bank and the President of Sierra Leone, Ernest Bai Koroma. During the speeches, all speakers, including the three mentioned, took the opportunity to push investors to do more in terms of local content: to hire more local people and to source material and services locally as much as possible. Not surprisingly, such statements, reflecting in popular terms what is outlined in the Sierra Leone Local Content Policy (GoSL 2012), trickle down to the local level, raise expectations and, when these are not fulfilled, may feed local disappointments, leading at times to friction. Moreover, the cry for more local content could be appropriated to support the enclave thesis that integration of the investor into the wider society is limited.

Scrutinising the limited linkages between foreign, large-scale mining operations and the local/national socioeconomic environments in which they operate can fruitfully highlight asymmetrical power relations and the dynamics of financial flows/hops, demonstrating the unequal division of benefits deriving from mining operations. It also allows us to examine how mining operations valorise nature, tap into pockets of usable space and skip what is regarded as unusable or disposable, processes which can even be plotted at the level of the securitisation of certain key parts of the concession (such as the mining pit, the processing facilities or the administrative buildings). Yet, despite its usefulness, the idea of the mining enclave may simultaneously obscure more nuanced dynamics on the ground. After all, an enclave calls forth an image of secured and isolated space, disconnected from its surroundings. However, even though considerable power inequalities are in play, this is not the impression one gets of the London Mining concession.

Interruptions and Cohabitation

During fieldwork I regularly conducted interviews while walking around, a research method known as 'the go-along' or 'the walking interview' (Kusenbach 2003). These walking interviews turned out to be productive in reading the landscape and getting a sense of place. As such, walking around in the London Mining concession and having ongoing conversations with different people, illuminated the diverse ways in which the concession was both formally and informally organised. In order to illustrate this, let me briefly recapitulate some observations and descriptions from my field research.

There were several points to enter the concession by road which were often marked by security checkpoints. Approaching the concession from the northern side, for example, security personnel counted the vehicles and individuals passing through the concession. The atmosphere around this checkpoint felt informal and friendly; women collecting firewood and producing charcoal sometimes left their products with the security to watch over it while they were busy with something else and friends of the security guards habitually passed by to greet them. Several hundreds of meters away from the gate, one could see the bottom of one of London Mining's two waste dumps[3] with rocks of different sizes being piled up. Several people collected rocks from this waste dump to sell to construction workers in neighbouring villages and towns. This activity was not without danger as the waste could start sliding, and, officially, the company did not approve of this activity, although this prohibition was hardly enforced. Passing along the waste dump one could take a road towards the administrative offices and the processing plant. Without invitation or company identification it was difficult to enter these areas, given that they were fenced and/or heavily securitised and off-limits for ordinary people.

Another road departing from the first security gate led to a lake called Matukia, which was created by DELCO, while passing by small farms. The lake was often a busy place, with women from surrounding villages doing their laundry, young men and boys offering car wash services to private individuals as well as company staff, and women and girls selling small food products. Whereas the concession had taken away certain livelihood opportunities, as farms were now part of operational sites, it also generated new ones, as the examples of the car-washing services and the new sales point for food products for women and girls show. Not far from here, along the road towards the eastern parts of the concession, a group of young men were preparing some land for agriculture. Their work appeared to be part of an agricultural livelihoods project for youth which was funded by London Mining and implemented by a local NGO within the concession area.

It may be clear that different activities and encounters between the company and local community members took place in the mining concession. Many of them were of a relatively relaxed nature, but others were tense and even led to conflict. A case in point was the situation of Maforki. During the 2013 rainy season, one of the lakes in the concession had flooded, for which London Mining was held responsible by the communities living around this lake. This not only destroyed many crops but also made travel, especially for schoolchildren, particularly difficult. Although a study by the Sierra Leonean Environmental Protection Agency (EPA) cleared London Mining of responsibility, many people living in the chiefdom testified that this was the first time the lake had flooded and some company employees confirmed that the flooding indeed occurred after they had altered the flow of the river in their operational area. The flooding issue became an important event in local resource politics. Especially in Maforki, located not far from the flooded lake, it caused heated conversations, heightened frustration and eventually resulted in a demonstration, during which some villagers entered the concession and damaged some company property. During the demonstration, all management-level staff were evacuated to the fenced and secured administrative compound (where I was present myself as well to conduct interviews). Moreover, discussions of London Mining management with the local unit commander of the police and the paramount chief, who had in the meantime arrived, swiftly started in order to quickly regain control over the situation. Allegedly, the strike was orchestrated by an influential person from Lunsar who often acted against the company by mobilising crowds of disappointed young men. During the 'demonstration' some people were arrested and in the next few days police officers visited Maforki several times (sometimes accompanied by the paramount chief or security staff of one of London Mining's contractors), which occasionally resulted in physical clashes. Eventually, the conflict remained unresolved and after months of adjourning court cases all parties seemed to have given up.

As the various examples above show, rather than being an isolated enclave, the London Mining concession was marked by the presence of a variety of people and activities, even seven years after operations had started. The economic activities that either continued (such as farming) or were newly developed (such as car-washing services or rock collecting) in the concession, as well as certain environmental changes which posed new challenges and problems for the area's inhabitants (like the flooding issue), illuminate that concessions are deeply integrated in the everyday lives of people living within and around this space. This observation resonates with other studies which emphasise the entanglement of various actors and activities in mining environments (see, for example, Luning and Pijpers 2017; Emel et al. 2011; Hilson 2002; Luning 2014; Panella 2010; Teschner 2013; Le Meur et al. 2013, as well as several of the other chapters in this volume). Moreover, the way in which certain areas are more securitised than others and company staff were taken to protected areas during the Maforki demonstration also illustrates how the total concession space consists of differently valorised and securitised space, thereby drawing attention to what is deemed usable and important and what is regarded as unusable, to apply Ferguson's (2005) and Reno's (1999) terms to this more micro-level situation. However, the extent to which the company can fence off the concession is influenced by, among other things, other forms of land use, the locations of sacred/spiritual sites and the history of DELCO's 'thick' integration into society (cf. Ferguson 2006; see also Pijpers 2018). Thus, even though the securitisation of concessions, the push for local-content policies and general perceptions that too few benefits derive from mining operations at the local level support the relevance of enclave theory, in the present case, applying the concept of the enclave does not fully acknowledge the integrated character and the negotiations that emerge around concession making.

Equally concerned with the materialisation of resource extraction projects at the local level, Emel et al. (2011) analyse territory making by discussing the idea of local interruptions of the territorial agreements between states and companies. They point out that the state's authority to give mining companies access to mineral wealth is based on its ultimate ownership of the subsoil mineral wealth, and that the interest of the state in extracting it may overpower the interests of local surface users. Meanwhile, the state's exclusive right to control and govern sub-surface wealth facilitates alliances with companies who are given permission to extract it. However, as Emel et al. (2011) clearly argue, even though extraction rights over a certain space can be negotiated at the national level, the territory of extraction materialises at the local level, where companies and states have to deal with local land-use practices and other activities that influence mining operations. Therefore, it is important to focus on 'the ways in which local populations living in the spaces of extraction are constantly interrupting state–capital sovereignty projects' (2011: 73). Building upon the understanding that local realities influence national-level territory making, Luning and Pijpers (2017) analyse how large-scale gold mining concessions in Ghana are governed. Typically, these concessions are characterised by the concurrence of a multitude of other activities and land uses resulting in a situation in which different stakeholders (Luning and Pijpers focus on the relations between the large-scale concession owner and small-scale artisanal miners) have to negotiate forms of cohabitation. By looking at 'in-depth geopolitics' – that is, the connection between three particular domains: the stage of a mining operation, the local social, political and economic history and the particular geological situation – Luning and Pijpers analyse how access and control within a gold mining concession is actively negotiated and particular forms of cohabitation are produced. As we have seen in the various examples discussed above, also in the case under study in this chapter, these local practices or interruptions – whether they already existed prior to the establishment of the concession, or emerged afterwards – and the efforts to negotiate some form of cohabitation are crucial in the practice of concession making.

A focus on cohabitation resonates with the idea of the minescape (Ey and Sherval 2016) and anthropological approaches to the production and dialectical character of landscape more generally (see, for example, Hirsch and O'Hanlon 1995; Stewart and Strathern 2003; Pine 2007; Liesch 2014). These studies stress that:

> landscape is never passive. People engage with it, rework it, appropri-
> ate and contest it. It is part of the way in which identities are created
> and disputed, whether as individual, group or nation-state. Operating
> at the juncture of history and politics, social relations and cultural per-
> ceptions, landscape is a concept of high tension. (Bender 2002: 488)

Consequently, landscapes, including those considered to be, or to include, mining concessions, can be seen as social configurations, inscribed with ideas of identity, history and religion, as well as the ownership, governance, use and organisation of land. Consequently, if concessions offer additional ways of configuring the landscape, how could we imagine (in greater detail than the examples discussed previously allow) such processes to take shape? How do mining concessions alter the way landscape is valorised and governed? How do they alter boundaries? And how do different people incorporate the dynamics of mining concessions into configurations of landscape? In order to explore these questions, we will now turn to several of the discussions that emerged during the resettlement process of the village of Chaindatha.

CHAINDATHA'S RESETTLEMENT: OVERLAPPING LAND GOVERNANCE AND NEW ALLIANCES

Chaindatha is a village located on the northern fringes of the London Mining concession. Since the arrival of London Mining, the village had been entangled in the company's operations: several villagers were employed, company traffic passed through the village and London Mining leased a considerable area of land from the Chaindatha landowning families, the Kamaras and the Kabias. Yet, in 2013, relations between Chaindatha and London Mining were taken to another level when the village's resettlement process began, due to its increasing proximity to a large waste dump. Resettlement may be typical for enclaving strategies, as it is geared towards clearing the concession area, but, if studied in detail, it also highlights how difficult it appears to disentangle mining from a 'local' landscape, how pre-existing forms of landownership continue to be crucial (even after the area had been part of the London Mining concession for several years) and how resettlement offers opportunities for creating new alliances and cleavages. During the resettlement process, a wide variety of stakeholders were drawn into the discussions at some point. Of course local landowners and land users were present, as well as the company staff and the consultants conducting the survey, but also one of the Lunsar town councillors, who happened to have kinship relations in Chaindatha, a national government representative, the chairman of the chiefdom's landowners association, the paramount chief, elders from other villages, landowners from other villages and, occasionally, in difficult times company staff members in management positions were called upon. Interestingly, these authority figures represent qualitatively different kinds of government – traditional and state-based – as well as people representing the 'enclaving strategy'.

The resettlement process, which lasted from November 2013 to March 2014, consisted of two main phases: a period of information sharing and various rounds of discussions and a period in which both external and internal boundaries (and therefore landownership) were surveyed. Most of the boundaries that needed to be indicated were located inside the concession and, at nearly all boundary points, fierce discussions arose between the different actors, as many of them had conflicting interests and some people tried to define boundaries in such a way that would increase the amount of land they owned. Below I will discuss two such instances. The first concerns a boundary dispute between Chaindatha and its neighbouring village Magbenthey, the second involves the boundary between the two landowning families of Chaindatha, the Kabias and the Kamaras.

'They Are Taking Advantage of the Company'

One of the main boundaries that had to be established during the survey was the boundary between Chaindatha and Magbenthey. At one point, soon after commencement of the survey, the leaders of Chaindatha were claiming a certain piece of land, to the frustration of members of Magbenthey village. Marie Tarawally, a woman from Magbenthey who had joined the survey, witnessed what was happening and started crying: 'The people of Chaindatha are taking advantage of our poverty. My father is the owner of this land; I know it very well here.' She explained that her family had worked the land when she was young. In those days, the boundaries between Magbenthey and Chaindatha were by the cemetery, but once, when people from Chaindatha came to demarcate the boundary, no one from Magbenthey was around and Chaindatha took their land. Apparently, the boundary had been surveyed before and her elder brother, who had just joined the conversation, added, 'Chaindatha is taking advantage of the company; some of them encroached on our land. Before, we lived peacefully with our brothers in Chaindatha, but since these white people came there have been conflicts about land, one after the other.' Marie continued, 'It would have been better if our children and husbands had been employed. But these white people haven't employed our children, nor our husbands; they just work on our land and cause confusion amongst us.' Her brother eventually concluded, 'Since they [Chaindatha] have claimed the land, let us forget about it.'

The vignette illustrates the ways in which concession-work renders old boundaries prominent and highly relevant. The concession does not erase the boundaries between these villages; it rather reinforces them and, especially in the wake of surface rent payment or land loss compensation, as is the case here, renders them more critical. It must be noted that this survey occurred well after the start of operations, and already for several years the land-lease payment to the landowners was conducted. However, time and again in the process of translating the concession map into practice, boundary disputes were brought up. The stakes involved in claiming certain areas are high. The more land Chaindatha landowners can claim, the higher their future compensation from London Mining. But the reverse is also true: the more land that people from Magbenthey manage to claim as theirs, the higher their potential future benefits. In discussions it became clear how people from Magbenthey felt they were on the losing end and connected this situation to the presence of mining: in their view Chaindatha used the company's interest in surveying their land to claim ownership of certain areas. Thus, according to people from Magbenthey, Chaindatha's leadership forged an alliance with London Mining against them. This alliance was made possible due to the process of concession making that took place at that time.

The DELCO Stream

Boundaries are contested not only between villages but also within villages, between the different landowning families, boundaries became contested. One such instance is our second case: a dispute regarding the boundary between Kabia and Kamara land. Central to the disagreement was the location of a particular stream. According to the Kamaras, this stream represented the boundary between the land of the two families.

However, PaSorie, a prominent member of the Kabia family, contested this, arguing that:

> The stream used to be the boundary, but it was shifted by the waste dump the DELCO people put here. When rain came, when erosion occurred, it started covering the stream little by little until it pushed the stream to where it is presently. The stream used to be where we are standing, but it was shifted by the waste dump.

The headman of Chaindatha, Abubakarr Kamara, responded that although PaSorie had spoken well, they, the Kamaras, used to work here and the boundary was supposed to run from a particular mango tree to the stream. The Kabias and Kamaras could not reach any agreement and eventually another prominent member of the Kamara family, PaYK, tried to end the discussion stressing that the families should not 'create too much confusion' and proposing to 'cancel the demarcation, sit down and find a peaceful solution'. After this statement, PaYK left, soon followed by the others.

The next day it appeared that there had been another reason for terminating the survey, in addition to the apparent one of the stream's recognised connection with the boundary. It emerged that the *condition* of the stream was an issue that was hotly contested, and with London Mining rather than between the Kabia and Kamara families. Since postponements had become a feature of the process, a London Mining community relations officer came to the village to talk about the ongoing disruptions. After a considerable group – including the key stakeholders from the Kabia and Kamara families – had gathered, the headman addressed the London Mining community relations officer and explained:

> After this survey [the external boundaries], if the issue with the stream is not resolved, nothing will happen. We have addressed this issue many times and we are tired of this. From the first day, the only reason that we have continued with the survey is because of this man [pointing at the consultant]. If it had been left with you [London Mining], nothing would have happened. We should first seek our own interest. Most of us have even fought our brothers for the sake of the company. We know what we suffer, what we give up for this LMC [London Mining] exercise. If the stream issue is not addressed, the survey will not go on.

From the statements and discussions, it transpired that Chaindatha was using the consultants and their survey – the concession-making process

– as a way of demanding a solution from London Mining for the dust and mud-polluted stream that runs behind the village. Until that issue was solved and London Mining shouldered its responsibility, the survey would not continue. Whereas several days earlier, Chaindatha allegedly used the concession-work to create an alliance with the mining company against one of the other villages, it now used the concession-work against the company and drew upon its ability to obstruct the survey in order to pose demands on the company. Thus, while the Kabias and Kamaras disagreed on the boundary issue, they had simultaneously formed an alliance in which the consultants had, unintentionally, ended up siding with Chaindatha against London Mining. More intentionally, however, the consultants had sought the support of London Mining in order to solve the stoppage in proceedings. For the community, this was a fine line to walk, as it may happen that chiefdom level authorities, such as the paramount chief, would back up the company and intervene (such as happened in the case of Maforki's demonstration).

The two cases from the Chaindatha resettlement process highlight the numerous discussions and negotiations over space and thus illuminate the ways in which landscape can be reworked, appropriated and contested (Bender 2002). Moreover, the examples also show that the lines of authority are not clear, since different sets of rules seem to apply simultaneously. Given that these two cases, as well as the examples in the previous section, were recorded in 2013 and 2014, several years after the start of operations, concession making does indeed resemble a process of ongoing negotiation. The different encounters that emerge in the process of concession-work show the power of the company and their efforts to organise space, but also their dependency on people's cooperation. They also show how certain parts of the concession are deemed valuable and in need of securitisation, such as the areas needed for administrative offices or the processing plant site, whereas other areas are more loosely controlled, giving access to people to deploy activities or even to local NGOs to implement company-funded development projects. Other areas are off-limits, yet this is not actively enforced, such as areas around waste dumps where local people gather rocks in order to sell them to local construction workers in neighbouring towns and villages. Moreover, especially in the Chaindatha cases, it becomes clear how the concession and its ongoing creation triggered different opportunities for shifting alliances and cleavages between different actors. In sum, it transpires that the concession does not erase, but rather alters and adds new layers of usage, governance and meaning. These new layers simultaneously pose new challenges as well as new opportunities.

CONCLUSION: MINING ENCOUNTERS AND THE MAKING OF CONCESSIONS

In this chapter I have discussed how mining concessions can be seen as dynamic social configurations which are negotiated in, and materialise through, numerous encounters. Building upon the concession map of London Mining (Map 5.1) and the Mining Lease Agreement between the company and the Sierra Leonean state, I have asked what this seemingly well-organised and well-defined concession looks like in practice and how different people face, challenge, influence and make use of the making of a concession.

In order to address these questions, I first discussed the 'enclave' approach as put forward by, for example, Ferguson (2005), Appel (2012) and Akiwumi (2012). While acknowledging the merits of such an approach, especially concerning power structures and territory making at the national-global level, I also argued that the notion of the enclave does not allow us fully to understand the micro-politics of large-scale mining (Pijpers 2018). Indeed, when looking at the mining concession of London Mining in detail, as has been done in this chapter, one can observe the presence of a multitude of actors and activities, such as women engaged in petty trade, farming activities, young men offering car wash services, villages located inside and on the borders of the concession and people collecting rocks from the waste dump. These ethnographic examples illustrate the dynamics in the process of making a concession; some of them reflecting enclaving strategies, clearly limiting the movement of people and strictly securing certain parts of the concession, with others highlighting the ways in which concession boundaries are contested, or how changes within the usage of different parts of the concession generate or block certain livelihood activities. This situation, which thus presents a more entangled image of mining concessions than the notion of the enclave does, resonates with studies that emphasise how forms of cohabitation are negotiated between different actors in these mining environments (see, for example, Bloch and Owusu 2012; Hilson 2002; Luning 2014; Teschner 2013; Le Meur et al. 2013; Emel et al. 2011 and Luning and Pijpers 2017). Consequently, even if mining companies aspire to create spatial and/or social enclaves, in practice they are confronted with dynamics that make enclaving difficult, impossible or even undesirable.

The two case studies taken from the Chaindatha case further illustrate these dynamics, but also foreground the dialectical and processual character of landscape (Hirsch and O'Hanlon 1995; Stewart and Strathern 2003; Pine 2007; Liesch 2014; Lentz 2006; Bender 2002), in this case a very particular kind of mining landscape. In addition, the changes in the environment and the process of concession making are appropriated by different actors in order to position themselves vis-à-vis others; for example, by Chaindatha leaders to appropriate land which Magbenthey inhabitants consider theirs or by the Chaindatha community to take a stance against London Mining and demand solutions for specific problems. In other words, these cases highlight how boundaries within the concession become more relevant as interests and stakes intensify, but also how concession-work produces opportunities for shifting alliances and cleavages between different stakeholders.

In sum, by taking a mining encounters approach (as suggested by Pijpers and Eriksen in the introduction to this volume) it becomes clear how mining concessions, and the maps and agreements in which they are presented, are not disentangled from their environment, but rather entangled in various social, economic and political dynamics, including local land use and governance practices. Consequently, studying a mining concession as a dynamic and connected social configuration that emerges out of a multitude of encounters is a fruitful approach; it allows focusing on the ways in which different (and unequal) actors enforce, challenge and negotiate mining concessions and, consequently, try to influence and shape the ways in which transnational mining operations affect local life worlds.

ACKNOWLEDGEMENTS

In addition to all my interlocutors in Sierra Leone, I would also like to thank the participants of the Mining Encounters workshop in Oslo (April 2015) for the discussions and their comments on an earlier version of this chapter. The research on which this chapter is based is funded by the European Research Council Advanced Grant 'Overheating', ERC grant number 295843.

REFERENCES

Akiwumi, F.A. 2012. Global Incorporation and Local Conflict: Sierra Leonean Mining Regions. *Antipode* 44(3): 581–600.

Appel, H. 2012. Walls and White Elephants: Oil Extraction, Responsibility, and Infrastructural Violence in Equatorial Guinea. *Ethnography* 13 (4): 439–65.

Bender, B. 2002. Landscape. In A. Barnard and J. Spencer (eds), *Encyclopedia of Social and Cultural Anthropology*. New York: Routledge, pp. 323–4.

Bloch, R. and G. Owusu. 2012. Linkages in Ghana's Gold Mining Industry: Challenging the enclave Thesis. *Resources Policy* 37: 434–42.

Bridge, G. 2009. The Hole World: Spaces and Scales of Extraction. *New Geographies* 2: 43–8.

Conteh-Morgan, E. and M. Dixon-Fyle. 1999. *Sierra Leone at the End of the Twentieth Century: History, Politics and Society.* New York: Peter Lang.

D'Angelo, L. 2015. The Art of Governing Contingency: Rethinking the Colonial History of Diamond Mining in Sierra Leone. *Historical Research* 89(243): 136–57.

Emel, J., M.T. Huber and M.H. Makene. 2011. Extracting Sovereignty: Capital, Territory, and gold Mining in Tanzania. *Political Geography* 30: 70–9.

Ey, M. and M. Sherval. 2016. Exploring the Minescape: Engaging with the Complexity of the Extractive Sector. *Area* 48(2): 176–82.

Ferguson, J. 2005. Seeing Like an Oil Company: Space, Security and Global Capital in Neoliberal Africa. *American Anthropologists* 107(3): 377–82.

—— 2006. *Global Shadows: Africa in the Neoliberal World Order.* Durham, NC: Duke University Press.

Forde, W. 2011. *The Story of Mining in Sierra Leone.* Bloomington, in: XLibris Publishing.

Gamble, D.P. 1963. The Temne Family in a Modern Town (Lunsar) in Sierra Leone. *Africa: Journal of the International African Institute* 33(3): 209–26.

GoSL (Government of Sierra Leone). 2009. Mines and Minerals Act. Government of Sierra Leone.

—— 2012. Sierra Leone Local Content Policy. Government of Sierra Leone.

GoSL and LMC Ltd (Government of Sierra Leone and London Mining Company Ltd). 2012. Mining Lease Agreement between THE GOVERNMENT OF SIERRA LEONE and LONDON MINING COMPANY LIMITED.

Hilson, G. 2002. An Overview of Land Use Conflicts in Mining Communities. *Land Use Policy* 19: 65–73.

Hirsch, E. and M. O'Hanlon. 1995. *The Anthropology of Landscape: Perspectives on Place and Space.* Oxford: Clarendon Press.

Jarrett, H.R. 1956. Lunsar: A Study of an Iron Ore Mining Center in Sierra Leone. *Economic Geography* 32(2): 153–61.

—— 1957. Mineral Developments in Sierra Leone. *Geography* 42(4): 258–60.

Kaniki, M. 1973. Economic Change in Sierra Leone during the 1930s. *Transafrican Journal of History* 3(1–2): 72–95.

Kusenbach, M. 2003. Street Phenomenology: The Go-along as ethnographic research Tool. *Ethnography* 4(3): 455–85.

Le Meur, P.Y., C. Ballard, G. Banks and J.M. Sourisseau. 2013. Two Islands, Four Estates: Comparing Resource Governance Regimes in the Southwest Pacific. In *Proceedings of the 2nd International Conference on Social Responsibility in Mining* (SRMining 2013, Santiago, Chile). Santiago: Gecamin, pp. 191–9.

Lentz, C. 2006. Land Rights and the Politics of Belonging in Africa: An Introduction. In R.L. Kuba and C. Lentz (eds), *Land and the Politics of Belonging in West Africa.* Leiden: Brill, pp. 1–34.

Liesch, M. 2014. Spatial Boundaries and Industrial Landscapes at Keweenah National Historical Park. *The Extractive Industries and Society* 1: 303–11.

Luning, S.W.J. 2014. The Future of Artisanal Miners from a Large-scale Perspective: From valued Pathfinders to Disposable Illegals? *Futures* 62(A): 67–74.

Luning, S. and R.J. Pijpers (2017). Governing Access to Gold in Ghana: In-depth Geopolitics on Mining Concession. *Africa* 87(4): 758–79.

Panella, C. 2010. Gold Mining in West Africa – Worlds of Debts and Sites of Co-habitation. In C. Panella (ed.), *Worlds of Debts: Gold Mining in West Africa as an Interdisciplinary Field of Study*. Amsterdam: Rozenberg Publishers, pp. 1–14.

Pijpers. R.J. 2016. Mining, Hope and Turbulent Times: Locating Accelerated Change in Rural Sierra Leone. *History & Anthropology* 27(5): 504–20.

——2018. *Navigating Uncertainty: Large-scale Mining and Micro-politics in Sierra Leone*. PhD Dissertation, University of Oslo.

Pijpers, R.J. and T.H. Eriksen (this volume). Introduction: Negotiating the Multiple Edges of Mining Encounters. In R.J. Pijpers and T.H. Eriksen (eds), *Mining Encounters: Extractive Industries in an overheated world*. London: Pluto Press.

Pine, F. 2007. Memories of Movement and the Stillness of Place: Kinship Memory in the Polish Highlands. In J. Carsten (ed.), *Ghosts of Memory: Essays on Remembrance and Relatedness*. Oxford: Blackwell, pp. 104–25.

Reno, W. 1999. *Warlord Politics and African States*. Boulder, CO: Lynne Rienner Publishers.

Scott, J. 1998. *Seeing Like a State: How Certain Schemes to Improve the Human Condition Have Failed*. New Haven, CT: Yale University Press.

Stewart, P.J. and A. Strathern. 2003. Introduction. In P.J. Stewart and A. Strathern (eds), *Landscape, Memory and History: Anthropological Perspectives*. London: Pluto Press.

Teschner, B. 2013. How You Start Matters: A Comparison of Gold Fields' Tarkwa and Damang Mines and Their Divergent Relationships with Local Small-scale Miners in Ghana. *Resources Policy* 38: 332–40.

van der Laan, H.L. 1965. *The Sierra Leone Diamonds: An Economic Study Covering the Years 1952–1961*. Oxford: Oxford University Press on behalf of Fourah Bay College, the University College of Sierra Leone.

NOTES

1. See, for a detailed discussion of Marampa's mining history and its contemporary situation, Pijpers (2018).
2. London Mining PLC went into administration per 16 October 2014. Although several developments indicate a potential restart by another company, the future of iron ore mining in Marampa remains, to date, uncertain.
3. The waste referred to here is the non-iron-bearing layer of soil that has to be removed before reaching the iron-bearing material that will be processed.

6. Drilling Down Comparatively

Resource Histories, Subterranean Unconventional Gas and Diverging Social Responses in Two Australian Regions

Kim de Rijke

INTRODUCTION

Recent large-scale developments of onshore unconventional gas resources, which typically include numerous wells and associated infrastructure dispersed over a large area, possibly also including the employment of extractive technologies such as hydraulic fracturing stimulation, have led to significant controversies in the United States, parts of Europe and Australia. These controversies have revolved around contested notions of economic development and the potential impacts of unconventional gas extraction on groundwater resources, agricultural land, the environment and climate more broadly, rural livelihoods and wellbeing, the adequacy of regulations and the distribution of rights, as well as envisaged energy futures, among others (e.g. McCrea et al. 2014; Mercer et al. 2014; Perry 2012; Willow and Wylie 2014). As the Organization of the Petroleum Exporting Countries (OPEC) maintained its level of oil production, the increase in unconventional oil supplies from the United States over recent years has contributed substantially to the rapid decline in global oil prices. In these ways, similar to the mining projects described in this volume, unconventional oil and gas developments may be seen to contribute to, and form part of, accelerated forms of change at various scales.

The extraction of coal seam gas (CSG, also called coal bed methane – CBM), a type of unconventional gas held in the dispersed cleats of underground coal seams, has rapidly expanded in the Western Downs region of southern Queensland, Australia, since about 2006. At the end of the third quarter of 2015, there were a total of 6,959 active coal seam gas wells in rural and regional Queensland (APPEA 2016). Using an extensive network of pipelines, many of these wells supply the liquefied natural gas plants built on Curtis Island, off the coast from Gladstone, where the gas is liquefied for marine transport to primarily Asian export markets (see

Map 6.1). While accurate and up-to-date figures are difficult to find, the relevant multinational joint ventures have invested approximately $70 billion[1] since about 2010 to develop and expand the Queensland unconventional gas industry. By contrast, in the region of the Northern Rivers, just across the southern border in the State of New South Wales (NSW), coal seam gas exploratory drilling activities in 2013 were met with significant opposition and site blockades. During escalating protests in May 2014, the New South Wales government initially prepared to deploy the riot police but then decided to suspend the relevant exploration licence on the basis of what it regarded as insufficient community consultation by the gas company, thereby halting drilling operations in the region. In April 2015, however, the NSW Supreme Court found this government action to have been unlawful, bringing back to the region potential unconventional gas developments. In response, the New South Wales government decided to offer to the gas company in question an exploration licence buy-back worth $25 million in November 2015, which was accepted by the gas company's shareholders in December 2015.

This chapter addresses the diverging responses to coal seam gas developments by residents in these proximate regions by taking a comparative approach to the regions' resource histories, their material environments and related economic and socio-political dynamics. In examining the mutually constitutive aspects of these factors, the comparison considers two extractive encounters (Pijpers and Eriksen, this volume) by drawing on the concept of 'resource environments' (Richardson and Weszkalnys 2014). Important to this concept is a view of resources as always 'becoming' within ever-changing human/non-human assemblages (Deleuze and Guattari 1987; Richardson 2014). The analysis thus focuses on the socio-material circumstances that allowed, as well as prevented, unconventional gas resources from 'becoming' in two Australian regions. Such an approach foregrounds the regionally specific and historically pertinent factors often absent from the ways cost–benefit analyses commonly seek to survey variables in diverging social responses to resource developments in a solely synchronic approach.

The chapter first outlines briefly some of the key demographic characteristics and 'resource histories' of the Western Downs and the Northern Rivers. These descriptions provide the groundwork for the comparative analysis, which addresses the diverging responses to contemporary unconventional gas extraction initiatives in these two proximate regions. The chapter concludes with a reflection on the utility of the historically informed comparative approach and proposes an understanding of the two extractive encounters and variously experienced forms of accelerated change in terms of an 'ontological politics of the future' (Ferry 2016: 187).

A BRIEF RESOURCE HISTORY OF THE WESTERN DOWNS, QUEENSLAND

The Western Downs is a local government area within the broader region of southern Queensland known as the Darling Downs. It is a fertile region of national and international 'black-soil' agricultural renown, producing cattle, vegetables, a variety of legumes such as chickpeas and soy beans, as well as crops such as cotton, wheat, sorghum and barley. More recently however, the local government council obtained a new trademark to market the region as a result of expanding unconventional gas and coal developments as 'the Energy Capital of Queensland' (Western Downs Regional Council 2015a). It covers approximately 38,000 square kilometres of largely flat to undulating land, including several rural towns with a total combined population of 33,653 in 2014 (population density 0.9 persons/km^2; Queensland Government Statistician's Office 2016).

The region struggled with rural decline over the last few decades, including diminishing employment opportunities and significant out-migration of young people (Measham and Fleming 2014; Everingham et al. 2015). Reflecting the recent resource boom, however, the unemployment rate in 2016 is relatively low. The broader statistical region of the Darling Downs – Maranoa, of which the Western Downs region is part – recorded 3.3 per cent unemployment in January 2016, compared to Queensland's average of 6.4 per cent and Australia's average of 6.0 per cent (Australian Government 2016b). In terms of relevant employment industries, the most significant sector is 'Agriculture, Forestry and Fishing', which accounts for 10 per cent of employment in 2016, while 'Mining' accounts for 2.8 per cent. Despite the relatively low number of mining jobs, the mining industry's contributions to gross regional product (GRP) increased by no less than 16.4 per cent per annum over the period 2010–15, making its annual share of $715.5 million the biggest contributor to GRP by far in 2013–14 (Western Downs Regional Council 2015b).

The subterranean unconventional gas resources currently extracted in the Western Downs are located in the coal seams of what is known in geological terms as the Surat Basin. This basin partly overlaps with the Bowen Basin to the north, which is also rich in coal and associated methane. The estimated coal seam gas reserves in

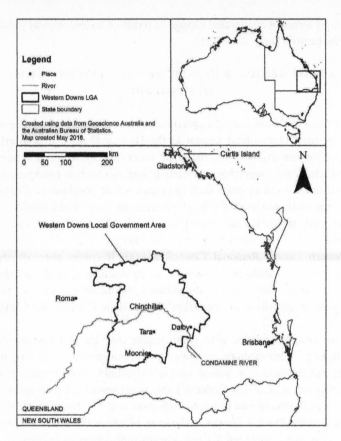

Map 6.1 The study region of the Western Downs in the State of Queensland, Australia

Source: Map created by the author with the assistance of Matthew Whincop, University of Queensland Culture and Heritage Unit.

Queensland are substantially larger than in New South Wales, and this explains why resource companies chose to develop these resources in Queensland first.

Notwithstanding some sandy soils less suitable for crop or cattle production, the fertile black-soil floodplains of the region first attracted the attention of European settlers after glowing reports of 'luxuriant pasturage' were received from the botanist explorer Allan Cunningham in 1827 (Cunningham, quoted in Hall 1925: 7). For the region's Aboriginal population these reports initiated a destructive influx of settlers, including the introduction of new animals and plants that quickly transformed the pre-contact landscape (French 1989a; 2002).[2]

Gold also figured in the hopes and dreams of the nineteenth-century settlers, some of whom politically exaggerated its abundance in their desire for a fresh supply of labour and economic investments in the region (French 1989b). Some gold was located by prospectors so enticed to the region, but gold mining was never developed successfully. Coal, however, was more easily found so that by 1925 the local resident Hall (1925: 4) wrote in hope:

> Some coal beds have been worked successfully for years, but there are many others lying as Nature made them, awaiting the power of Capital to vitalize the energy of man, so as to make the Darling Downs take its proper place as a coal mining area.

It was not until the latter parts of the twentieth century that coal mining became a serious undertaking. Paradoxically, at least one early coal mine played an indirect but important part in the agricultural history of the region. The coal mine at Warra, now a small and declining town on the floodplain between Dalby and Chinchilla, opened in 1915, but due to unprofitability and constant waterlogging it closed soon after in 1919. Former railway workers and coal miners were subsequently allowed to develop the surrounding land for agricultural purposes, laying the foundations of what is now one of the more productive cropping areas in the region (Heritage Consulting Australia Pty Ltd 2011: 95). Reflecting the importance of such extractive heritage to the region, a memorial surrounded by intensive cropping areas now stands at the former coal mine site (see Figure 6.1).

Figure 6.1   The Warra coal mine memorial
Source: Photograph by Matthew Petersen, 2014.

The process of regional settlement was also enabled by international advances in geological science and the introduction of a new technology in the late nineteenth century: water bore drilling. The Darling Downs is heavily reliant on groundwater resources, including the Great Artesian Basin (GAB), one of the world's largest aquifers which underlies about one-fifth of the Australian continent. De Rijke et al. (2016: 5) provide a brief overview of the manner in which the Great Artesian Basin became enrolled in the Australian settlement project:

> The GAB's first artesian bore was sunk in 1878, and, with government and private enterprise support, over the next 80 years landholders sank around 18,000 bores into the GAB, around 12,000 of which were in the state of Queensland (Powell 1991; Fairfax and Fensham 2002). Given the otherwise arid landscape of interior Australia, these water bores enabled the further expansion of the pastoral industry and permanent human settlements (Powell 1991; Gibbs 2009). Also premised on the violent dispossession of Aboriginal populations, the spatial and temporal distribution of settlers at the surface was thus directly linked to, and enabled by, increasing engagements with the vertical third dimension, its subterranean water, and access to capital intensive drilling technology.

Despite rapid reductions in groundwater pressure as a result of widespread extraction and wastage through free-flowing bores, groundwater resources continue to be a vital resource for the Darling Downs and inland Queensland more broadly today (see Map 6.2).

In 1900, drilling for subterranean water led to an unexpected discovery of natural gas near the town of Roma on the Darling Downs. The gas was used for local street lighting in 1906 but the well ran dry soon after (Wopfner 1988: 376). Natural resource development was, and continues to be, a matter of trial and error.

During the interbellum, when overall development of the region was strained already, the spread of prickly pear plants (*Opuntia inermis* and *Opuntia stricta*, but known among settlers as 'the green beast'; Waterson 1991: 17) was devastating – environmentally and economically as well as socially. Originally introduced to Australia in the Sydney area in 1788 to extract the carmine dye from an insect associated with it, as cattle fodder in times of drought and as an effective fence plant, it slowly moved north with cattle and settlers to its ideal growing locations in inland Queensland (Frawley 2007). While accepted in a domesticated setting, in the Darling Downs and other surrounding regions it came to be regarded as an invading enemy entirely out of place when it started to spread thickly

Map 6.2   Water bores (shown as circles) in the Queensland study region, March 2016

Source: Data provided by the Queensland Government, copyright Department of Natural Resources, Mines and Energy 2018, under Creative Commons Attribution 4.0 International (CC BY 4.0) licence.

and uncontrollably from the turn of the twentieth century (Frawley 2007). In 1920, it was spreading at an estimated rate of 100 hectares per day, forcing numerous settlers to abandon their properties. Prickly pear was threatening the pervading Queensland political project of 'closer settlement', a 'grandiose vision of an agrarian society … dominated by an independent and morally superior yeoman citizenry living on their own family farms' (Cameron 2005: 1, 4). A form of biological control – the introduction of a stem-boring moth from Argentina (*Cactoblastus cactorum*) – reversed the spread of prickly pear in the late 1920s. For that reason, the Cactoblastus Memorial Hall near the town of Chinchilla on the Darling Downs is possibly the only memorial in the world dedicated to an insect (Australian Government 2016a).

Now often simplistically regarded as a heroic battle of inland Australian settlers against nature, Frawley (2007) insightfully discussed the transnational networks involved in this conflict. Combined with concurrent developments in water bore drilling and subterranean extraction referred to above, these networks complicate the resource environment of the Darling Downs, 'which was not just a local place, but mobilised knowledge, plants, people and ideas from all over the world' (Frawley 2007: 388; see also Waterson 1991 for similar findings with regard to the development of agriculture in the region from 1920 onwards). This assemblage shifted again after the Second World War as resource exploration and extraction intensified further. In his overview of oil and gas development in Australia, the geologist Wopfner (1988: 379–80) noted:

> The introduction of the oil search subsidy by the Commonwealth Government induced a number of American 'independents' to join Australian companies in their search for oil ... [The] Moonie No. 1 [oil well] discovered 45° API oil late in 1961 ... After further appraisal and the construction of a pipeline to Brisbane the field started commercial production in 1964 ... It marked the birth of indigenous hydrocarbon production. The discovery of the Moonie field enormously stimulated oil search in Australia as a whole and especially in Queensland. Everyone wanted a slice of the cake!

The hydrocarbon histories of Moonie and Roma are now also celebrated as a form of local heritage, including the display of oil industry memorabilia in Moonie (see Figure 6.2) and The Big Rig Museum in Roma. Exemplifying that Darling Downs' resources had obtained internationally significant economic and political dimensions, a plaque was unveiled by Queen Elizabeth II in 1963 to commemorate the discovery of oil by the Australian-American conglomerate. Linking oil to an enduring settler ideology of nation building and progress, the Queen was reported to have said: 'the discovery of oil will open up new frontiers for industrial initiative and capital enterprise and point the way to a prosperous future for all the people of Australia' (*Dawn Magazine* 1963: 3; cf. Weszkalnys 2016: 127, on oil's futurity and 'lithospheric dreams of wealth, progress, and modernity'). Despite its opening being such a grand affair at the time, the oil field has now dried up and the plaque stands largely ignored in a small park among the struggling oil refineries at the port of Brisbane.

Older farmers recently interviewed about coal seam gas extraction remember clearly the changes in the region that have occurred since their youth. Farming increasingly involves large-scale agribusinesses, some of them owned by corporations rather than local residents, and dependent on large capital investments and advanced technologies. Depending on soil quality this may include expensive irrigation infrastructure, laser-levelled land to reduce water run-off, heavy machinery and farm activities guided by software programs, data management and global positioning systems. Chemical pesticides, herbicides and fertilisers are used, although genetically modified cotton has been introduced to reduce water consumption and chemical use. As a result of these developments, agricultural employment opportunities in the region, as elsewhere in Australia, have diminished. The costs of production have risen while international commodity prices have fallen, leading to the stark choice heard often among farmers: 'get big or get out'. A local woman with a farming background summed up her sense of the times during an interview:

> Growing up in Tara [a small rural town] was a very small town environment and everybody knew each other. We had farming communities and, when I was growing up [in the 1960s], oil in the district was … a big thing and it made the town prosper. During that time … the sheep prices were good and lots of people had wool, sold wool, and the farmers and graziers were doing very well because the commodity prices were pretty good for that time. And that's when the swimming pool was built, the hall was built; there was plenty of money about. And plus the oil … Tara was thriving when I was growing up … It is different now, because we are in drought, and we have been for such a long time, and the other thing is commodity prices – wheat, sheep,

Figure 6.2   Moonie oil memorabilia: public display of the drill bit that was used in the discovery of the Moonie oil field in 1961

Source: Photograph by Kim de Rijke.

cattle and all that – hasn't risen with the times. And so, lots of farmers, they are doing it real tough. (Interview, 5 December 2014)

Severe drought is an ever-present threat to agricultural production in Australia, leading to an enthusiastic uptake, as noted above, of water bore drilling technology, particularly as it became more affordable post-Second World War. Thousands of water bores have been drilled by landowners in the Darling Downs for crop irrigation, domestic use or stock water, bringing a sense of personal familiarity with drilling and subterranean resource extraction to many landholders in the region.

In summary then, this brief resource history illustrates some key moments in the shifting human/non-human assemblages of the Darling Downs. A number of factors can be seen to have combined to co-produce the region as it is known today: particular Anglo-Australian settler practices, politically sanctioned ideologies and rapid environmental changes; international advances in science and technology; the availability and extraction of subterranean water, hydrocarbons and coal; the particular quality and fertility of surface soils; the introduction of new animals and plants; and changing forms of global capital and economic enterprise. Analytically, this is an example of Richardson and Weszkalnys' (2014) 'resource environment', the 'ever-shifting assemblages comprising humans, organisms, substances, regulation, discourses, and technology' (Richardson 2014: 22) that allow certain substances to come into being as resources.

In the mid-2000s, when coal seam gas developments were introduced, a sense of economic malaise gripped the region: coal mining had not really taken off, the Moonie oil field had dried up, and the devastating 'millennium drought' was wreaking havoc among vulnerable farmers. Agriculture in any case was no longer providing the community service it once did given the reduced employment opportunities available as a result of the uptake of capital-intensive technologies and tight operations on deregulated international commodity markets. While the unconventional gas initiatives of multinationals were relatively new to the local population, the latter were accustomed to shifts in resource extraction practices and associated reconfigurations at various scales, and largely regarded this development as potentially opening up a new chapter in the rich resource history of the region.

A BRIEF RESOURCE HISTORY OF THE NORTHERN RIVERS, NEW SOUTH WALES

The Northern Rivers region is located in the north-east of the State of New South Wales. It is a region variously defined geographically, but for the purpose of this chapter I will equate it with the Richmond-Tweed Statistical Area used by the Australian Bureau of Statistics (see Map 6.3). The total population of the Richmond-Tweed region is about 240,000, spread over approximately 10,270 km^2 with a population density of 23.4 persons/km^2 (compared to 0.9 persons/km^2 in the Western Downs; ABS 2016, based on 2013 statistical data).

The physical environment of the Northern Rivers is very different from the Darling Downs: green rolling hills characterise the landscape, and higher volcanic plugs covered in subtropical vegetation are located in the northern border region with Queensland (see Figure 6.3). It is a region currently known internationally for its scenic and environmental attractions, beaches, and alternative lifestyles. Coastal centres such as Byron Bay in the east, and the counterculture town of Nimbin near Nightcap National Park about 50km inland, are well-known tourist attractions.

Despite the landscape differences, the early social and economic settler history of the region shares many characteristics with the Darling Downs: the dispossession of Aboriginal people, rapid environmental change and the creation of large pastoral properties by the powerful squattocracy, followed by increased land regulations and the introduction of smaller-scale agriculture and dairy farming foundational to many of the region's contemporary towns (Daley 1966). Logging, particularly of the abundant and valuable red cedar growing in forests known among settlers as the 'Big Scrub', was much more important in this region than it was on the floodplains of the Darling Downs (Daley 1966). The Northern Rivers never became widely known for sub-surface resource extraction, although a small underground coal mine for local use operated near Tyalgum during the 1920s and 1930s (Boileau 2004: 132–3). A few small collieries near Nimbin continued to operate until the 1950s (2004: 133; Mineralogy Database 2016). Internationally significant was the rutile, zircon and ilmenite mineral sand industry, which operated along the coast from the 1950s to the 1970s (2004: 133–6). Employing around a thousand people and using industrial methods, sand extraction significantly altered the coastal zones and increased the risk of wind and wave erosion (2004: 134, 136).

By the early 1970s most industries were struggling, with the decline in dairy and banana production hitting the region particularly hard. Unemployment rates have remained relatively high in the Northern Rivers ever since. In January 2016, the Richmond-Tweed Statistical Area had the second highest unemployment rate in New South Wales with 8.3 per cent, and the shared seventh highest unemployment rate in Australia.[3] The most important industry sector is 'Health Care and

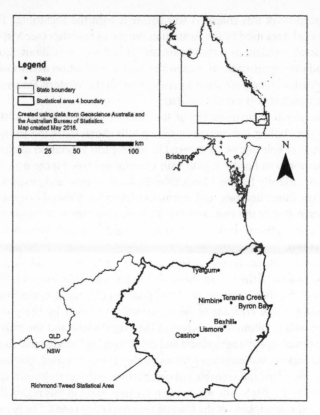

Map 6.3 The Northern Rivers region in north-east New South Wales, including selected places

Source: Map created by the author with the assistance of Matthew Whincop, University of Queensland Culture and Heritage Unit.

Social Assistance', which accounts for 12.6 per cent of all employment in 2016. Mining (largely building material quarries) provides just 0.8 per cent of employment in the region. Exploration for coal seam gas began in 1997, leading to a proposal for significant further development by the gas company Metgasco around 2010. The Kingfisher conventional gas field was developed near the town of Casino by Metgasco in the late 2000s. Given New South Wales' historical reliance on Queensland gas, further unconventional gas developments were at least initially promoted to avoid a predicted gas shortage; an argument that remains pertinent among gas industry proponents in that state today (e.g. APPEA 2014).

In the context of declining industries during the 1970s, two events came to define the Northern Rivers as it is known today: the 1973

Figure 6.3 Nightcap National Park often figures in Northern Rivers' tourist and marketing documents

Source: http://ozguidevisa.com.au/more-to-byron-bay/ (accessed 7 March 2016).

Nimbin Aquarius Festival, organised by the arts and cultural branch of the Australian Union of Students (Garbutt 2014: 4), and the subsequent Terania Creek rainforest anti-logging protests, which culminated in a direct-action blockade in 1979. The Aquarius Festival, attended by about 5,000 people, left 'an enduring countercultural presence in Nimbin and in its region to this day' (Garbutt 2014: 6), particularly by stimulating the influx of large numbers of newcomers to the declining region to pursue alternative lifestyles. The newcomers of the 1970s, often referred to as the 'new settlers' as opposed to the 'old settlers' involved in dairy farming and forestry, were instrumental in the Terania Creek logging protests. These protests became known as the Rainforest War, the first major rainforest protest in Australian history, which effectively launched the modern Australian conservation movement (Turvey 2006). Close to Nimbin, it was the rainforest environment that was among the reasons the new settlers had moved to the region in the first place (Foley 1991; Turvey 2006). Despite a foundational local settler history of logging, the protests were eventually successful and led to the creation of Nightcap National Park in 1983. Reflecting the 'emergence' of a new resource and reconfigured networks of knowledge and regulation, Nightcap National Park was inscribed as part of the Shield Volcano Group of the World Heritage Site 'Gondwana Rainforests of Australia' in 1986 and was added to the Australian National Heritage List in 2007 (Wilson et al. 2011; Australian Government 2016c). Both regional heritage and future aspirations in the Northern Rivers were thus increasingly infused by notions such as global biodiversity, environmental conservation and sustainability. New economic initiatives came to include eco-tourism, arts and crafts, and small-scale agricultural enterprises such as market gardens and orchards (e.g. Boileau 2004: 67).

Thus, the region around Nimbin is no longer known as the Big Scrub but is marketed today as the 'Rainbow region', and instead of the memorials celebrating sub-surface extraction observed in the Darling Downs, we find town welcome signs which declare that residents are 'living the village lifestyle' (see Figure 6.4). Seemingly appreciative of the various changes brought by the new settlers, the regional urban centre of Lismore temporarily changed its name to 'Lovemore' in 2013 to commemorate the fortieth anniversary of the Nimbin Aquarius Festival.

Given the influx of new residents with diverse interests over the past three to four decades, land use in the Northern Rivers as a whole has diversified; activities range from logging to sugarcane farming, beef cattle grazing, dairying, horticulture including fruit, nut and herb growing, natural oil extraction such as tea tree oil, and fishing industries. Farm sizes are generally substantially smaller than those in the Darling Downs, and agricultural land has become increasingly fragmented as a result of the rural residential subdivisions of previous farms. Many of the small farms are best regarded as non-commercial hobby farms, established by residents who moved to the region for lifestyle purposes (e.g. EnPlan Australia Pty Ltd 2013: 3).

DIVERGING RESPONSES TO COAL SEAM GAS

The brief outlines of the Western Downs and Northern Rivers regions above serve to illustrate the diverging historical trajectories of two regions in which contemporary responses to encounters with coal seam gas development can be understood. My aim is not to ascribe a form of causal primacy to any particular characteristic, but, rather, to highlight the mutually constitutive processes through which unconventional gas came into being as a resource in one region, and not in the other.

In their study of regional responses, Krieksy et al. (2013) conducted telephone surveys for comparative purposes in two adjacent Pennsylvanian counties with differing levels of shale gas drilling. They concluded that:

> We find that major support for shale gas drilling comes from individuals who stand to profit through negotiation of mineral rights leases, those who otherwise believe that this form of energy extraction is an economic opportunity, and those who believe the threats to the environment and public health are minimal. (Krieksy et al. 2013: 234)

Figure 6.4 Living the village lifestyle at Bexhill in
the Northern Rivers

Source: Photograph by Kim de Rijke, 2013.

Absent from this survey of variables, however, is a discussion that might
shed light on the ways in which 'economic opportunity' and 'belief' are
socio-historically grounded in these regions. Acknowledging the need
for synchronic context to their survey research, Willits et al. (2013)
argued that 'we must begin a systematic effort to monitor the patterns
of our studies *over time*. Shale-related drilling studies provide one ideal
opportunity for such efforts' (2013: 71, original emphasis). Similarly,
Brasier et al. (2011: 53) noted that '[e]xtractive history seems to affect
the perception of social and economic issues differently than perception
of environmental issues'. Nevertheless, much of the literature on unconventional gas developments in the United States and Australia to date has
reported on surveys of contemporary attitudes and perceptions among
local populations without substantial attention to mutually constitutive
socio-historical and materially transformative factors.

This chapter has discussed two proximate regions in Australia and
brings into relief the relevance of such an analysis in addition to those
studies based largely on surveys of contemporary attitudes. With regard

to the Western Downs region, where numerous coal seam gas wells have now been drilled, many residents were accustomed to, and comfortable with, industrial technologies and extraction of subterranean water, coal and hydrocarbons prior to the introduction of the coal seam gas industry. In this region, international extractive capital, export markets, global commodity prices as well as historical alterations of the landscape and struggles 'against nature' to transform material substances into viable resource industries are part of daily routine and the socioeconomic fabric of regional settler heritage. Combined with the (drought-proofing) economic benefits and regional revitalisation the new coal seam gas industry was hoped to deliver, unconventional gas resources 'came into being' relatively quickly and, compared to the Northern Rivers, without widespread opposition (see Map 6.4).

Thus, imbued with diverging notions of heritage and variously envisioned futures, temporality emerges as a key factor in the development of resource environments (e.g. Ferry 2016; D'Angelo, this volume). Ferry and Limbert usefully noted that resources:

> frame the past, present, and future in certain ways; they propose or preclude certain kinds of time reckoning; they inscribe teleologies; and they are imbued with affects of time, such as nostalgia, hope, dread, and spontaneity. (quoted in Rogers 2015: 367)

In the cases described above, the 'affects of time' were also relevant to opposition and protest. Unconventional gas and hydraulic fracturing became an international concern particularly after the release in 2010 of the Oscar-nominated activist film *Gasland* (carrying the subtitle *Can You Light Your Water on Fire?*) produced in the shale gas fields of the United States. It agitated against the gas industry by focusing on the harmful environmental and human impacts it was said to produce. Through imagery such as burning domestic tap water – one of the ultimate expressions of 'matter out of place' (cf. Douglas 1966) – it caused global consternation and opposition to the unconventional gas industry (de Rijke 2013). Developments in the Darling Downs had already started, however. Moreover, in terms of temporal dynamics at the regional level, some farmers described in recent interviews with me the 'trench warfare' they had fought over the last 20 years against environmental activists on issues of the introduction of genetically modified crops and laws to reduce tree clearing that were resented by many farmers in the region. Environmental concerns about the coal seam gas industry were thus interpreted through memories of recent disputes with 'Greenies'

Map 6.4 Registered water bores (shown as circles) and coal seam gas wells (triangles) in the Queensland study region, March 2016

Source: Data provided by the Queensland Government, copyright Department of Natural Resources, Mines and Energy 2018, under Creative Commons Attribution 4.0 International (CC BY 4.0) licence.[4]

who were seen as averse to rural visions of agricultural development. By 2012, activists in the Northern Rivers had organised multiple regional viewings of *Gasland* as well as bus tours to the gas fields of the Darling Downs. Such activists were digitally connected to global networks and this, in combination with reports of health complaints emerging from the Queensland gas fields, worked to strengthen their resolve to prevent the industry from entering their region. Of course, the Northern Rivers itself had been an activist base since the 1970s. Veterans of the Terania Creek rainforest blockade still live there, and a number of them became heavily involved in anti-coal seam gas activism. The Darling Downs was soon considered 'lost'. The Northern Rivers, by contrast, came to be regarded as the main battleground in setting a national precedent, and an activist movement mobilised rapidly in response to the exploratory drilling plans of Metgasco. With media savvy professionals, experienced environmental activists and organisers, 'old settlers', artists and folks living in local communes, Indigenous people, as well as urban residents uniting against it, the gas industry was clearly not going to develop in this region as it had in the Darling Downs. Despite the Northern Rivers' high unemployment figures, which might suggest a potentially more welcoming reception, the much higher population density and land use diversity, eco-tourism and discourses around 'village' lifestyles, as well as the prevalence of small hobby farms and future aspirations based on resources such as biodiversity and environmental heritage, were clear indicators the operating environment in the Northern Rivers was unlikely to be supportive. In these myriad ways, some of which are regionally specific, temporal relations informed the ways in which two Australian encounters with unconventional gas resources unfolded.

CONCLUSION

This chapter has taken on the call by Richardson and Weszkalnys (2014) to study the processes through which particular material substances come into being as resources. Using Australian case material about unconventional gas developments, I have conversely also described a set of circumstances which might prevent resource development. The chapter has employed an historical and regionally comparative approach to broadly trace the trajectories and socio-material contexts of two proximate regions in Queensland and New South Wales. While the key shifts in these regional resource histories can only be sketched here, they give context to contemporary responses often reported on in terms of quantifiable variables or cost–benefit considerations. The trajectories of human/non-human assemblages in the Western Downs and the Northern Rivers were seen to diverge in ways important to the manner in which contemporary resource encounters are regionally anticipated and assessed. Such assessments, imbued with future aspirations, hopes, fears, as well as notions of heritage and who and what belongs in the landscape, contain both regionally specific and historically persistent themes. They are part of what Mathews and Barnes (2016) describe as a 'prognostic politics' with co-constitutive material and sociocultural dimensions. Attentive to various temporal dynamics in such assemblages, the diverging regional responses to coal seam gas developments might thus be seen to result from an 'ontological politics of the future' (Ferry 2016: 187).

If the term 'overheating' can be said to capture various forms of accelerated change occurring in the world today (Eriksen 2016), it is appropriate that I conclude this chapter with an anecdote of recent events to illustrate this in Queensland. The Condamine River on the Darling Downs is a river at the headwaters of the largest surface water basin in Australia: the Murray-Darling Basin that covers parts of the States of Queensland, New South Wales, Victoria and South Australia. The basin has degraded significantly over recent decades, leading to increased societal and political debate about water extraction policy and agricultural irrigation practices, ecological integrity and the relevance of concepts such as Indigenous 'cultural flows' (e.g. Weir 2009). On 23 April 2016, news spread rapidly across Australia that the Condamine River was burning (Figure 6.5). While gas seeps in the river had first been reported in the media in 2012, the intensity of the fire at a particular gas seep was regarded by activists as evidence of the increasing environmental impact of nearby hydraulic fracturing activities. The relation between hydraulic fracturing and the gas seep, however, is questioned, or at least not regarded as straightforward, by scientists, government, as well as the relevant gas company. Mostly unqualified to evaluate the geological evidence, anthropologists might productively interpret the burning Condamine River in ways that shed light on the sociocultural dimensions of such an event: the widespread consternation and fear of danger resulting from perceptions of matter out of place and material boundary crossings (Douglas 1966), an increasing societal anxiety associated with environmental change, and more general readings of this event as materially and symbolically illustrating potential forms of overheating that might accompany the development of contentious unconventional gas resources around the world.

Figure 6.5   Overheating in the Condamine River in 2016
Source: Williams (2016).[5]

ACKNOWLEDGEMENTS

My gratitude goes to Maurice French AM, Emeritus Professor of History at the University of Southern Queensland, David Trigger, Professor of Anthropology at the University of Queensland, Dr Richard Martin, Research Fellow at the University of Queensland and Martin Espig, anthropology PhD student at the University of Queensland, for productive comments on earlier drafts. Matthew Whincop, former consultant archaeologist at the University of Queensland Culture and Heritage Unit, assisted in the production of Maps 6.1 and 6.3.

REFERENCES

APPEA. 2014. NSW Gas Shortage Will Hit Businesses First. Available at: http://www.appea.com.au/2014/02/nsw-businesses-will-be-hit-by-gas-shortage-first/ (accessed 22 April 2016).
—— 2016. Industry Statistics: Third Quarter 2015 CSG Statistics. Available at: http://www.appea.com.au/wp-content/uploads/2015/12/Q3-2015-Industry-Data.pdf (accessed 5 February 2016).
Australian Bureau of Statistics. 2016. Richmond – Tweed (SA4). Available at: http://stat.abs.gov.au/itt/r.jsp?RegionSummary&region=112&dataset=ABS_REGIONAL_ASGS&geoconcept=REGION&measure=MEASURE&dataset

ASGS=ABS_REGIONAL_ASGS&datasetLGA=ABS_REGIONAL_LGA&regionLGA=REGION&regionASGS=REGION (accessed 7 March 2016).

Australian Government. 2016a. Protecting Heritage Places – Boonarga Cactoblastis Memorial Hall, Queensland. Available at: http://www.environment.gov.au/node/19384 (accessed 10 May 2016).

—— 2016b. Labour Force Region (SA4). Available at: http://lmip.gov.au/default.aspx?LMIP/LFR_SAFOUR (accessed 21 April 2016).

—— 2016c. *Place Details: Gondwana Rainforests of Australia, Lismore, NSW, Australia*. Available at: http://www.environment.gov.au/cgi-bin/ahdb/search.pl?mode=place_detail;place_id=105704 (accessed 7 March 2016).

Boileau, J. 2004. *Community Based Heritage Study: Thematic History*. Report for Tweed Shire Council. Available at: http://www.tweed.nsw.gov.au/Download.aspx?Path=~/Documents/Planning/Heritage/TSC01930_Tweed_Thematic_History_2004.pdf (accessed 12 February 2016).

Brasier, K. J., M.R. Filteau, D.K. McLaughlin, J. Jacquet, R.C. Stedman, T.W. Kelsey and S.J. Goetz. 2011. Residents' Perceptions of Community and Environmental Impacts from Development of Natural Gas in the Marcellus Shale: A Comparison of Pennsylvania and New York Cases. *Journal of Rural Social Sciences* 26(1): 32–61.

Cameron, D. 2005. Closer Settlement in Queensland: The Rise and Decline of the Agrarian Dream, 1860s-1960s. In G. Davison and M. Brodie (eds), *Struggle Country: The Rural Ideal in Twentieth Century Australia*. Clayton: Monash University ePress, pp. 1–21.

Daley, L.T. 1966. *Men and a River: A History of the Richmond River District, 1828–1895*. Melbourne: Melbourne University Press.

D'Angelo, L. this volume. Diamonds and Plural Temporalities: Articulating Temporalities in the Mines of Sierra Leone In R.J. Pijpers and T.H. Eriksen (eds), *Mining Encounters: Extractive Industries in an Overheated World*. London: Pluto Press.

Dawn Magazine. 1963. Oil Strike: Flowing Gold Could Be Priceless Anniversary Gift to Nation. *Dawn Magazine* 12(6): 3–5.

Deleuze, G. and F. Guattari. 1987 [1980]. *A Thousand Plateaus: Capitalism and Schizophrenia*, trans. B. Massumi, Minneapolis, MN: Bloomsbury.

de Rijke, K. 2013. Hydraulically Fractured: Unconventional Gas and Anthropology. *Anthropology Today* 29(2): 13–17.

de Rijke, K., P. Munro and M.D.L.M. Zurita. 2016. The Great Artesian Basin: A Contested Resource Environment of Subterranean Water and Coal Seam Gas in Australia. *Society and Natural Resources* 29(6): 696–710.

Douglas, M. 1966. *Purity and Danger: An Analysis of the Concepts of Danger and Taboo*. London: Routledge.

EnPlanAustraliaPtyLtd.2013.*TweedShireCouncil,RuralLandStrategy:Community Discussion Paper*. Report prepared for Tweed Shire Council. Available at: http://yoursaytweed.com.au/rurallandstrategy/documents/12264/download (accessed 14 February 2016).

Eriksen, T.H. 2016. *Overheating: An Anthropology of Accelerated Change*. London: Pluto Press.

Everingham, J. A., V. Devenin and N. Collins. 2015. 'The Beast Doesn't Stop': The Resource Boom and Changes in the Social Space of the Darling Downs. *Rural Society* 24(1): 42–64.

Fairfax, R.J. and R.J. Fensham. 2002. In the Footsteps of J. Alfred Griffiths: A Cataclysmic History of Great Artesian Basin Springs in Queensland, Australia. *Australian Geographical Studies* 40(2): 210–30.

Ferry, E. 2016. Claiming Futures. *Journal of the Royal Anthropological Institute* 22(S1): 181–8.

Foley, G. 1991. Terania Creek: Learning in a Green Campaign. *Australian Journal of Adult and Community Education* 31(3): 160–76.

Frawley, J. 2007. Prickly Pear Land: Transnational Networks in Settler Australia. *Australian Historical Studies* 38(130): 373–88.

French, M. 1989a. *Conflict on the Condamine: Aborigines and the European Invasion*. Toowoomba: Darling Downs Institute Press.

—— 1989b. 'A Leaden Bullet Covered with Gold Leaf': Gold Discoveries on the Darling Downs Before Separation. *Journal of the Royal Historical Society of Queensland* 13(11): 417–27.

—— 2002. What Fate Awaits? The Indigenous Peoples of the Darling Downs in 1851–52. *Queensland Review* 9(1): 23–33.

Garbutt, R. 2014. Aquarius and Beyond: Thinking through the Counterculture. *M/C Journal* 17(6): 1–9.

Gibbs, L.M. 2009. Just Add Water: Colonisation, Water Governance, and the Australian Inland. *Environment and Planning A* 21: 2964–83.

Hall, T. 1925. *The Early History of Warwick District and Pioneers of the Darling Downs*. Toowoomba: Robertson & Proven Ltd.

Heritage Consulting Australia Pty Ltd. 2011. *Arrow Energy Surat Gas Project: Non-Indigenous Heritage Report*. Surat Gas Project Environmental Impact Statement, Appendix 20, prepared for Arrow Energy Pty Ltd. Available at: http://www.arrowenergy.com.au/__data/assets/pdf_file/0011/2702/Appendix20 R20-20Non-Indigenous20Heritage20Impact20Assessment.pdf (accessed 26 March 2013).

Krieksy, J., B.D. Goldstein, K. Zell and S. Beach. 2013. Differing Opinions about Natural Gas Drilling in Two Adjacent Counties with Different Levels of Drilling Activity. *Energy Policy* 58: 228–36.

Mathews, A.S. and J. Barnes. 2016. Prognosis: Visions of Environmental Futures. *Journal of the Royal Anthropological Institute* 22(S1): 9–26.

McCrea, R., A. Walton and R. Leonard. 2014. A Conceptual Framework for Investigating Community Wellbeing and Resilience. *Rural Society* 23(3): 270–82.

Measham, T.G. and D.A. Fleming. 2014. Impacts of Unconventional Gas Development on Rural Community Decline. *Journal of Rural Studies* 36: 376–85.

Mercer, A., K. de Rijke and W. Dressler. 2014. Silences in the Boom: Coal Seam Gas, Neoliberalizing Discourse, and the Future of Regional Australia. *Journal of Political Ecology* 21(12): 279–301.

Mineralogy Database. 2016. Mineral Collecting, Localities, Mineral Photos and Data. Available at: http://www.mindat.org/ (accessed 11 March 2016).

Perry, S.L. 2012. Development, Land Use, and Collective Trauma: The Marcellus Shale Gas Boom in Rural Pennsylvania. *Culture, Agriculture, Food and Environment* 34(1): 81–92.

Pijpers, R.J. and T.H. Eriksen. (this volume). Introduction: Negotiating the Multiple Edges of Mining Encounters. In R.J. Pijpers and T.H. Eriksen (eds), *Mining Encounters: Extractive Industries in an Overheated World*. London: Pluto Press.

Powell, J.M. 1991. *Plains of Promise, Rivers of Destiny: Water Management and the Development of Queensland 1824–1990*. Bowen Hills, Qld: Boolarong Publications.

Queensland Government Statistician's Office. 2016. *Queensland Regional Profiles: Western Downs Regional Council Local Government Area (LGA)*. Available at: http://statistics.qgso.qld.gov.au/qld-regional-profiles (profile generated on 4 March 2016).

Richardson, T. 2014. The Politics of Multiplication in a Failed Soviet Irrigation Project, Or, How Sasyk Has Been Kept from the Sea. *Ethnos: Journal of Anthropology* 81(1): 1–27.

Richardson, T. and G. Weszkalnys. 2014. Introduction: Resource Materialities. *Anthropological Quarterly* 87(1): 5–30.

Rogers, D. 2015. Oil and Anthropology. *Annual Review of Anthropology* 44: 365–80.

Turvey, N. 2006. *Terania Creek: Rainforest Wars*. Brisbane: Glasshouse Books.

Waterson, D.B. 1991. The Darling Downs: Changing Patterns and Altered Perspectives, 1920–1989. In B.J. Dalton (ed.), *Peripheral Visions: Essays on Australian Regional and Local History*. Townsville: James Cook University, pp. 8–24.

Weir, J.K. 2009. *Murray River Country: An Ecological Dialogue with Traditional Owners*. Canberra: Aboriginal Studies Press.

Western Downs Regional Council. 2015a. *Business and Industry*. Available at: http://www.wdrc.qld.gov.au/doing-business/business-and-industry/ (accessed 11 March 2016).

—— 2015b. *Western Downs Economic Annual*. Report prepared for Western Downs Regional Council by Lawrence Consulting. Available at: http://www.rda-ddsw.org.au/fileadmin/user_upload/Western_Downs_Economic_Annual.pdf (accessed 11 March 2016).

Weszkalnys, G. 2016. A Doubtful Hope: Resource Affect in a Future Oil Economy. *Journal of the Royal Anthropological Institute* 22(S1): 127–46.

Williams, P. 2016. Condamine River Set on Fire after Greens MP Lights Bubbling Methane Gas, Blames Fracking. *Australian Broadcasting Corporation*, 23 April. Available at: http://www.abc.net.au/news/2016-04-23/condamine-river-bubbling-methane-gas-set-alight-greens-mp/7352578 (accessed 27 April 2016).

Willits, F.K., A.E. Luloff and G.L. Theodori. 2013. Changes in Residents' Views of Natural Gas Drilling in the Pennsylvania Marcellus Shale, 2009–2012. *Journal of Rural Social Sciences* 28(3): 60–75.

Willow, A. and S. Wylie. 2014. Politics, Ecology, and the New Anthropology of Energy: Exploring the Emerging Frontiers of Hydraulic Fracking. *Journal of Political Ecology* 21(12): 222–36.

Wilson, E., K. Stimpson, D. Lloyd and W.E. Boyd. 2011. Promoting Gondwana: Presentation of the Gondwana Rainforests of Australia World Heritage Area in Tourist Brochures. *Journal of Heritage Tourism* 6(4): 297–308.

Wopfner, H. 1988. Oil and Gas in Australia. *GeoJournal* 16(4): 371–86.

NOTES

1. All monetary amounts are in Australian dollars.
2. While such characterisations must not be understood literally to imply the complete destruction of Aboriginal people and culture since early colonisation, the total Indigenous population in the Western Downs and the Richmond-Tweed statistical area was just 4.5 per cent and 3.8 per cent of the total populations respectively in 2011 (Australian Bureau of Statistics 2016; Queensland Government Statistician's Office 2016). The important analysis that examines the ways in which the settler region developed in relation to enduring Indigenous presence and relationships to land is beyond the scope of this chapter.
3. The New South Wales average is 5.5 per cent. Data by the Australian Government (2016) *New South Wales – Unemployment Rate by Labour Force Region*. Available at: http://lmip.gov.au/maps.aspx#layer=LabourForceRegions (accessed 1 June 2018).
4. Queensland Government data on registered water bores and coal seam gas wells obtained via 'Queensland Globe' (2016), available at: https://www.business.qld.gov.au/business/support-tools-grants/services/mapping-data-imagery/queensland-globe (accessed 1 June 2018).
5. The original caption for this photo was: 'Bubbling methane gas was set alight by Jeremy Buckingham'. Photo supplied to the Australian Broadcasting Corporation by Jeremy Buckingham, 23 April 2016.

7. Coal Trafficking

Reworking National Energy Security via Coal Transport at the North Karanpura Coalfields, India

Patrik Oskarsson and Nikas Kindo

INTRODUCTION

Increased energy generation is a key national policy goal in India. Energy is required by important voter groups among rural farmers and middle-class urban residents alike. It is seen as a core requirement for industrialisation to take off, as well as to prevent the recurring, paralysing power cuts which make it all too clear that India is yet to join the world of modern nations that its growing economy and improved self-confidence signals it should be part of (Lahiri-Dutt 2014). Electrical energy in India means coal power and this is not about to change in the coming years, despite air pollution in Indian cities reportedly being the world's worst, and concerns regarding climate change as well as protests relating to the major disruptions – to both the landscape and society –involved in the extraction and transport of enormous quantities of coal (Guttikunda et al. 2014; Lahiri-Dutt 2017).

The North Karanpura coalfields of the east Indian state of Jharkhand represent the most recently opened coal mining region in one of India's main mining states. Here, coal is available in large quantities from a number of open-cast mines for transport especially to the main cities of the north and west of the country. Although coal mining has been planned since the 1980s only limited infrastructure has been put in place. The region is known to have a number of armed insurgency groups and yet thousands of trucks pass through the surrounding forests each night. In addition to the lack of infrastructure and security concerns, a host of local, small-scale industries are supported by an informal supply chain of coal scavengers largely consisting of the mine-displaced who are left with few other work options. Thus, getting coal out of North Karanpura is far from straightforward, yet it sort of works. Millions of tons are moved out of the mines and enough of it is siphoned off or captured as rent to keep various local and state-level actors content enough to let things continue to operate.

This chapter uses coal transport as a way of understanding how national ideals of modernity, economic growth and the efficient use of minerals become implicated in local political economies and transformed, at least in part, into locally relevant resource worlds. It starts with a discussion on resource control and coal logistics in central India, followed by an overview of the coal mining region under study. The three transport options – railway, truck and cycle – are then discussed in detail before conclusions are drawn on the continued malleability of Indian resource governance in spite of increasing centralised control.

RESOURCE POLITICS AND COAL TRANSPORT

In eastern India coal is a key resource shaping the polity and society as well as nature. Coal is also closely aligned to dreams of future prosperity of the nation by influential groups (Lahiri-Dutt 2016). An important characteristic of Indian mining, and particularly coal mining, is its considerable insulation from global economic and social trends. In a world where mining has entered 'an unprecedentedly intense period, with fast growth and resource "booms and busts"' (Pijpers and Eriksen, this volume), Indian coal is instead characterised by a slow but seemingly unstoppable domestic expansion which largely lacks the dramatic up- and downturns of international mining markets. And while some international investors, suppliers and consultants are present, the coal market as well as the key actors and their sources of finance and governance are domestic, underpinned by the long-running deficiency in power nationwide. In this context, the world market price only has influence on the amount of coal that is imported. The main approach is to allow domestic production to expand as much as is possible. As the national government's Minister of Power, Coal and Sustainable Development expressed it 'coal is really an issue of energy security' (Centre for Science and Environment 2016) and the entire industry is run domestically in spite of increasing liberalisation within the country in many sectors.

Coal for sale in the general market can only be mined by the public sector since nationalisation of the industry in the 1970s. Liberalisation of the economy in recent decades has, however, seen a strong return of the private sector to take on outsourced activities from the public mines, including coal transport but also, at times, carrying out mining for its own needs. The national government regulates the main aspects of coal operations, sharing responsibility for this with the state government

(Lahiri-Dutt 2014). National security and the environment are concerns for the national government while the state government regulates land and issues documents to control the movement of the trucks and trains transporting the coal. Technological change in production is increasingly towards large-scale open-cast mining, resulting in a large land use footprint (Lahiri-Dutt 2014). The displacement of communities and related environmental degradation within the production of spaces in extractive industries has been frequently discussed (Fernandes 2009; Oskarsson 2014). But the transportation of large quantities of coal from the coal face to power plants, as well as to a wide range of other users ranging from steel plants, to small-scale industries, restaurants and even households has its own specific political economies as this chapter shows. Side by side with the formal coal industry there is a large informal one. Here, ad hoc solutions dominate in an informal mining and coal supply industry. Coal can be accessed in multiple ways, including some not officially sanctioned as legal, via entry into the mines directly, by accessing coal from loading points, or through manipulating the paperwork. Control over the resource is part of this but not the entire story. The ability to control key access points and routes also allows control over the coal (Oskarsson 2017).

A core challenge for national energy security is that coal is found mainly in central-eastern India, including in Jharkhand, while the main demand comes from the urban centres of the west and north of the country. Transport of hundreds of millions of tons of coal is required to bridge this gap between areas of supply and demand, accounting for as much as 50 per cent of the freight transported by rail nationally. Transport is crucial for overall energy security since the cost 'is often as much or more than the price of coal at the mine' (National Transport Development Policy Committee 2013: 376). The railway remains the favoured solution, in spite of increasing congestion and an outdated infrastructure, due to its lower cost and its ability to transport large quantities (National Transport Development Policy Committee 2013). The mineral-rich states of central-eastern India, of which Jharkhand is part, have for decades been vying for the unenviable position of being India's poorest state. As the rest of the country has been making progress, if often highly unevenly, these states are increasingly left behind with local politics focused on identity issues rather than human or other forms of development. State failure, or even absence in some places, has additionally opened up spaces for left-wing guerrilla Naxalite groups (Corbridge 2011). Some see local people as being sandwiched between left-wing militancy and government counter-operations, two forces both prone to the use of violence and not necessarily working in the interest of the region (Guha 2007). Others have provided a more integrated picture of how local people move between different roles for a wide range of reasons (Shah 2007b).

Just like political parties and other organisations in India, the Maoist groups too continue to be strongly shaped by local factors in the regions where they operate:

> The [CPI(Maoist)] party's politics and policies are not uniform across states – much depends on the shape of local class hierarchies, the past history of the area, geographic factors, the nature of the ruling regime and even the nature of local Maoist commanders. (Sundar 2014: 473–4)[1]

It is well known that '[t]he Maoists finance their state through levies ... [E]veryone working in Maoist areas has to pay them taxes' (Sundar 2014: 478). So widespread is this practice in Maoist areas that Sundar concludes that they 'do not pose an alternative to advanced capitalism as a whole' (2014: 478). Since the economy of Maoist-influenced regions depends on the natural resource base so do the main levies, which have tended to come from forest products, for example, but also from minerals. Other actors, including the local state, have long acted as a resource extraction entity. And this rent extraction is not necessarily competitive between Maoist insurgency groups and the local state, but rather a form of cooperation (Shah 2006). '[T]he Naxalite movement is spreading through greater control over a market of protection controlling the informal economy of state resources, conventionally called the systems of corruption' (Shah 2007b: 1818). Politically influential groups can control certain routes across the forested terrain relying on a combination of muscle power and political connections to ensure access to a share of the coal transport; at the same time they risk leaving traces of their illegal activities. Encounters (cf. Pijpers and Eriksen, this volume) between mining company, security forces, guerrilla groups, political representatives, party workers and coal mafias have been worked out over years of mining activity to ensure a certain balance of power and, seemingly, an informally settled share of the returns.

On the margins of the violent groups and the key political and bureaucratic interests that have the possibility of extracting rents from coal sits an impoverished population with few alternatives other than to become part of the local coal economy. This means either joining one of the armed groups, obtaining a truck licence or scavenging for coal along transport routes and at dumps and loading points. A highly visible phenomenon in Jharkhand are the coal cycles detailed by Lahiri-Dutt and Williams (2005). These are reinforced bicycles providing coal to households and smaller businesses within 40–50 km of a mine. The coal cycles may be informal, they are however usually dependent on the main roads and thus also exposed to similar forces as those controlling other means of coal transport.

Uncertain political relations in Jharkhand state have prevented a coherent approach to security, with national forces propping up the local security apparatus but often being prevented from intervening by influential state leaders (Shah 2007a). This chapter explores these and related arrangements as they appear in coal transport, whether for monetary gain by key political interests at local and state levels, in support of left-wing insurgency groups, or for mere survival for those dispossessed by the mines.

THE NORTH KARANPURA COALFIELD OF JHARKHAND STATE

North Karanpura is part of the Chotanagpur *adivasi*[2] region of Jharkhand state. Here rebellions have been fought for centuries against various outsiders, including the British, feudal princes and the modern Indian government (Bates and Shah 2014), resulting in strong land protection on paper but, in practice, continued support of extraction for the benefit of outsiders via coal mining and forest plantations (George 2010). *Adivasis* dominate numerically, especially in rural areas, while the mining settlements tend to experience an influx of various other groups of mainly lower and middle caste Hindus who come both for the manual work and the more technical and managerial positions offered in relation to the mines.

Jharkhand has an extensive history of coal mining stretching back more than a century and some of India's first larger mines were established in and around Dhanbad and Jamshedpur in the eastern part of the state (Lahiri-Dutt 2014). Mining has continued to expand in these locations but also moved into new territories further west along the Damodar River valley. The North Karanpura coalfield represents the most recent expansion in one of India's main coal regions. Since the 1980s this region has become a major coal supplier operated by Central Coalfields Ltd (CCL), a subsidiary of the public sector company Coal India. The annual accounts of CCL from the fiscal year 2015–16 presents sizeable coal deliveries of 59 million tons (Central Coalfields Limited 2016).

The Piparwar mine was the first 'modern' mine in the North Karanpura coalfield when it was established in the late 1980s with World Bank funding and Australian technologies. It was supposed to ensure efficient, mechanised mining via open-cut technologies, unlike other Coal India mines, long plagued by low productivity. Environmental mitigation and reclamation activities were also supposed to follow international best practices (Advance Environmental Planning Group 1987). The technically efficient mining envisaged by the World Bank and its consultants relied on a dedicated railway link to take coal directly to major north Indian cities for power generation (Advance Environmental Planning Group 1987). But a 30-year delay in the construction of the railway line has created a continued need for thousands of Tata trucks making use of a number of formal and informal roads through the forests for its coal transports.

Twenty-three additional coal mines have been planned in the North Karanpura coalfield (Bharat Jan Andolan and Nav Bharat Jagriti Kendra 1993) and, while often facing significant delays, new mines continue to open. The mining expansion has created a set of mines with highly variable extraction and transport technologies, but also with frequent outsourcing as well as informal operations (Oskarsson 2017). Lahiri-Dutt (2016) explains the setting as containing multiple resource worlds of coal based on entirely different logics of extraction within officially nationalised extraction. In North Karanpura this means that mines officially operated by the public sector using open-cast extraction can have some or all of their operations outsourced to private contractors. And informal coal, extracted via coal scavenging, ensures a separate coal world operating side by side with several official ones. The formal and informal coal worlds use highly variable transport solutions. Some mechanised mines have a direct railway connection while others use manual loading and trucks that travel along bumpy forest roads. And alongside large-scale operations are underground mines, operating today in ways very similar to those of 50 or more years ago. The open-cast mines and the official transport routes are particularly open to scavengers adept at slipping in unnoticed to take away significant amounts of coal, and transporting these to similarly informal customers.

The presence of left-wing groups in the mining areas has heightened calls for increased presence of security staff in the area, but also for technical improvements including GPS tracking to ensure coal dispatches reach officially intended customers (Central Coalfields Limited 2016; National Transport Development Policy Committee 2013). The CPI(Maoist) is the main insurgency group operating in the state, but the South Asia Terrorist Portal (2015) mentions four other groups active in the state. At the North Karanpura coalfields three of these were found to operate, including the CPI(Maoist), JLT (Jharkhand Liberation Tigers, now also called People's Liberation Front of India), and TPC (Tritiya Prastuti Committee). The JLT is a group almost entirely interested in blackmailing money from industrial operations rather than working towards revolutionary ideals. The TPC is a group of lower-caste and *adivasi* Maoists who broke off from the CPI(Maoist) since they did not want to be led by middle- and upper-caste comrades. Its main reason to exist has become to fight the CPI(Maoist) group, but also to extort money from mines and other sources to fund operations. The national government's Central Industrial Security Force (CISF) is in charge of security in the central industrial areas of the coalfields. Operating from camps in nearby forests are Special Forces like the state-level Jharkhand Jaguars and the national Central Reserve Police Force (CRPF) and the army Cobra (Commando Battalion for Resolute Action) force. These forces have special training and equipment to target Maoist groups and to protect important industrial facilities and yet appear unable to significantly reduce the Maoist presence even in the immediate vicinity of the coal areas. Blurred lines between the security establishment and Maoist groups appear to explain this. One example, as mentioned by Das (2013), is the JPC (Jharkhand Prastuti Committee) group which has been fighting the CPI(Maoist) with support from the Jharkhand government. Another, from an interview with a journalist, is the story of how an elected Congress party member of the state assembly chose to start his own left-wing militant group a few years ago, presumably in order to be able to extract local rents over resources.[3] Future realignments are to be expected between different entities of the state and Maoist groups.

COAL TRANSPORT AT THE NORTH KARANPURA COALFIELDS[4]

In North Karanpura three different modes of transport ensure that the coal can leave the area in large quantities; railway, truck and cycle. Railway is for large customers, typically public or private power or steel plants. Trucks can serve big industries in a highly flexible manner, depending on demand, but are also used for small and medium-sized businesses. Households and smaller businesses rely on cycles for coal, usually over short distances since the roads are not well developed in the region.

During the day the coal area was characterised by virtually open access, which could be seen as surprising given the high presence of Maoist groups and various security forces. Anybody can take a car, motorbike or cycle and drive straight into the mines, and even walk around and take photos, as long as you know which turns to take on the very poor and often temporary mud roads. The coal is of course neither ungoverned nor unguarded. It is just that, as a coal trader expressed it, 'all government officials who are posted here are for money, their prime motive is to earn money, as they have given someone money for their posting here. So they have investment too.'⁵ Indicating that significant sums are involved in the collection of levies, one source with insights into left-wing operations estimated that the value for insurgency groups per year in Jharkhand amounted to about 2 billion Indian rupees (approximately US$30 million).⁶ Governance in the area is thus, according to informants, directed by money coming from the coal trade. Consequently, the security guards of the coalfields and the special police forces roaming nearby forests largely stay away from direct control. Written laws are at the same time not entirely absent. In the midst of the apparent chaos of the coalfields, hundreds of trucks line up all day to clear the paperwork that will allow them to use the official transport routes. The law thus has an influence and a role, although it is highly malleable. Those who engage in coal trade in contravention of the rules refer to this as doing No. 2 business (in Hindi: *do number ka dhandaa*). No. 2 business is not in opposition to legit No. 1. business since, as a coal trader expressed it, '[h]ow can you do No. 2 without their [the government's] permission, at one shot you will get caught.'⁷ In this situation, the legal and formal does not stand in clear opposition to the illegal and informal, but merely becomes part of a wide spectrum of practices.

Railway

Railways have never been quite developed in Jharkhand as the region was bypassed when metropolitan cities were connected around the country. But it was only via rail that it would be possible to move large amounts of coal out of the mine and then on to the main cities in the north and the west of the country (Advance Environmental Planning Group 1987). The area has a railway link running just south of it but a wide range of concerns has continued to hold up the actual connection, despite only a few kilometres of track being needed to connect the mainline to the North Karanpura coalfields. The Maoist presence in nearby forests has certainly not helped with the completion of the railway but frequent protests against land acquisition is another reason for delays.

Coal is loaded at so-called sidings, railway loading points for coal. At Khalari within the North Karanpura coalfields is a major siding with a new train leaving every two hours. There are also sidings in two nearby towns, a couple of hours away by truck transport. Lacking in advanced infrastructure these sidings are often little more than yards where coal can be dumped and later lifted on to railway carriages. Each train has 52 rakes, or carriages, with each rake capable of carrying about 50 tons of coal. This means that 2,600 tons can leave the Khalari siding on the railway every two hours, or 31,200 tons per day. The railway siding lacks protective walls and security, allowing criminal gangs – usually referred to as the coal mafia – to extort money. Coal mafias were understood in interviews as people with guns and some amount of support from within the administration and other influential groups. Using this power, they were capable of establishing domination over a particular area and of exerting control over the movement of coal.

Centrally located railway sidings have become key areas of control for the different coal mafia groups operating at North Karanpura. Two influential Rajput (warrior) caste members were identified by informants as being in charge of coal transport based on their historical influence as labour and truck contractors. The main gangs are considered too powerful for other groups to interfere with. Indeed, shootings do take place and one previous head of a coal mafia group was killed in 2014. The Congress party has been close to coal mafia leaders and it has been noticed that political leaders of the party would always visit them when in the area.[8] During field investigations 70,000 rupees (about US$1,100) per train was quoted as the regular fee charged by the mafia to allow a train to leave the siding. Fees are likely to vary however as these are arranged over the phone from time to time like so many other business transactions in this region. Little is known so far about the exchange of these large sums of money. The money will be exchanged far away from the coal face. If the train goes to a private company then a steep fee will have to be paid. At the same time, the public sector customers appeared not to be forced to pay. Efforts to counter the extortion attempts include building so-called super sidings, in which access can be strictly controlled via gates. This kind of siding additionally increases the efficiency by loading a train in just one hour. Only a few such sidings have been built to date and the main one in Bachra in North Karanpura is of the old, open variety.

The close relationship between the power of guns and of politics in the local political ecology of coal is understood to shape the possibilities for extorting money from the railways. Private companies will simply not get coal for their power plants unless they pay. The threat to stop the trains from leaving the siding works in spite of the central location in the coal town, with security staff, police forces and paramilitary units in the vicinity. With state and central government police forces in the area officially to combat Maoists it would not have been a problem to dedicate a small force to secure the railway as well. Close links between the coal mafia and key politicians in the area appear as the only possible explanation otherwise this form of extortion would not be allowed to continue. The coal mafia focuses on controlling the railway sidings but this is not the sole focus of their extortion work. They can and do take up work together with various groups from time to time as the coal transport business inevitably goes through changes in terms of the routes that are profitable. Diverting trucks meant to carry coal from the mines to nearby railway sidings is one profitable business. As each company has 50 to 200 trucks running all day long on these short routes it becomes possible to send a few of them off to a side location to unload the coal and sell it at a greater profit on the black market.[9] The coal mafia is also known to at times work with one of the main Maoist groups to extort money from coal trucks.

Truck

The delay in completing the railway link has enabled a virtual armada consisting of thousands of trucks to operate on the two very bumpy roads which lead out of the North Karanpura coalfields, one to the south towards the capital Ranchi and one to the north. The trucks typically line up for large parts of the day at a particular coal mine to clear paperwork and fill up, and then travel at night to minimise the disturbance in villages which have to be passed on the way to customers for the coal. The possibility for local political and business interests to own even just a few trucks and run these for personal gain would appear to be a motivating factor for why the railways have not been completed. At the same time, it is clear that there is a technological upgrade ongoing from smaller to larger trucks, including larger truck operators who own more trucks per company. In interviews this was seen as benefiting the larger business houses and bigger politicians at state level as opposed to those operating in the area. From time to time there will be new regulations issued for truck transport. While early 2014 saw thousands of trucks regularly move coal out of the North Karanpura area, these had virtually been stopped towards the end of the year. Then the newer, larger, Tata trucks started to replace the old, orange ones. Depending on market demand, the operations of the railway, as well as political and security conditions, trucks may be used by the thousands or made to wait idle for weeks in unpredictable ways.

While not completely open to transporting coal anywhere, the system of issuing delivery orders for truck transport is highly malleable towards supporting particular interests. Getting hold of a DO, Delivery Order, is key to official passage out of the area. These are issued by the local transport authorities and guarded even among close friends once obtained. If you have the DO it tells you how much you are going to transport, from where to where and for what price. Based on these details, a lot of things can be figured out in terms of which route you will be taking and how much levy can be extracted, including the possibilities for leakage of additional amounts of coal. This is why everyone guards their DOs. Before the 1990s it was easy for smaller traders to get DOs. Anyone who wanted coal could weigh their loaded truck, make a bank draft and submit it to the Coal India local office. In one or two hours the trader would receive DO papers. Nowadays, the minimum DO is for 500 tons and under this arrangement only larger companies can afford to enter into business.[10] Similarly, for the e-auction larger traders are preferred.[11] A number of options exist to leak coal based on a single DO. The first option is to run 2–5 trucks on a single DO. In this arrangement one trip will be legal and the rest will go to other destinations. Another arrangement is when a truck is registered to enter into a coal siding with a validity of 10 to 15 days. If it completes the DO delivery in five days then it will have another five days to enter a coal depot and arrange forged papers to receive coal. The third arrangement is the duration of one DO with specification of delivery deadlines at, for example, a faraway destination like the city of Varanasi for 10 days, but in reality taking three loads from the coal depot. When questioned about the late delivery the truck owner can make an excuse of truck breakdown, something which in any case occurs frequently on very bumpy roads.[12]

Lacking in other livelihood opportunities, and also not having the educational qualifications and the cultural capital required to be employed in the formal coal company positions, truck driving has become a key source of employment for local people. Though a licence is required this can be acquired on the black market, at which point getting hired as a helper provides the actual training to manoeuvre a truck loaded with coal, and crucially also how to navigate the different coal transport routes which exist and the various gatekeepers who control each of them. To be a truck driver is a challenging position given the many authorities which have to be navigated. And almost all the transports take place at night given the pollution of thousands of trucks moving with heavy loads of coal through villages and towns on often poor roads. In the end a driver will receive about 500 rupees for one truck delivery, a paltry sum when navigating control points, paying the right amount of bribes, and frequently having to ensure that the full payment for the coal is returned to the truck owner. Some informants mentioned the existence of a varied levy between the three left-wing groups in the area; the CPI(Maoist) charges 40 rupees, TPC 20 rupees and JLT 10 rupees per ton of coal for safe passage. Another informant stated that fees are charged per truck load. One coal mafia member stated that:

Money is fixed of around 300 to 500 Rs per truck according to truck loading capacity for every trip leaving the coal region. This money is divided among three operating Naxal groups in this region i.e. TPC, JLT and MCC [now part of the CPI(Maoist)] as well as to police. These groups including police have secret meetings at different secret locations and have drinks together over the settlement of money shares. (Interview with coal mafia member, 26 November 2014)

Prices have tended to be decided in meetings outside of the mining area.

The key image of gatekeepers at North Karanpura is of men hanging out on their motorbikes for no apparent reason along forest backroads. But even children along the road function as gatekeepers. A child waving a flag to stop will be obeyed by a driver since the consequences of not doing so can be to meet an armed gang further down the road. And members of the Regional Transport Office (RTO) and the Maoists may also stop drivers. To keep track of vehicle flows requires constant communication to determine which trucks are moving, whether they have paid their fees, and when they should be stopped or allowed to continue. The number plates of the trucks are the key identifiers in this informal transport control since the plates are fixed while drivers and other things can change. The transport controllers will remember the last four digits on the plate. Knowing how many trucks a certain owner has will then allow them to discover if payment has been received in total or not. Conversations take place on the phone using codes. Routes have identifiers like C which only they know. The RTO officers operate along the main roads at night. Any little excuse, such as when something is broken on the truck, can be used to get some money. But if you have paid in one check post you can tell them your name and get off paying again. The Maoists often stop trucks in the early morning, at about 3 or 4 a.m. when they are returning empty back to the coal areas. They too will only charge once. You mention the name of the person who took your money and the next Maoist will let you go. In this case you might think that calling to check would be harder since mobiles are likely to be tracked but according to interviews it works.

Illegal coal is usually transported to smaller plants and brick-making units. And the payment is of course in cash since nobody would want their bank transactions to be traced. About 20,000 rupees for a truck load of coal was the going rate during fieldwork. This money has to be transported back to the truck owner by the drivers, which requires strong trust in the driver but also ingenuity enough to hide the cash should the driver face a raid by the authorities, left-wing guerrillas or others. Truck drivers were using a number of ways to hide money in little stashes here and there around their trucks. They might pack 10,000 rupees into knapsacks and then keep them in the driver's compartment or on top of the petrol tank for example. It appears to be a very risky way of living which puts a lot of stress on the individual drivers to bring back money to the owners.

Cycle

The displaced who are unable to qualify for formal jobs in the coal industry often find scavenging for coal to be the best livelihood option as land has been lost, polluted or drained of irrigation water. One 'koyala chori' (Hindi for coal thief), or informal coal collector, explained that: 'We feel that this is the only work available here. People were thrown out of mining work, then from manual loading sites, big contractors don't want to give work to women, so what will people do?'[13] The work can be much more remunerative than manual labour jobs in the area but also comes with great danger, relying as it does on accessing coal from the mines without security services noticing, or taking it from moving railway carriages. Another coal collector explained how 'in front of me people have died under the train, or because of overhead wires'.[14] Coal cycles have become the main vehicle for supplying informal coal and are a very visible feature along the main roads in Jharkhand's coal belt. Given that millions of tons of coal are involved each year and the need for multiple, manual steps from the actual carrying, to burning off impurities, then packaging and transporting coal, the extent of labour involved is significant, often occupying a large number of people in coal-side villages (Lahiri-Dutt and Williams 2005).

North Karanpura has poor roads and is a long distance away from any major towns. Consequently, household and restaurant supplies have been avoided in favour of local, small-scale industry. In particular, small-scale brick kilns and steel plants utilise informal supply options via coal cycles, or at the very least coal initially scavenged by coal cycles and then handed over to trucks along informal supply routes through the forests. Coal, as for the trucked coal above, becomes available for scavengers in many locations across the coalfields, although in this case it is fully within the informal industry. Loading points for trucks and the railway are scattered across the area from right next to the mines to various reloading points, including some deep in the forests; all these become potential access points for the coal scavengers. And once in transit coal spills over from trucks travelling along bumpy roads or can be thrown off when people climb on to slow-moving trains. The mines themselves are often surprisingly lacking in security, allowing people to walk into them, especially early in the morning before guards arrive, to lift coal.

Once coal has been secured it might be taken away if a security patrol discovers it. To overcome this problem, coal is better left somewhere in common areas, along the railroad for example. Coal left in the open cannot easily be tied to an individual unlike if it is found in large quantities in a home. Patrols along the railway lines do not have the means to transport coal on a daily basis from where it is found, scattered throughout the area, to the legal storage points, and they cannot easily fine anyone. The scavengers will naturally have to protect their piles of coal against other scavengers, but can otherwise leave these quite safely. At the same time, there is no reason to think that coal scavengers are allowed to operate without similar demands for rent to those demonstrated above for railway and truck transport. Hundreds of people operate coal cycles and others carry out forms of informal coal scavenging in each of the main coal mining areas of Jharkhand every day, giving possibilities for the extraction of significant levies. In this sense, the coal cycles become similar to the other forms of coal transport.

CONCLUSION

This chapter has outlined the impressive multiplicity of approaches and groups involved in the movement of coal at the North Karanpura coalfields as a way of understanding how coal transport rearranges national energy security into locally relevant 'resource worlds' (Lahiri-Dutt 2016). National policy preferences are increasingly decided in close collaboration at the top between domestic big business and political leaders (Chandra 2015). Increased mechanisation has followed intense efforts to secure energy supply to large-scale customers in the nation's industrialised mega-cities, which have faced a crisis in power supply for years. These strong incentives for an industrialised supply chain have been backed up by significant funds and yet, as this chapter shows, there is a multiplicity of interest groups able to rework national politics to allow for highly varied transport solutions, and thereby local political economies.

Opportunities in coal transport exist for guns for hire supported by political interests, but also for left-wing guerrillas who are supposed to be interested in a socialist revolution rather than money. In this study, the insurgency groups appeared as yet another collaborator in the extraction of rents from coal by powerful groups much in line with the existing literature. Meanwhile, security forces at the coalfield remain inactive, indicating some form of political understanding under which attacks are not made by any of the sides involved. An informal but well-defined coal trade appears to exist to exert control and extract rents with complicated rules for how to keep track of who makes payments and how much. And, despite the informality with a lack of receipts and ledgers, there appears to be some degree of possibility to not get charged several times for the same trip. More detailed investigations are required to understand whether the informal market for coal transport contains similarly detailed rules to those identified by Wade (1985) in a classic account of how rents became formalised in Indian irrigation water governance, with payments distributed far up the chain of command in the state bureaucracy. Initial accounts indicate similar arrangements in the coalfields of Jharkhand, with an added element of militarisation to indicate the higher stakes at play in this key resource for the nation.

High-level planning, including long-running deficiencies in coal infrastructure, has not been followed through with on-the-ground attention to resource movement or the many local residents not included in present plans. And yet the poorest are able to find ways to survive via coal scavenging and cycle transport where few alternative means of living exist. The present compromise evident in the transport of coal in the North Karanpura coalfields in part fulfils national goals of energy security while providing opportunities for rent collection and support for populations not included in official plans. India may be increasingly authoritarian at the top but its various interest groups are still able to rework resource uses to better suit their needs.

ACKNOWLEDGEMENTS

The authors would like to thank Robert Pijpers and Thomas Hylland Eriksen for the invitation to the Overheating mining conference in Oslo where the initial draft of this chapter was presented. Patrik Oskarsson would also like to acknowledge the support of Formas via grant number 2013-1965.

REFERENCES

Advance Environmental Planning Group. 1987. *Advance Environmental Management Plan for North Karanpura Coalfield of Central Coalfields Ltd.* Delhi: Ministry of Coal, Government of India.

Bates, C. and A. Shah (eds). 2014. *Savage Attack: Tribal Insurgency in India.* New Delhi: Social Science Press.

Bharat Jan Andolan, and Nav Bharat Jagriti Kendra. 1993. *Social Impact: Piparwar and the North Karanpura Coalfields.*

Central Coalfields Limited. 2016. *Annual Report and Accounts 2015–16.* Ranchi, India: Central Coalfields Limited.

Centre for Science and Environment. 2016. Coal Is All About Energy Security, Says Coal Minister in CSE's Global Conference. Press release. Available at: http://cseindia.org/content/coal-all-about-energy-security-says-coal-minister-cse%E2%80%99s-global-conference (accessed 18 March 2016).

Chandra, K. 2015. The New Indian State. *Economic and Political Weekly* 50(41): 46–58.

Corbridge, S. 2011. The Contested Geographies of Federalism in Post-Reform India. In S. Ruparelia, S. Reddy, J. Harriss and S. Corbridge (eds), *Understanding India's New Political Economy: A Great Transformation?* London: Routledge, pp. 66–80.

Das, S. 2013. Supporting Tritiya Prastuti Committee Likely to Backfire for Jharkhand. *The Times of India* 5 April. Available at: http://timesofindia.indiatimes.com/city/ranchi/Supporting-Tritiya-Prastuti-Committee-likely-to-backfire-for-Jharkhand/articleshow/19388641.cms (accessed 9 May 2018).

Fernandes, W. 2009. Displacement and Alienation from Common Property Resources. In L. Mehta (ed.), *Displaced by Development: Confronting Marginalisation and Gender Injustice*. New Delhi: Sage, pp. 105–32.

George, A.S. 2010. The Paradox of Mining and Development. In N. Sundar (ed.), *Legal Grounds: Natural Resources, Identity, and the Law in Jharkhand*. Oxford: Oxford University Press, pp. 157–88.

Guha, R. 2007. Adivasis, Naxalites and Indian Democracy. *Economic and Political Weekly* 42(32): 3305–12.

Guttikunda, S.K., R. Goel and P. Pant. 2014. Nature of Air Pollution, Emission Sources, and Management in the Indian Cities. *Atmospheric Environment* 95: 501–10. Available at: https://doi.org/10.1016/j.atmosenv.2014.07.006 (accessed 9 May 2018).

Lahiri-Dutt, K. 2014. Introduction to Coal in India: Energising the Nation. In K. Lahiri-Dutt (ed.), *The Coal Nation: Histories, Cultures and Ecologies*. London: Ashgate, pp. 1–36.

—— 2016. The Diverse Worlds of Coal in India: Energising the Nation, Energising Livelihoods. *Energy Policy*, 99, 203–213. https://doi.org/10.1016/j.enpol.2016.05.045

—— 2017. Coal for National Development in India: Transforming Landscapes and Social Relations in the Quest for Energy Security. In K.B. Nielsen and P. Oskarsson (eds), *Industrialising Rural India: Land, Policy, Resistance*. London: Routledge, pp. 85–106.

Lahiri-Dutt, K. and D.J. Williams. 2005. The Coal Cycle: Small-scale Illegal Coal Supply in Eastern India. *Resources, Energy, and Development* 2(2): 93–105.

National Transport Development Policy Committee. 2013. *India Transport Report: Moving India to 2032*. Delhi: Government of India.

Oskarsson, P. 2014. The Political Ecology of Coal in the South Indian State of Andhra Pradesh. In K. Lahiri-Dutt (ed.), *The Coal Nation: Histories, Cultures and Ecologies*. London: Ashgate, pp. 197–218.

—— 2017. Producing 'So-So' Infrastructure for National Energy Security at the North Karanpura Coalfields in Eastern India. *South Asia: Journal of South Asian Studies* 40(4): 1–15. Available at: https://doi.org/10.1080/00856401.2017.1375042 (accessed 9 May 2018).

Pijpers, R.J. and T.H. Eriksen (this volume). Introduction: Negotiating the Multiple Edges of Mining Encounters. In R.J. Pijpers and T.H. Eriksen (eds), *Mining Encounters: Extractive Industries in an Overheated World*. London: Pluto.

Shah, A. 2006. Markets of Protection. *Critique of Anthropology* 26(3): 297–314.

—— 2007a. 'Keeping the State Away': Democracy, Politics, and the State in India's Jharkhand. *Journal of the Royal Anthropological Institute* 13(1): 129–45.

—— 2007b. The Dark Side of Indigeneity? Indigenous People, Rights and Development in India. *History Compass* 5(6): 1806–32. Available at: https://doi.org/10.1111/j.1478-0542.2007.00471.x (accessed 9 May 2018).

South Asia Terrorist Portal. 2015. Jharkhand Assessment 2015. Institute for Conflict Management. Available at: http://www.satp.org/satporgtp/countries/india/maoist/Assessment/2015/Jharkhand.htm (accessed 9 May 2018).

Sundar, N. 2014. Mimetic Sovereignties, Precarious Citizenship: State Effects in a Looking-glass World. *Journal of Peasant Studies* 41(4): 469–90.

Wade, R. 1985. The Market for Public Office: Why the Indian State Is Not Better at Development. *World Development* 13(4): 467–97. Available at: https://doi.org/10.1016/0305-750X(85)90052-X (accessed 9 May 2018).

NOTES

1. The CPI(Maoist) is the Communist Party of India (Maoist).
2. Adivasis, meaning the original inhabitants, are seen as people who inhabited the Indian subcontinent preceding the arrival of other groups. Adivasis are identified in the Indian Constitution by the name Scheduled Tribes as in need of special protection though not recognised as indigenous. They are also referred to as tribals.
3. Interview with a journalist, Hazaribagh, 5 December 2014.
4. This research relies on a combination of ethnographic fieldwork in North Karanpura, key informant interviews at state level and document analysis carried out by the two authors. Two periods of fieldwork have been completed, including a scoping trip in April 2014 and detailed fieldwork in November–December 2014 and June–August 2015.
5. Interview, North Karanpura, 29 August 2015.
6. Interview, North Karanpura, 29 July 2015.
7. Interview, North Karanpura, 29 August 2015.
8. Interview with truck operators, 26 November 2014.
9. Interview with a coal trader, 29 August 2015.
10. The older 6-wheel trucks carry 9 tons, or when overloaded, as they frequently are, up to 12 tons. The newer 12-wheel trucks carry 22 tons and up to 28 tons when overloaded.
11. Interview with JMM party official North Karanpura, 2 December 2014.
12. Interview with truck operators, 26 November 2014.
13. Interview, North Karanpura, 17 July 2015.
14. Interview North Karanpura 17 July 2015.

8. Diamonds and Plural Temporalities

Articulating Encounters in the Mines of Sierra Leone

Lorenzo D'Angelo

In uno tempore, tempora multa latent.
—Lucretius, *De Rerum Naturam,* IV[1]

INTRODUCTION

As the most famous and seductive slogan of the main diamond company in the world – 'diamonds are forever' – suggests, buying diamonds is a way to gain certainty and a sense of the eternal in a world of uncertainty, a way to possess a unique and glittering fragment of time beyond time. Susan Westwood (2002) coined the expression 'diamond time' to express how the use of time in marketing strategies erases the 'scurrilous history' of 'blood diamonds' mined in Angola, the Democratic Republic of Congo, Liberia and Sierra Leone from the diamond industry. The most consolidated marketing strategies for diamonds are based on and presuppose the separation between consumption and production. The way time is used or evoked by the precious gems industry helps to construct and maintain this separation. By analysing the complex articulation of the different time frames of 'diamond time' ('natural time', 'authentic time', 'romantic time', and 'identity time' or 'timing the self'), Westwood highlights not only the polymorphism of time consumption (see Appadurai 1996), but also how each of these frames contributes to the separation of 'marketing time' and 'labour time' (see Westwood 2002: 33). The limit of Westwood's analysis, however, is that it does not precisely investigate the 'labour time' of production 'at the beginning' of the diamond-commodity chain. Therefore, it does not consider the diachronic processes of labour time and the temporal views of those directly involved in diamond extraction. Moreover, Westwood (2002) does not consider whether or how the labour time of diamond extraction is linked to other temporalities. In other words, Westwood's analysis is unable to show how 'diamond time' is a set of temporalities 'without history' (cf. Tomba 2012) that are not created only by the separation between producers and consumers but also by the continuous historical processes of the articulation and disarticulation of capitalist and non-capitalist temporalities and modes of production (Bair and Werner 2011; Zack-Williams 1995).[2]

As little is known about the views and working conditions of diamond miners, this chapter not only theorises the relationship between this particular mineral resource and time (cf. Ferry and Limbert 2008), it also addresses the issue of time from the perspective of the miners themselves, specifically the artisanal miners operating in Sierra Leone. Most of these miners do not know or are not particularly interested in how Western consumers actually make use of diamonds (D'Angelo 2014; see Smith 2011; Walsh 2004). However, they know that with the money obtained from the sale of the precious stones they can increase their ability to plan a future in which their income depends on what they consider to be more reliable and consistent economic activities (e.g. finding a job in Europe, buying a taxi or a little shop, and so on). Like the Kivutiens living in the eastern region of the Democratic Republic of the Congo who mined the so-called 'digital minerals' (tantalum, tungsten, tin), Sierra Leonean miners also often wish to convert the minerals that they extract in their country into individual or family projects, durable goods and long-term profitable activities (cf. Smith 2011: 30). Among these miners, this capacity for the conversion of money is also expressed in terms of velocity. Indeed, money from diamonds is often defined as 'fast money', large amounts of money (in cash form) that are ideally – but not necessarily – obtained in a short time (D'Angelo 2011; Pijpers 2011). Given the high commercial value of these most precious stones, 'diamond money' is capable of bringing accelerated change to local household economies which is perceived as both incremental and exponential. For this reason it is actively sought: it allows desired futures imagined by the miners to become present in reality in ways that other activities do not guarantee for ordinary people. The velocity and the accelerated change of 'diamond money' presuppose the slowness of money coming from other economic activities, and contrast with the formation of the minerals exploited that are the result of geological processes as old as they are slow.

By examining and comparing different kinds of extractive activities in a Sierra Leonean village, I argue that (1) miners' sense of time is linked to the ways people perceive and relate to specific resources in particular market contexts; (2) miners' ideas about fast money are key to understanding temporal perceptions of resources and to highlighting a temporal economy based on the articulation of different modes of production; and (3) what Smith (2011) calls 'temporal dispossession' is just one aspect of a more complex and extended process of exploitation set in motion by the global mining industry in its efforts to (de)synchronise a plurality of heterogeneous spatio-temporalities (cf. Bestor 2001; Miyazaki 2003; Mezzadra 2008). In doing so, this chapter offers an ethnography of encounter (Faier and Rofel 2014; Pijpers and Eriksen, this volume) focused on temporal aspects of mining and defines the partial and contingent results of synchronisation efforts in terms of 'temporal encounters'. Thus, artisanal diamond mining is considered as a transformative practice that seeks to accelerate the encounter between a variety of speeds, rhythms and temporalities.

By referring to time in the plural, I mean to emphasise the need to go beyond a temporal model based merely on the juxtaposition of multiple temporalities – a model in which there is, implicitly, a fundamental temporality against which it is possible to recognise the multiplicity of the others.[3] To use the plural is to emphasise that these temporalities are *already* plural and heterogeneous, and they can only be understood in relation to each other within a specific socioeconomic context (cf. Tomich 2004: 94).

The goal of this chapter is to highlight the relationship between the velocity of mineral money, commodity markets and mining temporalities. To this end, it highlights the layers of processes occurring on different time scales: from the long-term geological processes of diamonds – what I call the 'deep time of resources'[4] – to the medium- and long-term historical and cultural processes that characterise the specific West African region where I carried out my fieldwork, that is, in a particular mining village in Sierra Leone located along the Sewa River.[5] Lastly, this chapter focuses on the temporal perspectives of artisanal miners, comparing the views of diamond miners with those people who search for gold and break stones for a living.

MINESCAPES AND DEEP TIME

Geologists estimate that the oldest diamonds that exist in the world result from geological processes that began more than 3 billion years ago (Shirey and Shigley 2013). For this reason, in the eyes of contemporary geologists, diamonds represent privileged witnesses of unexplored territories and eras in which our planet was very different to the way we know it today. Diamond deposits have been found on every continent, but that does not mean that they can be found anywhere. Their location, in fact, is not entirely random. The locations of diamond deposits correspond with the oldest and most stable regions of continents, called cratons. The diamondiferous deposits of Sierra Leone, as well as those of neighbouring countries Guinea and Liberia, are part of the West African Craton, which formed during the Precambrian era more than a billion years ago. At that time, the African and the American continents had not yet completely separated (Skinner et al. 2004).

It is only under certain conditions of pressure and temperature, usually present at depths of about 80–100 km, that coal crystallises and turns into diamond. However, just as coal that formed on the surface can be swallowed into the earth's depths, so diamonds and other kinds of stones and minerals can emerge transported by volcanic magma. As it rises, the magma forms conduits that gradually solidify and become rock. This type of rock is called kimberlite and it can contain diamonds. Usually, kimberlite diamond deposits are positioned vertically and are therefore spatially circumscribed on the surface. For miners, this facilitates the demarcation of working areas and the estimate of the deposits. Investors who possess enough financial capital can employ large-scale mining technology capable of crushing the kimberlite and extracting the diamonds. This is what happens, for example, in the diamond mines of South Africa.

In Sierra Leone, artisanal miners exclusively extract alluvial diamonds. These types of diamonds are derived from the millennial erosion of kimberlite pipes. Kimberlite is much less resistant to atmospheric agents and other erosive forces than diamonds, which are the hardest minerals that exist in nature. In this way, over millennia, diamonds originally present in kimberlite pipes have been dragged and scattered to places more and more distant from their original sources, mainly by rains and rivers. Continual and imperceptible shock and friction have bevelled corners and shattered the oldest stones. Thus, the imperfect and less resistant gems have been reduced over time. The gems that survived have continued on their paths, driven by the inexhaustible energy of rain and rivers, as well as the ever-present force of gravity. Some have ended their journey sitting for centuries, and perhaps millennia, at the foot of large boulders; others were deposited in holes in riverbeds where they remained trapped for extended periods of time. The river that carried them may have since changed course, its precious cargo ending up in a hole or beneath a rock, covered by layers of soil and vegetation over the centuries. Rivers can diverge, but they can also return to older paths and add further layers to the existing gravel and soil. As a result, alluvial diamonds become buried several metres deep for thousands and thousands of years.

In Sierra Leone these long-term hydro-geological processes have distributed diamonds over an estimated area of about 20,000 square kilometres through the south-eastern region of the country that is crossed by the Sewa River and its tributaries (Morel 1976). As far as is known, no human being was particularly interested in these minerals, which emerged millions of years ago from the deepest regions of the lithosphere, until 1930.

In the late 1920s, British geologists identified important deposits of iron and some alluvial gold deposits in the northern regions of the Protectorate of Sierra Leone. In Kono, and along the valley created by the Sewa River and its tributaries, they discovered rich deposits of alluvial diamonds in 1930. A few years later, in 1934, the Sierra Leone Selection Trust (SLST) obtained an exclusive licence to explore and extract diamonds throughout Sierra Leone. In the following years, British colonial authorities tried their best to protect SLST's monopoly, but they failed to prevent the illicit trafficking of gemstones. Despite the surveillance of colonial security forces, the activities of illegal diamond seekers expanded.

In the second half of the 1950s, the mines of Kono district were filled with a large number of African migrants who started what van der Laan (1965) defines as Sierra Leone's 'diamond rush'. In this tense and complex period, many miners moved further south along the Sewa River's path in order to avoid both clashes with security forces and competition with their local colleagues. Thus, 'legitimate trade' based on agricultural produce competed with and at the same time benefited from new forms of illegal – but more profitable – activities, thus generating contrasting imaginaries and ideas about wealth and morality (D'Angelo 2015).

In the early 1960s, the stretch of the Sewa running through the districts of Kono, Kenema and Bo was considered by local miners to be a sort of El Dorado, attracting the attention of large investors such as the Diamond Exploration Company (Sierra Leone) Ltd (DEC).[6] In 1961, this company bought a mining licence from the government to explore a 3-mile stretch of the Sewa. A year later, a huge and expensive dredge began swallowing and sifting the gravel of the Sewa riverbed without pause, through all seasons and water conditions. Miners were organised into shifts: three 8-hour shifts from Monday to Friday, and two shifts on Saturday of which one was dedicated to maintenance. Despite the intensity of these activities, the investment turned out to be an unsuccessful gamble. Diamonds were found wherever they moved the dredge, but the total value of the stones did not cover the cost of staff and the maintenance of the expensive machinery. The DEC's managers commissioned a study (DEC 1965) that highlighted some of the deeper reasons behind this failure. They realised that, beyond the value of each stone, the particular conformation of the riverbed did not allow for the existence of large and uniform diamondiferous deposits. Cliffs, holes, rocks, waterfalls and other irregular geo-morphological obstacles did not offer optimal conditions for an intensive and profitable exploitation of the river within a reasonable time. It was estimated that it would take at least 20 years to complete the work of sifting the 3-mile stretch. Despite a gain of about £33,000 obtained by selling 3,288 carats of diamonds mined in the four years of activity, the company's expenses for the entire project were about £500,000. In 1965, the metallic structure that scratched and sucked out the Sewa riverbed was abandoned (DEC 1965).

More than half a century after the so-called 'diamond rush', and after several attempts to exploit the gravel of the Sewa with small- and large-scale machinery, the Big River was still one of the main sources of income for the villages that had sprung up along its banks when I visited the region (2008–16). Despite the variety and intensity of the mining activities, its waters were still full of fish. And, despite many failures, the river had given some satisfaction to gem-seekers from various regions of the world, including Russians, Israelis, British, Dutch, South Africans and Swedes. Like their local colleagues, these international miners were concerned with both gold and diamonds, and some of them were not deterred by Sierra Leone's civil war (1991–2002). On the contrary, in those years, some foreign miners and other international actors took advantage of the chaotic situation in the country to make substantial profits.

Located along the Sewa River, Lembima[7] was a village whose long history and experience of mining encounters (see Pijpers and Eriksen this volume), dating from 1950s, were at least partially remembered by the local population and inscribed in the landscape itself. Thus, this landscape can be read in the same way as Ingold (2000) analyses Bruegel's painting *The Harvesters*, that is, as a timescape in which traces and memories of past experiences are juxtaposed in a complex mosaic which informs miners' current activities.

In the small stretch of the Sewa River where I carried out most of my field observations, each area had a different name. For example, *ITP* was the nickname miners gave to a site on the riverbank where a mining company owned by a European operated in the late 1980s. After the war, the only remaining traces of this company were the foundations into which large-scale machinery had been placed, as well as some fragmentary and tragic rumours about the fate of one of its European managers. Another area on the same riverside was nicknamed *Jelyad* ('Jail yard') because – as was explained to me by the inhabitants of the nearby mining village – police had arrested a great number of illegal miners there in the past, particularly during the so-called 'Robin Hood time'. Miners remember that period in almost mythic terms as being a time when it was very easy to find diamonds and become rich overnight in Sierra Leone. However, during the same period – usually temporally located between the 1930s and 1960s – many miners operated illegally and were consequently targeted by colonial police as well as the security forces belonging to the main diamond mining company operating in Sierra Leone before the civil war, the SLST (D'Angelo 2016). Thus, *Jelyad* reminded miners of the potential richness *and* risks of the area.

Lastly, to offer another example, adjacent to *Jelyad*, there was another area that miners had dubbed *UN* – because, as a villager told me, 'If you find diamonds there, [you become so rich that] you can go to the United Nations!' However, an experienced miner that lived in the same village told me that during the civil war, the area was occupied and had been fenced in by ECOMOG troops.[8] These soldiers searched for diamonds and gold in collaboration with local miners. Hence, the *UN* reminds the people of Lembima of the ambiguous relationship between the military forces who intervened during the civil war and the extraction of minerals in their village.

As these examples show, in Lembima mining landscapes can be read as socio-historical maps in which local and global, past and present conflate and overlap thereby creating non-homogeneous spatio-temporal mosaics of local anachronisms and global synchronicities. Paraphrasing Bender (2002: 103), a minescape is 'time materializing'. Like all landscapes it does not just *tell*, but *is* a story (Ingold 2000: 189), or better, is a multitude of stories and different intertwined temporalities. In order to unravel some of these plural temporalities, it is necessary to focus on some of the main activities carried out by artisanal miners in this particular West African region.

ARTICULATING PLURAL SPATIO-TEMPORALITIES

Lembima played host to many miners whose efforts were concentrated around different kinds of extractive activities. These workers considered diamonds to be the most profitable resource, and therefore the most desirable. However, many miners were also engaged in gold, stone and sand mining, activities that offered gains that were smaller but more consistent than those obtained from unpredictable diamonds. Each of these mining activities was organised or influenced by a multitude of heterogeneous temporalities, including the cycle of the seasons, the subsequent phases of the river's changing water level, and the economic cycles of local and international gemstone markets. Artisanal miners considered the dry season to be the best time for any type of mining activity. The river's water was lowest between February and April. When

the water level was low, the currents were weaker and water temperature higher; as a result, the conditions for divers were less dangerous and
more profitable. During the dry season, sand and diamond divers could
reach and work in parts of the riverbed that would have been dangerous
during the rainy season when the water levels were high. Even the stone
miners benefited from the low water level of the river because they
could split the numerous boulders found along its banks and transport
them to nearby routes frequented by customers. In contrast, during the
rainy season they had to seek boulders far from the river. Moreover,
the rainfall in July and August was an obstacle to splitting boulders as
stone miners employed fire to break them. As in other mining areas of
Sierra Leone, in Lembima the temporal organisation of artisanal mining
was also conditioned by the cycles of farming – whose activities peak
during the rainy season (Maconachie 2011) – and trends in local and
international markets for metals and precious stones (cf. Nyame and
Grant 2012). In this regard, Pijpers (2011) highlights how the international crisis of 2007/8 and the consequent 'diamond crisis' persuaded
some Sierra Leonean miners to shift from diamond to gold mining, or
to alternate between mining and farming during their working day, so
that 'after searching for diamonds until 1 or 3 o'clock in the afternoon,
many individuals work the land for the remainder of the day' (Pijpers
2011: 1070). To emphasise the economic relevance of these livelihood
strategies in many Sub-Saharan rural areas (see Hilson 2016) as well
as the complex coexistence of different kinds of activities in the same
places, Pijpers (2011, 2014) employs the notion of co-habitation (see also
Luning 2008, 2009; Panella 2010: 6), which he defines as the 'idea that
places are not single and bounded spaces, but rather areas of intertwin-
ing actors and activities, not only at one specific moment, but also over
time' (Pijpers 2011: 1078).

Rather than employing the notion of *co-habitation*, which considers
the interconnectedness of mining and non-mining activities to be a
primarily spatial coexistence that evolves over time, I propose the use
of notion of *articulation* in the sense employed by Althusser and Balibar,
as 'the joining together of diverse elements' or levels (Hart 2007: 91;
see also Foster-Carter 1978: 53–4). In what follows I suggest that this
notion better explains mining activities and their combination, not only
in spatial but also in temporal terms, specifically as complex processes
of synchronisation of different rhythms and cycles that intersect
various ontological levels. Further, speaking of articulation is – to use
Zack-Williams' words – 'to emphasise that the presence of a particular
mode of production is not sufficient to secure the reproduction of its
conditions of existence' (Zack-Williams 1995: 2). It is precisely by artic-

ulating the work in the mines with the work of other economic activities – usually carried out by members of miners' extended families – that workers create the conditions for extracting diamonds. Thus, the notion of articulation points to a paradox that deserves attention: while working to secure a better future, miners contribute to their own exploitation.

Some vignettes from my fieldwork offer examples of these processes and, at the same time, an understanding of the ways artisanal miners perceive specific mineral resources in relation to time.

'Diamond Mining Has No Time'

At the beginning of the dry season, miners seeking diamonds in or near the Sewa riverbed began to prepare the relevant equipment for mining: sieves, shovels, buckets and water pumps for the alluvial open-cast mines; canoes, ropes, air-compressors and sieves for the riverine mining. This was also the period in which they tried to synchronise the timing of their work with the spatio-temporalities of their local and international funding networks. As a miner explained:

> When the dry season arrives is the time when you look for the money and prepare things. You go to someone asking for help, to finance you. 'I have a place where there are diamonds' […]. The other says, 'Ok, I'll help you, but wait first.' Meanwhile, time is passing and you go back: 'Now, it's time to work, I want to work.' And he replies: 'Ok, now I'm ready to help you, but wait, I have no money. I have a brother who has gone to Freetown' or 'I have a brother who has gone to Guinea' or 'I have a son who is abroad' – in Canada, Holland, or America – when he will send me the money I will help you.' After a week, you go back to him and he says: 'Ok, you can start working.'[9]

Waiting for a response from a sponsor was often nerve-wracking because receiving the money too late meant running the risk of jeopardising the success of operations that could last several weeks or months. With the arrival of the rainy season, in fact, diving in the turbulent water of the river became very risky. The work also became more complicated and more expensive in the open-cast mines as the rain water flooded the pits and water pumps were needed to empty them. Thus, waiting meant giving up or spending more money and reducing profit margins.

In Lembima, diamond, sand and stone miners often worked side by side along the same stretches of the river. In some cases, mining activities were so spatially and temporally intertwined that it was hard to determine where one began and the other ended. Indeed, working side by side or mixing one activity with the others produced reciprocal economic advantages. For example, the sand excavated by diamond miners to reach the gravel, instead of being discarded, could be resold to sand miners at relatively low prices. The gravel itself could be resold. Once the diamond miners completed their washing and sieving operations, gold miners – mostly women – scoured the same gravel again with their pan in search of gold dust. Thus, diamond mining not only coexisted with sand and gold mining but was also intertwined. As a result, these activities were not always clearly distinct from one another.[10]

Moreover, all these operations could be carried out within a single household unit, as was the case in Momodu's extended family. Momodu was a Muslim miner in his fifties, born and raised in the village of Lembima. As a member of one of the main ruling families, he was also a landowner. As such, he had privileged access to the land. Strangers were required to ask his permission, as well as the permission of other local authorities, before working on the land in Lembima. Strangers were also expected to offer tributes for benefiting from this land. In the south-eastern region of Sierra Leone, no artisanal mining activity could be carried out without the authorisation of landowners. Momodu had two wives and several children and grandchildren. He lived with his extended family in a group of houses near the Sewa River. Each member of Momodu's family was engaged in one or more working activities. The women were mainly engaged in agriculture and gold mining. The children and grandchildren supported the work of adults and senior members of the family.

While discussing the temporality of each of these activities with Momodu, he noted that agriculture was clearly linked to the seasonal cycles of rainfall, just as sand mining was linked to the flooding of the river. The extraction of diamonds was an exception. Compared to agriculture, 'diamonds have no time', he told me. Then, he added: 'There is not a [specific] time, unless you say: "I am tired."'[11] In his view, the only limit to diamond mining was the money available for financing the extraction of gemstones in different environmental conditions.

Often, gold mining followed or was carried out alongside diamond mining. The gravel extracted and sieved by gem-seekers was always sifted again by women in search of gold or small diamonds that had escaped the attention of previous operations. Gold mining decreased in intensity during the rainy season, but diamonds were still sought throughout the year, albeit at sites distant from the river. As acknowledged by miners, gold was easier to find than diamonds: 'You can find gold every day', although in small quantities. For Momodu, gold money was important because it financed the extraction of diamonds. However, it was diamond money he aspired to because this kind of money allowed him to dream of a better life, possibly as a rich man. As Momodu once told me: 'With diamond money you can think of going to London and do business.' With the money earned from agriculture, or gold, this possibility was not even imaginable.

Fast and Slow Money

The mining site where Momodu and his family worked was close to *UN* and was called 'The bank' by Lembima's inhabitants because, years before, a small-scale mining company had created an embankment to drain a portion of the river and pull the gravel more easily. Playing on the double meaning of the word 'bank', some of Momodu's colleagues told me that the bank of the river was Momodu's bank, that is, the deposit from which he regularly withdrew money in the form of extracted sand, gold, and diamonds.

Not all forms of money are the same. For diamond miners, diamonds generate fast money. In Lembima, however, stone miners also considered the money from their work to be fast money. How can it be explained that the same term can be attributed to money generated by two very different materials such as stone – easy to find and relatively cheap to buy – and diamonds, which are, by definition, rare and expensive? Common sense would suggest that talking about diamond money as 'fast money' is, in fact, paradoxical. To some extent, miners themselves agreed by saying that in the past – that is, before the civil war – finding diamonds was much easier than in the present. According to older workers, it was enough to possess a shovel and a sieve to be sure to come home with a diamond by the end of a single working day. On the contrary, most of the miners I knew during my fieldwork, complained of having to wait a long time before getting something. Why did they continue to talk about fast money? What did they mean by 'fast'? What then was 'slow'? To answer these questions it is important to remember that in Lembima diamond mining was a job performed mainly by men while gold mining was carried out almost exclusively by women. The extraction of stones was instead an activity that engaged both men and women – usually workers more economically vulnerable than diamond miners. For men, discourses on velocity were ways of emphasising their masculinity and stressing their roles of breadwinners despite the fact that women have always had important but unrecognised economic roles in mining (Rosen 1981). To explore other reasons why miners spoke of velocity with different meanings depending on the type of the material they extracted, it is useful to compare their activities and views more closely.

The fast money earned by a stone or a sand miner was generally perceived in Lembima as money related to very hard and strenuous work. The building sector was quite active in the period following the civil war, and it was capable of absorbing increasing quantities of production. It follows that the greater the labour time, the greater the potential profits for stone miners. Indeed, the heavy physical work was the main limit to labour time and stone miners' profits. In this context, 'fast' was thus synonymous with the short time that usually elapsed between the end of the production cycle of stones and the time of their actual sale. In short, this is a case in which 'time is money' (Adam 2003). What is worth stressing is that this reduced time – what miners defined as 'fastness' – relied on the synchronicity achieved by these workers with the seasonality of the river and the temporalities of the market for local building materials. This synchronicity resulted, in turn, in regularity in miners' gains and in the possibility of obtaining cash within a reasonably short time. It should be emphasised that this kind of 'fast money' was linked to stone miners' need for small but consistent amounts of income by which to cover their everyday expenses. Unsurprisingly, these miners were mainly recent immigrants, or workers with limited symbolic and material capital, usually unable to face the relatively high costs (and potentially long waits) of diamond mining.

In artisanal diamond mining, the dominant temporalities were qualitatively different from those experienced by stone miners. For diamond miners, labour time was not bound to gains in the same way as in the extraction of stones. The more diamond miners worked to achieve their objective (finding diamonds), the greater their losses. The time of artisanal diamond production was dotted with potential but unpredictable discoveries. The shorter the production cycle, the luckier it was considered to be for a miner. Discovery resulted in significant earnings to the extent that miners did not have to excessively consume their symbolic and material resources in the process. What mattered above all else was, therefore, the lucky (and blessed) find, and the qualitative time marked by what some miners defined as 'God's time' (D'Angelo 2015).

Similar to stone mining, gold mining offered a relatively regular income. By working hard with a gold pan, a miner could get from 1 to 2 carats a day. Nevertheless, as diamond miners noticed, the money one could obtain from the sale of these small quantities of gold, as well as from the sale of stones, was very little. Although I objected that gold could be found almost certainly, every day, while there was no guarantee of finding diamonds even after several months of hard work, diamond miners still claimed that the money from diamonds was fast money. 'It is true that it may take a long time before you can find them' – my interlocutors admitted – 'however, once you find a good diamond, like a 2-carat white diamond, the money you earn is much more than that earned with the gold day by day.' To support their claims, they compared the possible gains of both types of mining. Using a gold pan, a miner can get up to 30 karats of gold in a month. By contrast, with just a 2-carat diamond, 'I've got much more money than a gold miner', a diamond miner told me multiple times during our conversations.

In other words, the cycle of diamond production when it is measured as clock time, or in quantitative terms, is (usually) slower than the cycle of gold production (or, slower than stone production). Indeed, a long time can elapse between the time of the beginning of operations and the time of the actual discovery of a (good) diamond. However, the time of diamond production cannot be measured by the clock. To borrow Momodu's words, 'diamond mining has no time', that is, it does not matter how much time is spent working, what is important is the chance of encountering (at the right time, chosen by God) a good-quality diamond. This type of diamond generates 'fast money' – as much money as to be worth many cycles of gold and stone production. Thus, fast is no longer synonymous with speed, as it was for previous generations of miners, but is synonymous with large quantity. It is this fast money that diamond miners aspire to make. Indeed, only this kind of money makes possible an encounter between their desired futures and their present realities.

Given the difficulty in finding the most precious gems and their high commercial value, it is not surprising that miners described the excitement of discovering a good-quality diamond as a 'shock'. With this term they highlighted the intensity of a complex mix of emotions that was difficult to conceal from others, to the point that it was said that mining supervisors were capable of determining whether a worker had or had not found a diamond in the sieve just by observing his uncontrollable bodily expression of surprise.

If each discovery is a node of encounters between a plurality of spatio-temporalities, the result of intertwined historical processes that involve not only human but also non-human agency (stones and God included), then a diamond miner's shock can be seen as surprise in the face of holding a crystal of time which contains all or some of their desired futures.

FINAL THOUGHTS

If labour is a crucial source of value embedded in commodities, and if labour is also time, then commodities are forms of crystallised time.

Thus, gems may *appear* valuable because they are built by 'diamond time' (cf. Westwood 2002: 36) but, in fact, they gain *value* because they are the result of the (dis)articulation and (de)synchronisation of different modes (and temporalities) of human and non-human production. Articulating and disarticulating different modes of production and heterogeneous temporal levels is one of the crucial problems of contemporary capitalism (Mezzadra 2008) – and, therefore, also a problem of the global diamond industry. As the case of Sierra Leone shows, this problem falls back on local production contexts (Zack-Williams 1995).

The 'diamond time' upon which the global marketing of these precious stones is based not only alienates consumers from producers by concealing the miners' working time; it makes invisible a plurality of non-capitalist temporalities and non-human rhythms that actively contribute, in various ways, to the production of diamonds. Mining capitalism does not impose a single model of economic production. It subsumes existing ones by trying to (de)synchronise them – by using violence or through obtaining the consent of a multitude of social actors, miners included – in accordance with its needs. It follows that the kind of exploitation at stake here is far more extensive and comprehensive than what is suggested by Westwood's analysis (2002). The 'scurrilous history' of diamonds is more than a story of alienation or dispossession and violence; it is a story of heterogeneous and intertwined forms of exploitation that require non-capitalist social relations to be effective.

'Diamonds are forever' and 'diamond mining has no time' are two sides of the same coin. On one hand, a temporality that claims to contain all temporalities, that goes beyond the physical limits of existence in the direction of eternity. On the other, a time without time, a temporality that, in the absence of better alternatives, impels a never-ending search limited by bodily capacity. Both obscure the fact that diamonds, like all capitalist commodities, are 'simultaneously capitalist and non-capitalist' (Tsing 2013); the result of a layered and interwoven set of plural temporalities.

ACKNOWLEDGEMENTS

I am grateful to Thomas Hylland Eriksen and Robert Jan Pijpers for their useful suggestions on different versions of this chapter as well as to the participants of the workshop 'Mining Encounters: Extractive Industries in an Overheated World' (University of Oslo, Norway, 2015) for their comments on the first draft. Thanks also to David M. Rosen and Michael T. Taussig for reading and commenting on an early draft. A fellowship awarded by the Italian Academy for Advanced Studies in America at

Columbia University in New York, allowed me to concentrate on writing during spring 2015. As usual, I am the only person responsible for any inaccuracy or error this text may contain and the views it expresses.

REFERENCES

Adam, B. 2003. When Time is Money: Contested Rationalities of Time in the Theory and Practice of Work. *Theoria: A Journal of Social and Political History* 102: 94–125.

Althusser, L. 2006. *Philosophy of the Encounter: Later Writings, 1978–1987*. London: Verso.

Althusser, L. and E. Balibar. 1970. *Reading Capital*. London: New Left Books.

Appadurai, A. 1996. *Modernity at Large: Cultural Dimensions of Globalization*. Minneapolis: University of Minnesota Press.

Bair, J. and M. Werner. 2011. Commodity Chains and the Uneven Geographies of Global Capitalism: A Disarticulations Perspective. *Environment and Planning A* 43: 988–97.

Bair, J., C. Berndt, M. Boeckler and M. Werner. 2013. Dis/articulating Producers, Markets, and Regions: New Directions in Critical Studies of Commodity Chains. *Environment and Planning A* 45: 2544–52.

Bender, B. 2002. Time and Landscape. *Current Anthropology* 43: 103–12.

Bestor, T. 2001. Supply-side Sushi: Commodity, Market, and the Global City. *American Anthropologist* 103(1): 76–95.

Bhambra, G.K. 2007. *Rethinking Modernity: Postcolonialism and the Sociological Imagination*. New York: Palgrave.

Chambers, S.A. 2011. Untimely Politics *Avant la Lettre*: The Temporality of Social Formations. *Time & Society* 20(2): 197–223.

D'Angelo, L. 2011. Il duro lavoro e i soldi veloci: l'economia occulta dell'estrazione mineraria in Sierra Leone. In A. Voltolin (ed.). *L'ideologia del denaro: tra psicoanalisi, letteratura, antropologia*. Milano: Bruno Mondadori, pp. 97–130.

——2014. Who Owns the Diamonds? The Occult Economy of Diamond Mining in Sierra Leone. *Africa: Journal of the International African Institute* 84(2): 269–93.

——2015. Diamond Mining Is a Chain: Luck, Blessing, and Gambling in Sierra Leone's Artisanal Mines. *Critical African Studies* 7(3): 243–61.

——2016. The Art of Governing Contingency: Rethinking the Colonial History of Diamond Mining in Sierra Leone. *Historical Research* 89(243): 136–57.

DEC [The Diamond Exploration Company (Sierra Leone) Ltd]. 1965. *A Report on the Sewa Dredge Experiment*. Freetown, Sierra Leone: DEC.

Eisenstadt, S.N. 2000. Multiple Modernities. *Daedalus* 129(1): 1–29.

Faier, L. and L. Rofel. 2014. Ethnographies of Encounter. *Annual Review of Anthropology* 43: 363–77.

Ferry, E.E. and M. Limbert (eds). 2008. *Timely Assets: The Politics of Resources and Their Temporalities*. Santa Fe: School for Advanced Research Press.

Foster-Carter, A. 1978. The Mode of Production Controversy. *New Left Review* I(107): 47–77.

Hart, G. 2007. Changing Concepts of Articulation: Political Stakes in South Africa Today. *Review of African Political Economy* 11: 85–101.

Hilson, G. 2016. Farming, Small-scale Mining and Rural Livelihoods in Sub-Saharan Africa: A Critical Overview. *The Extractive Industries and Society* 3: 547–63.

Ingold, T. 2000. *The Perception of the Environment: Essays on Livelihood, Dwelling and Skill.* London: Routledge.

Irvine, R.D.G. 2014. Deep Time: An Anthropological Problem. *Social Anthropology* 22(2): 157–72.

Luning, S. 2008. Liberalisation of the Gold Mining Sector in Burkina Faso. *Review of African Political Economy* 117: 387–401.

—— 2009. *World of Debts, Encounters for Co-habitation: Gold Mining Sites in West Africa.* WOTRO Integrated Program.

Maconachie, R. 2011. Re-agrarianising Livelihoods in Post-conflict Sierra Leone? Mineral Wealth and Rural Change in Artisanal and Small-scale Mining Communities. *Journal of International Development* 23: 1054–67.

Mezzadra, S. 2008. *La condizione postcoloniale: storia e politica nel presente globale.* Verona: Ombre Corte.

Miyazaki, H. 2003. The Temporalities of the Market. *American Anthropology* 105(2): 255–65.

Morel, S.W. 1976. *The Geology and Minerals of Sierra Leone.* Freetown: Fourah Bay College Bookshop.

Morfino, V. 2014. *Plural Temporality: Transindividual and the Aleatory between Spinoza and Althusser.* Leiden: Brill.

Morfino, V. and P.D. Thomas. (eds). 2017. *The Government of Time: Theories of Plural Temporality in the Marxist Tradition.* Leiden: Brill.

Nyame, F.K. and A. Grant. 2012. From Carats to Karats: Explaining the Shift from Diamond to Gold Mining by Artisanal Miners in Ghana. *Journal of Cleaner Production* 29–30: 163–72.

Panella, C. 2010. Gold Mining in West Africa: Worlds of Debts and Sites of Co-habitation. In C. Panella (ed.), *Worlds of Debts: Interdisciplinary Perspectives on Gold Mining in West Africa.* Amsterdam: Rosenberg Publishers, pp. 1–14.

Pijpers, R. 2011. When Diamonds Go Bust: Contextualising Livelihood Changes in Rural Sierra Leone. *Journal of International Development* 23: 1068–79.

—— 2014. Crops and Carats: Exploring the Interconnectedness of Mining and Agriculture in Sub-Saharan Africa. *Futures* 62: 32–9.

Pijpers, R.J. and T.H. Eriksen (this volume). Introduction: Negotiating the Multiple Edges of Mining Encounters. In R.J. Pijpers and T.H. Eriksen (eds), *Mining Encounters: Extractive Industries in an Overheated World.* London: Pluto.

Rosen, D.M. 1981. Dangerous Woman: 'Ideology', 'Knowledge' and Ritual among the Kono of Eastern Sierra Leone. *Dialectical Anthropology* 6: 151–63.

Shirey, S.B. and J.E. Shigley. 2013. Recent Advances in Understanding the Geology of Diamonds. *Gems & Geology* 49(4).

Skinner, E.M.W., D.B. Apter, C. Morelli and N.K. Smithson. 2004. Kimberlites of the Man Craton, West Africa. *Lithos* 76(1): 233–59.

Smith, J.H. 2011. Tantalus in the Digital Age: Coltan Ore, Temporal Dispossession, and 'Movement' in the Eastern Democratic Republic of Congo. *American Ethnologist* 38(1): 17–35.

Tomba, M. 2012. *Marx's Temporalities*. Leiden: Brill.

Tomich, D.W. 2004. *Through the Prism of Slavery: Labor, Capital, and World Economy*. Lanham, MD: Rowman and Littlefield.

Tsing, A. 2013. Sorting Out Commodities: How Capitalist Value Is Made Through Gifts. *HAU: Journal of Ethnographic Theory* 3(1): 21–43.

van der Laan, H.L. 1965. *The Sierra Leone Diamonds*. Oxford: Oxford University Press.

Walsh, A. 2004. In the Wake of Things: Speculating in and about Sapphires in Northern Madagascar. *American Anthropologist* 106(2): 225–37.

Westwood, S. 2002. 'Diamond Time': Constructing Time, Constructing Markets in the Diamond Trade. *Time & Society* 11(1): 25–38.

Zack-Williams, A. 1995. *Tributors, Supporters and Merchant Capital: Mining and Underdevelopment in Sierra Leone*. Aldershot-Brookfield, USA: Avebury.

NOTES

1. Eng. trans.: 'In one moment lie hidden a plurality of temporalities'. I thank Vittorio Morfino for pointing out this passage by Lucretius. For a philosophical reading of time and contingency in Lucretius and, more generally, of the 'underground currents of the materialism of the encounter', see Althusser (2006) and Morfino (2014).

2. Since the late 1960s, the concept of articulation has been reworked in several theoretical debates. Both the controversy over modes of production in the 1960s and 1970s (see Foster-Carter 1978), and the more recent debate about the perspectives on disarticulation in the analysis of commodity chains (e.g. Bair and Werner 2011; Bair et al. 2013) refer to the concept of articulation developed by Althusser and Balibar (1970) (which has since been re-elaborated in slightly different ways by other thinkers, including, for example, Pierre-Philippe Rey and Stuart Hall). Regarding the recent literature on commodity chains, the concept of disarticulation has been used to highlight how capitalist processes of production are not just based on the logic of incorporation, but also on that of exclusion (Bair and Werner 2011: 988). In my view, this latter reading of the concept of disarticulation relies heavily on spatial metaphors, while Althusser and Balibar (1970) offer insights for a temporal reading of social formations and capitalist economies (Chambers 2011). For this reason, Althusser's reading of capital is an important source of inspiration for this chapter.

3. This temporal model emerges, for example, in the analysis on 'multiple modernities' (e.g. Eisenstadt 2000) and it is effectively criticised by postcolonial scholars such as Bhambra (2007). Taking this critique into account,

I prefer to use the term 'plural temporalities' or 'plural times' rather than 'multiple temporalities' (see Morfino and Thomas 2017).

4. On the notion of 'deep time' see Irvine (2014).

5. I visited this village four times between 2008 and 2016 for periods that ranged between two and four months.

6. In the early 1960s this company was known as the Sierra Leone State Development Company (DEC 1965).

7. Name changed to protect the anonymity of my interlocutors.

8. Sierra Leone is a member of the Economic Community of West African States (ECOWAS). During the civil war the ECOWAS intervened with its multilateral armed force, the Economic Community of West African States Monitoring Group (ECOMOG). In 1998, the United Nations established the United Nations Observer Mission in Sierra Leone (UNOMSIL), followed a year later by a larger mission, the United Nations Mission in Sierra Leone (UNAMSIL).

9. Interview with Ibrahim, Bo District, 12 January 2009.

10. It is not the case the other way around. In fact, sand miners use only shovels and buckets. Similarly, gold miners use the gold pan, which allows the recovery of gold dust and only rarely of diamonds, which are often of varying of sizes.

11. Interview with Momodu, Bo District, 8 January 2009.

9. Risky Encounters
The Ritual Prevention of Accidents in the Coal Mines of Kazakhstan

Eeva Kesküla

Outside the window spring was hiding its fangs
From underneath the crust of earth appeared the green lush steppe
Underground, we were gnawing with our sharp-bladed spades

But on one of those dark shifts the ceiling did not hold out
Grief came to our mini-towns
Dead miners in the rubble were carried to heaven

Absolutely nothing changed, people perished for Mittal
Only a spoon tinkled against a cup of London tea[1]

INTRODUCTION

In a song called 'London Tea', the local punk-rock group Nomady from the Karaganda area in Kazakhstan sings about a mining accident that turned the underground into a mass grave. The author of the song, a miner himself, believes that despite the grief that shook all the 'mini-towns' erected around the mines, nothing was done to make the mines safer. To the management of the company ArcelorMittal, whose headquarters are in London, the lives of Kazakhstani miners are little more than the sound of a spoon tinkling against a cup of English tea.

Accident prevention is a particularly tense field where mining encounters (cf. Pijpers and Eriksen, this volume) take place. Rather than being a localised practice, accident prevention is tied to global flows of capital in the raw materials market, international risk management systems and safety regulations, as well as relations with the national government and the histories and cosmologies of the particular place. An accident in Kazakhstan is produced by, or causes a tinkle in, a tea cup in London, and the insignificance of that sound is acutely sensed in the Central Asian steppe. Following Pijpers and Eriksen's conceptualisation of mining encounters in the introduction to this volume, accident prevention in mining involves frictions, tensions and negotiations between different global actors regarding the cost of lives and is a particularly rich site in which to explore the overheated world.

The causes or triggers of mining accidents, similarly to natural disasters, are becoming harder to identify and predict due to globalisation, as the cause of the accident might be far from the disaster location. The challenge is to understand how past human actions, conscious decision making to further specific political economic interests in society and deeply embedded cultural predispositions all produce vulnerability to disasters (Jones and Murphy 2009). As anthropological research into disasters has emphasised, vulnerability is not linked only to natural conditions – disasters also highlight inequalities in capitalist societies where disadvantaged groups are more vulnerable in the disaster and its aftermath.

In industrial production, all actors (owners, management and employees) wish to prevent accidents and make more profit or earn a higher salary. Their motivations for preventing accidents, as well as their rituals for avoiding them, are different, however. Health and safety is not a neutral technocratic regulation to save human lives but rather an outcome of the struggle between capital, labour and politics (Nichols 1997). In the everyday social relations of production, meeting the production quota, or the *political economy of speed* (Carson 1982, cited in Woolfson 2013) always hinders safety improvements (Nichols and Armstrong 1973; Nichols and Walters 2013). Management's problem is 'how to achieve higher levels of exploitation without producing or constructing health or safety problems at levels which undermine the political, economic, and technical conditions necessary to that exploitation' (Hall 1993: 3). In these mining encounters, players at different levels come together to balance the political economy of health and safety (H&S) and the political economy of speed, in a situation where the simultaneous increase of efficiency and safety is rarely possible. All such balancing acts can be seen as the performance of prevention rituals, following Victor Turner, who defines a ritual as 'a stereotyped sequence of activities involving gestures, words, and objects, performed in a sequestered place, and designed to influence preternatural entities or forces on behalf of the actors' goals and interests' (Turner 1973: 1100). The efficiency of such prevention is not always known and the outcome not always what was intended.

This chapter brings together the literature of political economy of accidents and industrial health and safety and the ethnographic tradition of studying rituals of accident prevention in mining. What are the implications of a global corporation privatising Soviet mines and how does it affect the health and safety regime? What are the rituals that both the company and miners undertake in order to prevent accidents? Why do miners feel that accidents lead to nothing more than a spoon tinkling against a teacup in a distant city? I argue that undertaking rituals in order to prevent accidents is important also in contexts where there is no coherent local cosmology. Nevertheless, as it is with ritual sacrifice, one can never be entirely sure whether this helps to prevent accidents, as the global political economy is so central in influencing local outcomes and sometimes rituals serve an unintended purpose.

THE POLITICAL ECONOMY OF ACCIDENT PREVENTION

The Karaganda coal mines in Central Kazakhstan were of crucial economic significance in the Soviet period. They produced coal for power generation and coking coal for steel production in Central Asia's largest steel plant in nearby Temirtau, as well as the star of Soviet steel production in the Urals, Magnitogorsk. In the Soviet period, coal mining was heavily subsidised by the government, rather than a profit-making enterprise. After the break-up of the Soviet Union in 1991, the newly independent Kazakhstani government did not have the means to keep subsidising the production, salaries were not paid, and repair and main-tenance work in the mines was minimal. Furthermore, the infrastructure of mining towns was falling apart, including heating, electricity and water as well as social and medical services. To pull the industry and region out of crisis, foreign investment was needed.

In the 1990s, Kazakhstani industries were privatised *en masse*, very quickly and with little transparency. In the mineral sector, instead of encouraging market competition, privatisation in Kazakhstan led to the re-establishing of very large integrated enterprises more typical of the Soviet era (Peck 2002). The privatisation of the coal mines, together with the steel plant in Temirtau nearby, shows a general trend in the volatile steel market where companies tend to acquire their own raw material sources in order to be less dependent on external providers (Humphreys 2011).

The vision of ArcelorMittal's mining business is 'to create shareholder value through operational excellence and profitable growth while caring for the environment and our people'. Its aims are, among others, to 'focus on mine safety, mine planning, quality, expansion, cap[ital]ex[pansion] and logistic[s]'. However, it has been noted that the company priori-tises productivity over the environment, communities and labour rights (Global Action on ArcelorMittal 2008: 6). Between the ArcelorMittal takeover in 1996 and 2009, the number of deaths in the steel and coal operations in the Karaganda area was 191. Besides individual accidents, around 100 miners' lives were lost in methane gas explosions. Workers allege that Mittal has done little to improve labour and safety conditions since taking over ArcelorMittal Temirtau (AMT, the company branch in Temirtau and Karaganda), most of the problems being the result of outdated equipment, such as ineffective methane detectors, and a mutual agreement to ignore H&S rules by both workers and management (Global Action on ArcelorMittal 2008). After major mine explosions in 2004 and 2006, ArcelorMittal said the Karaganda miners' concerns were being addressed, with significant sums being spent on modernisation and new H&S equipment. This was followed by a massive gas explosion in 2008, taking the lives of 30 miners.

Mine workers remember that H&S regulations were breached regularly in the Soviet period (Kesküla 2013). One human life for a million tonnes of coal was a commonly known and accepted rule. Nevertheless, the number of accidents in relation to production volume increased significantly after privatisation.[2] In 2004–9 explosions were frequent. The press, independent trade unions and the miners themselves associated these explosions with the privatisation of the mines by ArcelorMittal and the irresponsibility of the new owner.

The company claimed to have made significant improvements 'to introduce a new health and safety culture'.[3] This involved hiring DuPont, a global leader in industrial safety management systems, to introduce risk management systems, including safety training. In 2013, DuPont appointed AMT the winner for the DuPont Safety and Sustainability Awards 'owing to the company's achievements in driving a cultural evolution in safety and sustainability'. According to DuPont the company's Central Kazakhstani branch 'embarked upon a comprehensive revamp of health and safety processes at its facilities ... Most importantly, in concrete terms the ensuing cultural shift saw an impressive reduction in the number of recorded industrial accidents, which declined from 1475 in 1996 to 34 in 2011' (E.I. Dupont de Nemours and Co. 2013). Thus, from a global perspective, health and safety had significantly improved. When it came to profit making, things were not as positive.

At the time of my fieldwork in 2013, the company had not made a profit for several years and there was constant talk of 'crisis' in both the company and the steel market that meant no new hiring, fewer investments and frozen salaries. Besides the drop-off of some steel markets and difficulties competing with steel production in Russia and China, the management indicated that the price of coal had dropped 35 per cent globally. Foreign management was comparing the efficiency levels with Poland, where AM took over steel works (Trappmann 2013), indicating a much higher labour efficiency there. Whereas before the 2008 economic crisis, the coal was just used internally for steel production in Temirtau, now it was sold also to external consumers to reduce financial risks. For workers, this meant a 10 per cent increased production target, but little investment in equipment and no new hiring. In a situation which I call *exhaustion capitalism*, miners felt that the last strength was squeezed out of their bodies as they were working with ageing equipment and decreasing staff numbers.

After fatal accidents, nevertheless, the management made efforts to avoid further accidents in various ways, following common international practices in industrial health and safety. Just as miners engage in certain rituals which might or might not be effective, nation states, corporations and local enterprises also apply accident prevention rituals that can take various forms. In mining, both national laws and international standards regulate accident prevention. In coal mining, a large proportion of accident prevention is related to avoiding methane gas explosions. For this, gas levels are measured and recorded periodically and gas drainage and ventilation systems are operated as part of coal extraction. To avoid coal dust explosions, rock dust is spread over coal dust to create an inert dust mixture, which makes it more difficult for shock waves from methane explosions to blow up coal dust. Any electrical or diesel equipment is checked to avoid fire hazard. All these measures are, to an extent, followed in the AMT mines in Kazakhstan, including a new British gas monitoring system installed after the explosions of 2004–8. Nevertheless, according to an international audit team that checked the safety of the mines in 2014, detection, monitoring and prevention systems needed significant improvement.

Other rituals of accident prevention at AMT were more strongly linked to the 'human factor', for example teaching workers to prevent accidents, in accordance with the system implemented by DuPont. Various pedagogical tools included training and exams that miners had to undertake; weekly meetings where H&S messages and information about the latest accidents in the company were delivered. All workers were expected to know the H&S rules and support the 'journey to zero': the company's ambitious plan to reduce the number of accidents to zero in their operations globally.

Aggressive visual messages were displayed around the mining operations, in the form of posters and placards displaying H&S messages. 'Stop, think and act safely', was the main message, depicting workers following the rules in different situations at work and at home. Another poster, available in different variations, read 'Father, take care of yourself' or 'We are waiting for you at home', displaying miners' children. The posters started at the car park, where miners disembarked from the workers' buses, followed them to the changing rooms and became especially dense in the area where miners collected their lamps and took the lift down to the mine. Numerous audits by government inspectors, management and independent consultants took place. Thus, H&S policy was much more hands-on, aggressive, inspection-heavy and visually intense than it had been before the explosions. Additionally, miners themselves and middle management had their own ideas on how to prevent accidents while working.

THE COSMOLOGY OF KAZAKHSTANI MINERS

Anthropologists have described workers' attempts to manage risk and avoid accidents particularly in mining, a dangerous work activity riddled with the potential for rock falls, tunnel collapse or explosions caused by dynamite or methane gas. Even when miners have to work in extremely hard and dangerous conditions, they do what they can to stay alive. Nash (1979) has documented how Bolivian miners believe that the under-ground is the realm of the Tio, the devil, a bloodthirsty creature who needs to be satisfied for miners to find ore and stay safe. To satisfy Tio, miners hold periodical rituals where they sit together around the statue of the devil, sprinkle alcohol on the ground, chew coca. When accidents do happen, it means that Tio has not had proper ritual offerings and has desired the blood of miners instead. He then has to be pacified with the ritual sacrifice of llamas, with the help of a shaman (Nash 1979: 229–30). This classical literature mostly focuses on miners' rituals in the context of a strong indigenous cosmology.

Soviet miners were labour migrants rather than indigenous people, and therefore had a different relationship to the surrounding environment. Instead of talking about reciprocity with nature, they usually echoed the Soviet discourse of conquering nature. The steppe of Central Kazakhstan, where the mines were located, was seen by the miners as having been 'empty' (despite being inhabited by nomadic Kazakhs) and only their grandfathers who came to the area as Gulag prisoners or youth construction brigades built anything worthwhile to fill the emptiness. Soviet miners could be seen as a slight disappointment to the anthropol-ogist searching for the exotic, the esoteric, the superstitious. Questions about the potential of risk and explosions were often answered in an impersonal scientific discourse, repeating what the miners had learned in the mining college. As Zonabend (2007) notes about technicians of a nuclear power plant, workers in high-risk industries rarely talk about their own personal experiences and sound more like a scientific brochure in a formal situation. Kazakhstani miners might have had Christian

Orthodox icons or scriptures from the Koran decorating their cars, as traffic accidents were frequent, but would take no particular precautions when going underground. On the contrary, Muslims were known to eat pork fat underground because God cannot see what is going on in the belly of the earth. Older people, both Kazakh and Russian, often openly stated that they were communists and atheists; middle-aged people often had a vague belief that there was a God but did not actively participate in religious rituals. Younger people rarely cared about spirituality.

At the same time, stories about near misses were very common in the area. Just as everyone knew someone who had died in the explosion, everyone also seemed to know someone who had escaped death. In these stories, a vague mention of God was mixed with ideas of being lucky and Azande-esque explanations that the rock falling has to do with geological conditions while the precise moment when it happens was related to higher forces (Evans-Pritchard 1937). The local cosmology was an assemblage of geological factors and the exhaustion capitalism AMT practised mixed with questions of *Why me? Why here?*

Dima, a Russian-speaking miner in his late forties rarely spoke about the explosion and what it felt like to be one of the few who was brought out when tens of others died. He would look at his fire-damaged hands with regret and say that the only good thing about this was that he did not have to work in the mine again. He was saved only because his friend further ahead shouted 'Fire!' and he lay down immediately. I asked whether he thought it was fate that he stayed alive.

> This is a good question. You know how much I have thought about this?! Were we just lucky, or [was it] because we were older and walking more slowly, or really fate? He ran, warned me, we lay down and because we lay down the shock wave could not kill me. If we had been standing, we would have been killed immediately. There are three factors. The shock wave should have killed us immediately but it did not. The fire did not burn me completely. Then I should have been poisoned by the gas, laying there for three hours. The ventilation was not working, I was breathing in carbon monoxide. Half an hour more and I would have probably been dead but then the rescuers found me. What do you think it was? It seems to me that it was fate after all.

Dima was aware of the physical and chemical processes that were taking place in the mine during the explosion and what effect they should have had on him. The fact that they did not kill him had to be explained by something else, but even years later he was not quite sure what it was. When telling me his story, he often struggled to find the precise words, expressing his frustration that he did not know whether I was able to grasp his feelings. There were gaps that words could not fill in his narrative; this lack of words characterised the whole community. No one liked to talk about explosions and it was always difficult to find a tactful and sensitive way to ask about it. People I knew would talk about it with the help of vodka. It seems that the main reason for the silence was the sheer inability to deal with the human pain of past events when knowing that the same thing could happen again.

While the political economy approach is useful in looking at the global struggles between labour and capital, it gives little ethnographic insight into how accidents really happen in the workplace and how people explain accidents in a situation where they have little power over their own lives and labour. Laura Bear (2014: 74) is right to point out that besides questions of political economy situated outside the workplace, H&S is intimately tied to questions of skill and workmanship, inviting ethical reflections on rights and responsibilities in the workplace and pushing workers 'to relate acts of work to a universe of productive powers. They provoke speculation on the relationships and boundaries between the human and non-human' (Bear, 2014: 4). Kazakhstani miners like Dima would link accidents to the employer, geology, their own experience and skills in keeping themselves safe, as well as supernatural powers.

The cosmology of Kazakhstani miners did not constitute a coherent set of beliefs about who was responsible for mining accidents and what to do about it. While for the Bolivian miners, the devil was the representative of a market economy that did not correspond to local ideas of reciprocal exchange (Taussig 1980), for the Kazakhstani miners, there was no one symbol or frame of beliefs that signified the arch-enemy. Perhaps it was about luck or fate, as well as the poor conditions in the mine or management shortcomings, but this did not provide a straightforward solution such as a ritual sacrifice to deal with the problem. Also, the juxtaposition of miners versus the management in accident prevention at the local level was not as clear cut as one would expect. The pedagogy of accident prevention, as a poignant example, can be seen simultaneously as a meaningless ritual and as a tool for community mobilisation.

GLOBAL BOX-TICKING AND COMMUNITIES OF COMPLAINING

In the Burannaya mine, Andrei Sergeevich, a former miner in his sixties, was in charge of training. Andrei Sergeevich had not only been a respected miner and brigade leader but also a successful cyclist and a communist, fulfilling political roles in the mine. Although the regime had changed, he continued to hold important positions in the mine, such as running the 'Study point', a unit that organised training and exams that miners had to undertake. This year, all the miners of Burannaya and nearby mines had to participate in a training exercise about team building. The logic behind the exercise was that if people worked as a team, without conflict, looking after each other, they would work more safely.

Andrei Sergeevich was talking to a classroom full of mine workers, men from their twenties to sixties, with heavy dark circles of coal around their eyes.

> Today we are talking about working in a group, which is why we have gathered you together here as a brigade. We are going to do several exercises, for example how to keep wooden poles standing up when you are moving from one pole to the next one in a circle, it requires team work.

The miners, some tired from the night shift that they had just finished, looked at the trainer with scepticism or indifference. One young man, 30-year-old Marlen, was especially unhappy with the exercise. He complained: 'Why are we doing this study? You know very well that underground we do not have time to observe the rules of health and safety. Do you know how many people we should have in the tunnelling team?' 'Ideally four, minimum three', Andrei Sergeevich replied.

> But we have two! We do not have enough people, you know it yourself! … If two people are supposed to do a certain task, but there is just one doing it and he gets hurt, then they just say that that he wasn't careful enough, right? And it takes us half a shift before we can even start working if we start with assessing the level of risk. We just need to spit on H&S, do the work that we were given and that's it. And what are we paid for? For metres [of tunnelling]. If we observe H&S, we are not paid!

One of the main reasons why miners thought that explosions and other accidents happened was connected to the working conditions. Miners blamed the insufficient number of people employed in the mine – as headquarters had forbidden hiring new staff in order to reduce staff costs, fewer people had to do the same amount of work. With fewer people, miners' bodies wear out more quickly and accidents are more likely to happen. Engineers as well as miners grumbled about the lack of investment and mechanisation of work, stating that human labour was considered cheaper than machines. Miners described the situation as squeezing the last power out of the equipment and the workers.

The company's production plan was constantly prioritised over health and safety. Miners were aware that accident prevention through checking methane gas levels and drilling gas drainage boreholes was not done as frequently as required since it slowed down tunnelling and long-wall mining work. The gas detectors were switched off to avoid work stoppages. One miner who had worked in the area where an explosion happened, said that everyone knew that it was only a question of time before something happened. But not fulfilling the plan meant punishment and a significantly smaller pay cheque for all mine staff. Rather than standing up against the double standards where everyone was supposed to follow H&S, which was impossible in reality, miners would comply, after having let off steam the way that young Marlen and his colleagues were doing. They knew very well that Andrei Sergeevich did not have the answer. The company's strategy was to invest in training that was cheaper than slowing down production. 'Sergeevich, you are speaking as if you did not work in the mine yourself! Why do we have to do the training if we know that there is no way of following the rules?'

The instructor explained that it was still good to study: if people did not learn from their mistakes, they needed to keep studying in order to avoid making the same mistakes again. He took out a book, the Soviet code for safety in mines, and explained that its red cover represented the blood of miners. 'Shame that the new code has white covers', he said somewhat nostalgically. Despite the miners' complaints, Sergeevich kept on speaking. About different accidents, men who could not work in teams but were excellent workers by themselves, his own past. He named the people he talked about and miners recognised their former workmates, fathers' friends and neighbours in the stories, relating to the accidents, sometimes chipping in, talking about the dangerous situations they themselves had faced in the mines. The miners understood very well that Andrei Sergeevich was a proper miner who had done the work himself and understood the problems, that he had to follow the corporate discourse and the best he could do was to tell stories about local men, rooted in the history of the place where mining had taken place for three generations and the tensions between machismo and carefulness, production and health and safety were ingrained in the bodies of the miners.

The training continued with a series of films illustrating team-building exercises in a corporation in Russia. Young office workers of both genders were doing numerous exercises such as walking from one concrete block to another along a narrow plank of wood. The miners watched the film as if it was a reality show, their eyes glued to the screen. A couple of them dozed off a few times, but there was no fidgeting, no checking their watch or cell phone, or looking around. Then Andrei Sergeevich assigned them some practical exercises. The miners were given two planks of wood and the person standing on them at the front attached the planks to his feet. The task was to move from one end of the room to another, with everyone having one foot on each of the planks, holding on to each other. The person in the front had to get the people standing behind him to lift up their right or left foot simultaneously, shouting 'left', 'right'! The men did the exercise without any questioning, having fun and messing around.

After the training session, some miners admitted that there was always something good in studying. Marlen, the young and vocal one said: 'Tomorrow, Sergeevich, we are going to tie the planks of wood under our feet and march to the coal face like that. If someone comes and asks if we are stupid, we say, "No, we are a team."' 'Production plan, what production plan? We are a team!', added another. Miners knew very well that the training exercises were a farce. Doing American team-building exercises with miners who have worked together for decades, have been through challenging situations in a real workplace and have a very strong culture of camaraderie and respect towards each other is simply another performative, even cynical aspect of the new H&S culture introduced after the explosions. Nevertheless, sharing stories and complaining together was a ritual that miners were happy to endure.

The vocal critique expressed by Marlen and his colleagues during the training was even more pronounced in the private gatherings of miners, but basically available for any empathic soul who was willing to listen. When first working with miners in Estonia in 2010, I encountered a repeated refrain of angry complaining by miners mostly concerning the danger and harsh conditions in a particular job, low pay, poor health, general economic conditions in the region and the negative consequences of the reorganisation of the company. Nancy Ries (1997), who studied the discourse of Muscovites during the Perestroika era, identifies a genre that she calls litanies or laments. 'Litanies were those passages in conversations in which a speaker would enunciate a series of complaints, grievances, or worries about problems, troubles, afflictions, tribulations, or losses ... a sweeping, fatalistic lament about the hopelessness of the situation, or an expressive Russian sigh of disappointment and resignation' (1997: 84).

Ries explains litanies as a vehicle through which people conveyed their social concerns, a culturally patterned way of expressing fear, anxiety, disappointment and frustration (1997: 110), dividing society into two, the victim and the villain. The speakers' group of victims was depicted as morally superior and innocent due to the suffering that they had to endure. This also indicated their strength and stamina in the face of hardships but also reinforced the feeling of despair and cynicism and powerlessness among the speakers, separating people from the political process and strengthening the sense of hopelessness and the futility of trying to change anything (1997: 115). David Kideckel (2008: 16) who studied post-socialist Romanian miners, noted that narratives of getting by were replaced by collective 'narratives of complaint about the circumstances of worker lives and labour'. He notes how the miners' *plângere* (complaint) unifies miners with others in Central-Eastern Europe who complain of hard times.

While both of these authors see the futility of post-socialist complaining, the lamenting around the kitchen table, the garage or the bus stop can also be seen as the foundation of framing miners' cosmology. As Nash (1979) and Taussig (1980) have pointed out, the ritual of miners sitting together to give sacrifices to Tio is not only about making peace with the supernatural but a community bonding moment. A trade union leader, for example, tells Nash that there is no communication more intimate, more sincere or more beautiful than the moment when the workers chew coca together and offer it to the Tio. Furthermore:

> There they give voice to their social problems, they give voice to their work problems, they give voice to all the problems they have, and there is born a new generation so revolutionary that the workers begin thinking of making structural change. This is their university. (Nash 1972: 231–2)

While the revolutionary spirit is nowhere to be found among the Kazakhstani miners, complaining together or to those who are their superiors but are still considered members of their community, such as Andrei Sergeevich, allows Kazakhstani miners to describe what they consider to be fair or unfair and express their critique of capitalism, without the symbol of the devil. Following Durkheim (1976), like religious rites, the rites of complaining together strengthen collective consciousness and conscience, making more explicit a shared moral and ethical way of how the world is imagined. Such sacred ritual awakens the feeling of support, safety, the sense that they are part of society because they practise the ritual together (1976: 421). Thus, while the usefulness of the training as a mining encounter where the global corporate ideology of team building and local workers meet was questionable in terms of H&S, it reinforced miners' local community-based consciousness, acting as an exercise in building a team *against* the global political economy of speed, even if it failed to create any direct political action in the process.

INTERNATIONAL, REGIONAL AND LOCAL MANAGERS: THE RITUAL OF INSPECTION AND PUNISHMENT

The inspection of health and safety measures illustrates the performativity of the H&S rituals and the particular organisational culture that led to rituals of fear, cover-up and pretence, a particular post-Soviet version of H&S. AMT local management, while receiving orders from the headquarters in London, was based in the steel town Temirtau, some 70 kilometres from the mines. The senior management in Temirtau was mostly foreign, consisting of Indians and some Eastern Europeans who had experience of management of post-socialist enterprises. The direct management of mines was executed by the headquarters of the Coal Division of Karaganda. Each mine had its own management, with a director, chief engineer and the deputy of the chief engineer who dealt with H&S questions. Besides that, there was a whole layer of engineer-technical staff (*inzhenerno-tekhnicheskie rabotniki*, ITR in Russian), responsible for running different departments. This formed a long command chain where everyone had to report to their (feared) superior and a chain of auditing where the superiors constantly checked on production numbers as well as accident prevention.

Regular internal inspections of production and prevention equipment and work practices are a common practice in industry and should ensure that rules are followed and support given in case of shortcomings. In the tension between safety and productivity, their meaning and ritual functions become much more multi-layered.

By way of illustration, let us look at the visit of Schmidt, Head of Health and Safety, to the Burannaya mine, where Chief Engineer Sergeev and the young head of a tunnelling section, Valeri, were waiting for him. We took the lift down to about 800 metres below sea level, the underground train to a point closer to the area Schmidt was to inspect and then started a long hike through the muddy tunnel going up a rather steep incline, with the conveyor belt to our left. The group was checking gas meters and large blackboards where gas content was recorded every few hours and marched upwards until they saw two young miners shovelling fallen rock back onto the conveyor belt. The visitors discovered that the miners had ignored the lockout procedures of the conveyor belt, meaning that any other passer-by could turn on the belt and potentially injure other workers. Schmidt started talking to the men, telling them off for not following the rules. Other questions followed, checking whether the pedagogy in the mine had any effect. 'Which standards do you know? When was the last accident in the mines and what happened?' The young men were not particularly well-informed and mumbled something nervously. Schmidt asked if they were married and when one of the men said that he was, Schmidt reminded him that his wife and children were waiting for him at home. He told them to be careful and moved on.

Only now did the real telling off start. The chief engineer of the mine stayed behind and asked what the names of the young men were.

Right, so both of you have fathers working in this mine too, haven't they taught you anything!? What were you thinking, not locking the conveyor belt, where is your lock and key for it? And why are you not wearing your vests with reflectors? And why did you not know the standards properly?! You have a higher work grade so you should actually know the standards, but you know nothing!

The angry chief engineer stormed off as he saw that the young men had little to say in response, anxious about what Schmidt might find next. One thing was clear – the miners would lose their H&S bonus, while the section head and the chief engineer would also be punished. Such inspections were always a cat-and-mouse game as the local engineers tried to take inspectors to tidier places and to workers who followed H&S regulations more closely. Keeping perfect order everywhere was impossible, due to the pressure of speed, staff shortages and the unorthodox work habits of miners whose fathers and grandfathers had taught them to cut corners. Sometimes inspectors could be tricked, but often they were experienced miners themselves and knew these games all too well. Gathering in the meeting room on the surface later, Schmidt indicated that since ArcelorMittal had bought mines that were in a miserable state, employees should be thankful and play according to the rules of health and safety.

Engineers whose sections had not done well, had to stand up while being spoken to, like naughty schoolboys. Not following the new global standards and the newest technologies of risk management were dealt with through the old Soviet practice of the public spectacle of punishment, where engineers and miners would be shamed, fired or their bonuses cut.

Following global rules of health and safety was translated into a complex local mix of inspections and check-ups, with repercussions and punishment when the rules were not followed. Everyone was aware of the global standards, admitted that many of the procedures made sense and that they indeed had children waiting for them at home, but they were also aware of the mismatch between the ideal and the local situation of staff shortages, inadequate equipment, low morale and the lack of trust in the company that was in constant 'crisis'. Such check-ups could be seen a stereotyped sequence of words and actions designed to prevent accidents by trying to influence the almost preternatural force of exhaustion capitalism, the positive outcome of which was just as unpredictable as miners' behaviour.

CONCLUSION

The Kazakhstani miners, raised as Soviet heroes of labour, often see injustices in the current labour and market regime where jobs are rare, and they are indebted and have to work hard in dangerous conditions while spending a considerable amount of their work time on something that they consider a farce. Due to low prices on the global steel and coal market that restrict investment and recruitment in the company, the miners sensed a heightened and potentially more dangerous workload. While on paper significant improvements in the local health and safety culture were made, with the help of a global risk management system, in reality this was often a show for both managers and miners. In the global political economy of mining encounters, the tensions are no longer just between profit and safety or indigenous cosmology and the logic of the market. The global and the local, together with the history of the place, come together in new configurations.

Even the most secular community needs its rituals to create order in the world and recreate faith in the morals of the community. The miners, with little power over their actual work conditions and safety, organise their world through collective complaining about their labour conditions. The ritual of joint complaining might lead to improvements in working conditions when given a political opportunity, as it forms the basis of miners' collective morality. As Bear (2014) has stated, workplace accidents provide an opportunity for the shared ethics of a workplace and workmanship to be manifested.

The local management, caught between the demands from London and the reality of the everyday running of the mine, are trying to meet the production plan as well as perform the health and safety ritual. If the miners' ritual of complaining must be at least to a certain extent satisfactory as it creates a feeling of a community with a shared moral base, the ritual of H&S meetings provides little satisfaction to those who have to perform it. The local mine management attempt to fulfil their duties to the global corporation but at the same time to indicate that they really are part of the local community forced into the global mining encounter that makes them perform in a particular way. In the tension between profit and H&S, global standards, national legislation, local history and traditions come together, each with its cultural baggage. While production numbers have decreased compared to Soviet times, the extreme intensity of exhaustion capitalism makes the steel and coal markets, production, machinery and workers' bodies increasingly overheated, seeking for new potential rituals to keep producing and stay alive.

Nevertheless, I would not write off the performative side of H&S management completely. Not all training is useless and indeed, there is plenty of laddish recklessness that miners could do without. The constant visual propaganda that surrounded me for ten months definitely made me cross the street and use my kitchen tools more carefully. When a miner friend had an accident in the mine, I was very angry at his care-lessness and shouted at him. 'What were you thinking? You should have first stopped and thought what you were doing and done it more safely! You have a wife and two young children at home!' Only later, I realised that I was using the words on the posters, because they simply are the most effective words you can use in the circumstances. But posters do not replace investment in modern equipment.

These global mining encounters bring together local cosmologies and rituals as well as global political economies and risk management rituals. Like environmental disasters caused by mining, large accidents can destroy communities and livelihoods where those already vulnerable in the corporate hierarchy are most likely to suffer. The everyday negoti-ation of risk, the small decisions that might not look like more than the tinkle of a teaspoon against a cup of London tea, can lead to accidents where rituals have lost their power in the everyday struggle of safety against profit.

ACKNOWLEDGEMENTS

I would like to thank the miners of the Karaganda area for sharing their stories with me. My thoughts are with the mining families that have lost members in mining accidents, the latest of which took place in August 2017, leaving three families to grieve for the dead. This research has been supported by the Max Planck Institute for Social Anthropology and Estonian Research Council grant PUT1263. I would like to thank the editors of this volume, Nancy Ries and colleagues at the Disaster Research Unit in Berlin for commenting on the earlier version of this chapter.

REFERENCES

Bear, L. 2014. 3 for Labour: Ajeet's Accident and the Ethics of Technological Fixes in Time. *Journal of the Royal Anthropological Institute* 20(S1): 71–88.

Durkheim, E. 1976. *The Elementary Forms of the Religious Life*. New York.

E.I. du Pont de Nemours and Co. 2013. *ArcelorMittal Termitau JSC*. Available at: http://www2.dupont.com/DSS_Executive_Forum/en_US/assets/documents/ArcelorMittal_comp_600px.pdf (accessed 6 June 2017).

Evans-Pritchard, E.E. 1937. *Witchcraft, Magic, and Oracles among the Azande*. Oxford: Clarendon.

Global Action on ArcelorMittal. 2008. *In the Wake of ArcelorMittal: The Global Steel Giant's Local Impacts*. CEE Bankwatch Network.

Hall, A. 1993. The Corporate Construction of Occupational Health and Safety: A Labour Process Analysis. *Canadian Journal of Sociology/Cahiers canadiens de sociologie* 18(1): 1–20.

Humphreys, D. 2011. Emerging Miners and Their Growing Competitiveness. *Mineral Economics* 24(1): 7–14.

Jones, E.C. and A.D. Murphy. 2009. *The Political Economy of Hazards and Disasters*: Lanham, MD: AltaMira.

Kesküla, E. 2012. *Mining Postsocialism: Work, Class and Ethnicity in an Estonian Mine*. PhD thesis, Goldsmiths, University of London.

—— 2013. Fiddling, Drinking and Stealing: Moral Code in the Soviet Estonian Mining Industry. *European Review of History: Revue européenne d'histoire* 20(2): 237–53.

Kideckel, D.A. 2008. *Getting by in Postsocialist Romania: Labor, the Body, and Working-class Culture*. Bloomington, IN: Indiana University Press.

Nash, J.C. 1972. The Devil in Bolivia's Nationalized Tin Mines. *Science & Society* 36(2): 221–33.

—— 1979. *We Eat the Mines and the Mines Eat Us: Dependency and Exploitation in Bolivian Tin Mines*. New York: Columbia University Press.

Nichols, T. 1997. *The Sociology of Industrial Injury*. London: Mansell Publishing.

Nichols, T. and P. Armstrong. 1973. *Safety or Profit*. Bristol: Falling Wall Press.

Nichols, T. and D. Walters. 2013. *Safety or Profit? International Studies in Governance, Change and the Work Environment (Work, Health and Environment)*. New York: Baywoor Publishing.

Peck, A.E. 2002. Industrial Privatization in Kazakhstan: The Results of Government Sales of the Principal Enterprises to Foreign Investors. *Russian and East European Finance and Trade* 38(1): 31–58.

Pijpers, R.J. and T.H. Eriksen, R.J. (this volume). Introduction: Negotiating the Multiple Edges of Mining Encounters. In R.J. Pijpers and T.H. Eriksen (eds), *Mining Encounters: Extractive Industries in an Overheated World*. London: Pluto.

Ries, N. 1997. *Russian Talk: Culture and Conversation during Perestroika*. Ithaca, NY: Cornell University Press.

Taussig, M.T. 1980. *The Devil and Commodity Fetishism in South America*. Chapel Hill, NC: University of North Carolina Press.

Trappmann, V. 2013. *Fallen Heroes in Global Capitalism: Workers and the Restructuring of the Polish Steel Industry*. New York: Palgrave Macmillan.

Turner, V.W. 1973. Symbols in African Ritual. *Science* 179(4078): 1100–5.

Woolfson, C. 2013. From Piper Alpha to Deepwater Horizon. In T. Nichols and D. Walters (eds), *Safety or Profit? International Studies in Governance, Change, and the Work Environment*. New York: Baywood, pp. 181–205.

Zonabend, F. 2007. *The Nuclear Peninsula*. Cambridge: Cambridge University Press.

NOTES

1. 'Londonskii Chai', song by Nurik Nurkeev from the group Nomady, my translation.
2. In 2004–9 the accidents were much more frequent given that coal mining had dropped from 43.6 million tonnes of coal in 1980 to 10.2 in 2010. In 1990, the coal basin consisted of 26 working mines and 100,000 people employed in the coal industry, compared to eight mines and 18,000 people in 2010.
3. European Bank for Reconstruction and Development spokesman told to EurasiaNet by email. http://www.eurasianet.org/departments/insight/articles/eavo20708a.shtml (accessed 26 April 2016).

Notes on Contributors

Catherine Coumans coordinates the Asia-Pacific programme at MiningWatch Canada. She holds a MSc (LSE) and a PhD (McMaster) in Cultural Anthropology and carried out postdoctoral research at Cornell University. Her publications on mining appear in, among others: *Canadian Journal of Development Studies* (2017); *UBC Law Review* (2012); *Journal of Sustainable Finance & Investment* (2012); *Current Anthropology* (2011).

Lorenzo D'Angelo completed his PhD at the University of Milano-Bicocca, Italy in 2011. His ongoing historical and ethnographic research focuses on the economic and religious aspects of artisanal mining in Sierra Leone. His interests also include the colonial history of West Africa, anthropology of extraction, political ecology and ethnographic theory. He is a member of the Italian Society of Labour History (SISLAV) and co-convenor of the EASA (European Association of Social Anthropologists) Anthropology of Mining Network.

Alex Golub is an Associate Professor of Anthropology at the University of Hawai'i at Mānoa. His book, *Leviathans at the Gold Mine*, won the annual book award of the Political and Legal Anthropology section of the American Anthropological Association. He studies the Porgera Gold mine in Papua New Guinea, American players of the video game 'World of Warcraft', and the history of anthropology.

Thomas Hylland Eriksen is Professor of Social Anthropology at the University of Oslo and was Principal Investigator of the Overheating project. His work on globalisation and identity politics was rewarded with the University of Oslo Research Prize in 2017. He is former president of EASA (European Association of Social Anthropologists) and the author of many books, including the textbooks *What Is Anthropology?*, *Ethnicity and Nationalism* and *Small Places, Large Issues*, and the Overheating books: *Overheating: An Anthropology of Accelerated Change* and *Boomtown: Runaway Globalisation on the Queensland Coast*.

Eeva Kesküla is a Senior Researcher at Tallinn University, School of Humanities. She has done fieldwork in Estonia and Kazakhstan on work, industrial health and safety, gender and class in mining communities. She has recently published in *History and Anthropology* and *Work, Employment and Society*.

Nikas Kindo is a PhD researcher at the School of Development Studies, Tata Institute of Social Sciences, Mumbai, India. His research interests are resource politics and political economy. Prior to studying for his PhD, he worked with Ministry of Rural Development, Government of India as a research associate.

Sabine Luning is Senior Lecturer at the Institute of Cultural Anthropology and Development Sociology, Leiden University. She teaches economic anthropology, with specific attention to environmental debates. Her research on goldmining landscapes in West Africa and South America focuses on mobilities and issues of scale – operational and temporal as well as spatial.

Patrik Oskarsson is a Researcher at the Department of Rural and Urban Development at the Swedish University of Agricultural Sciences. His work relates to resource politics in relation to Indian extractive industries including its land use, environmental governance and growing international footprint.

Robert Jan Pijpers is a postdoctoral researcher at the Institute of Social and Cultural Anthropology, University of Hamburg. His research focuses on the micro-politics of (large-scale) mining and processes of social, economic and political change in West Africa (Sierra Leone and Ghana). He is co-convenor of both the AEGIS Collaborative Research Group 'Resource Extraction in Africa', and the EASA Anthropology of Mining Network.

Kim de Rijke is a Lecturer in Anthropology at the University of Queensland. His most recent work has addressed the societal debates about onshore unconventional gas developments and fracking technologies in Australia. He has also undertaken applied research for Indigenous native title claims in both remote and more settled regions of Australia since 2003.

Marjo de Theije is an Associate Professor of Social and Cultural Anthropology at Vrije Universiteit Amsterdam. She has worked on small-scale gold mining, migration, and identity in the Guianas, and the cultural, social, economic and environmental aspects of this activity in the wider Amazon region. Currently she is involved in the socioeconomics of a Brazilian national inventory of small-scale mining.

Index